THE JURY SUMMATION AS SPEECH GENRE

Bridget Falconer-Salkeld

BENJAMINS PAPERBACKS

8

BENJAMINS PAPERBACKS

THE JURY SUMMATION AS SPEECH GENRE

AN ETHNOGRAPHIC STUDY OF WHAT IT MEANS TO THOSE WHO USE IT

Bettyruth Walter, Ph.D.
University of Pennsylvania

JOHN BENJAMINS PUBLISHING COMPANY
AMSTERDAM/PHILADELPHIA

1988

Library of Congress Cataloging-in-Publication Data

Walter, Bettyruth.
The jury summation as speech genre : an ethnographic study of what it means to those who use it / Bettyruth Walter.
p. cm. -- (Pragmatics & beyond. New series ; 1)
Bibliography: p.
Includes index.
1. Summation (Law) -- United States. 2. Forensic oratory. I. Title. II. Series.
KF8924.W35 1988
347.73'75 -- dc 19
[347.30775] 88-10125
ISBN 90 272 5010 3 (Eur.)/1-55619-034-4 (US) (hb.;alk. paper) CIP
ISBN 90 272 2107 3 (Eur.)/1-55619-035-2 (US) (pb.; alk. paper)

DEDICATION

To the most special people in my life

Donald, Caroline, Richard,
my Mother and Father

ABSTRACT

The American courtroom trial is a speech situation. Everything occurs through the spoken word. The 'summation', a speech event embedded within the trial, which is the chronological and psychological culmination of it, is one of the few opportunities for the lawyer to communicate directly with jurors. But the speech genre summation involves preliminaries as well as the event itself; and it can affect the aftermath of the trial, for the decisions of the jurors may be influenced by this discourse.

This ethnographic study considers the summation from three perspectives: (1) That of the producer. How he learns this way of speaking, how he prepares for and delivers it. Data was obtained from interviews with 34 trial lawyers who are considered to be extremely effective during this speech event. (2) From the point of view of the ethnographer who observed and analyzed sixty-six actual summations. (3) From that of the receivers of the speech event who must act upon it. Information was obtained from post-deliberation questionnaires completed by 223 jurors, plus 35 alternate jurors.

Results: 1) Seventy-five percent of the lawyers interviewed believed that the closing speech could make a critical difference in 'a close case'.

2) The ethnographer as participant-observer determined closing speeches are most effective when speakers appear to be most credible, and when they inform the listeners about the case while holding their interest. Significant features were: knowledge of the law, ability to select appropriate content, awareness that summation is a performance.

3) The jurors, with statistical significance, indicated that they remembered, believed, and found more interesting the closing speeches of the prosecutor; that they preferred knowing the prosecutor better; that the defense attorney spoke too long.

4) No relationship was established between hearing a summation and changing one's opinion.

Conclusions: 1) Lawyers as senders of the summation believe their message to be far more effective than do jurors as receivers.

2) There is a connection between summation and reputation among others in the community, and reputation in one's own mind.

3) The immediate response to summation seems to be mitigated during jury deliberation.

4) The summation, traditionally considered to be a monologue, is in fact a two-way communication.

TABLE OF CONTENTS

PREFACE

> A description of a culture derives from an ethnographer's observations of the stream of the activities performed by the people he is studying. As a first step toward producing an ethnographic statement, the investigator must segment and classify the events of this behavior stream so that he can say, for example, of two successive events, that one is "different" from the other and, of two nonsuccessive events, that they are repetitions of the "same" activity.....Information about what is the "same" and what is "different" can only come from the interpretations of events made by the people being studied.
>
> Charles O. Frake (1969)

The culture which is being observed in this study is the American legal community, and the people being studied are some of those who belong to that culture — lawyers. The activity which will be segmented and classified is the linguistic event 'summation'. Information about what is the same and what is different about this speech event which occurs in the space of the courtroom trial will come from the words and observations of those lawyers who participated in the study.

The sociolinguistic analysis of the speech event summation, which is the focus of this book, will be of interest to more than one audience. First of all, to students of language who concern themselves with the social use of language within one of our primary democratic social institutions — courts of law.

A second audience will be the trial lawyers who use language in the legal arena of the courtroom to obtain what they believe is fair and just for those whom they serve, be it private citizen or the government. As well as to the practitioners, it will be of interest to other lawyers, judges and law students who wish to learn more about how the spoken word can be used for good or for ill within the legal context.

This study will also demonstrate a method of language research within a specific social setting where strict legal rules usually preclude open and frank language sampling. However, it is possible to do, and should be done — and this is one way. As the courts gain more confidence in social science research, and realize that this work can go forward without disruption to or effect on the judicial process, language researchers will be allowed more precise techniques of data collection than was possible for this study. This is a good beginning.

Because this study of summation addresses two diverse reader groups, there may be some limitations and frustrations for both. Although legal and linguistic terms and concepts will be explicated so that the text will be meaningful for both, linguists may wish that some of the language issues were discussed more completely, with greater attention given to linguistic detail. Lawyers may wish that certain legal issues were more thoroughly dissected and discussed. This might mean, perforce, that in some instances terms or issues will appear too elementary for some of the readers, and too complex for others.

However, if I have done my job well, through the reading of this book both audiences will be able to learn about and exchange information about another discipline — one with which their own intersects.

ACKNOWLEDGEMENTS

Having always been fascinated by language, and spending most of my life in the company of those who studied and/or practice law, it is all together reasonable that I would embark on a study of the intersection of law and language. In the course of completing this research, there were many persons who increased my knowledge and guided my efforts, and to whom I owe much.

Of special note is my husband, Donald J. Goldberg, who contributed hours to serving as my sounding board for ideas, as information source on innumerable legal issues, and as fascinating subject for the study.

To my children, Caroline Virginia Walter Goldberg and Richard Walter Goldberg, who always enlarge my understanding of any issue.

To Dell H. Hymes, who has inspired so many who have been fascinated by the interaction of language and social setting.

To William M. O'Barr, whose own explorations into the interaction of language and law have given linguistic evidence of the effects of the spoken word in the courtroom.

To Michael H. Long, outstanding linguist and teacher as well as student of law, who has instilled in so many a deep commitment to the scientific method in linguistic research.

Special appreciation is expressed to the judges who permitted me open access to their courtrooms so that I could collect the data necessary for the successful completion of this project:

Hon. Marvin R. Halbert
Hon. David N. Savitt
Hon. Eugene Gelfand

But the persons to whom I owe the most are the attorneys who are the heart and soul of this entire research enterprise. Without them, not only would there be no book — there would be no closing speeches.

Sincere thanks and appreciation are extended to the following courtroom lawyers who participated in this study. They generously shared their valuable opinions and precious time — as well as their good company — and it is through their words that the speech event summation springs to life.

Those words fill many of the pages which follow. When the lawyers were interviewed, they all most graciously gave permission to be quoted, and in many instances their quotations have been given name credit. However, sometimes I chose not to identify the speaker on the slight chance that a frank comment might prove embarrassing to the informant. The decision to identify the speaker or not was always my own.

All of the lawyer/informants listed on the next page practice their art primarily in Philadelphia unless otherwise noted.

Ainslie, Elizabeth K.
Bailey, F. Lee — Boston, Massachusetts
Bergstrom, Thomas A.
Brown, Raymond A. — Newark, New Jersey
Carroll, John Rogers
Carroll, Thomas Colas
Christie, Barbara L.
Dershowitz, Alan M. — Cambridge, Massachusetts
DeSimone, Frank E.
Fahringer, Herald Price — New York, New York
Fitzpatrick, F. Emmett — Former District Attorney of Philadelphia
Goldberg, Donald J.
Haynes, Richard — Houston, Texas
Kidd, Ronald F.
King, Roger E.
La Rossa, James M. — New York, New York
Levy, Elwood S.
Litvin, S. Gerald
Lytton, William B.
Magarity, Gregory T.
Maguigan, Holly
McGill, Joseph J.
Meyer, Stephen P. — Charleston, West Virginia
Peruto, A. Charles
Preiser, Stanley E. — Charleston, West Virginia
Purnell, Jean

Rubino, Judith
Rudovsky, David
Rutter, Thomas B.
Sprague, Richard A.
Temin, Carolyn E. — Now Judge in the Philadelphia Court of Common Pleas
Toro, Eugene F. — Providence, Rhode Island

And two special interviews:

Higgins, Pamela W.
Nast, Diane M.

LIST OF TABLES

1 . Introduction

The American courtroom trial can be divided into six segments: the voir dire[1] during which prospective jurors are interviewed and selected; opening statements presented by opposing counsel; evidence as introduced by witnesses; closing statements as spoken by opposing counsel; the charge to the jury by the judge; and the verdict rendered by the jury following deliberation. All of these parts of a trial are events which occur through speech.

It is the closing speech to the jury, or summation, which is the focus of this study. Within the legal community, summation is defined as a speech by the lawyer to the jurors which is an "exercise in persuasion" (Jeans 1975), and for which law students are instructed as to the very definite restrictions on its form and content. As one legal textbook states, "Closing arguments are the chronological and psychological culmination of a jury trial. They are the last opportunity to communicate directly with the jury" (Mauet 1980).

In the Pennsylvania Criminal Practice, the closing argument is defined as:

> . . . a critical stage in a trial. In it the lawyer has the opportunity to marshal the evidence and to present it, along with the permissible inferences arising therefrom, to the jury in the best possible light on behalf of his client, and to attempt to explain away the evidence which is unfavorable (Wasserbly 1981: Chap. 27-Page 40).

According to linguists, and following a model developed by Hymes (1972), the trial can be considered as a speech situation which takes place in the setting of a courtroom, and in which there are observable 'ways of speaking'. The language used is integral to that particular setting.

The summation is a 'speech event' which is delivered within the context of the trial. In order to define speech event, Hymes (1962) suggests that we use the ethnographic technique of looking at words which name it, such as: sunday morning sermon, inaugural address, pledge of allegiance;

or colloquial expressions: salestalk, bull session, cocktail conversation. Although there is no common structural analysis to be made of these different speech events, what we do know is that each event is governed by its own rules of use, and that each is a culturally recognized social activity in which language plays a specific role.

In order to develop a linguistic understanding of summation, it is important to consider and associate the following terms: speech act, speech event, persuasion and genre. These notions are interrelated and form a structure with the speech act serving as minimal unit, and the genre as maximum unit, each higher term incorporating the ones below. Therefore, the speech act is a constituent factor of the speech event summation, which is used for the function of persuading a jury when a summation is spoken by a lawyer during a trial within the social setting of a courtroom.

"A speech act is a bit of speech produced as part of a bit of social interaction" (Hudson 1980). Within the Speech Act Theory developed by Austin (1962), bits of speech, or utterances, in addition to meaning whatever they mean, perform specific actions. They have a particular force. For example, the utterance "Have a nice day", can have the force of wishing you a pleasant day, or be used to close a conversation in lieu of "Goodbye." (For a more complete discussion of Speech Act Theory, see pages 149-151.)

Within the speech event summation, one may find many speech acts each with its own force, such as: opening statement, "Ladies and Gentlemen of the jury"; imperative, "Find my client innocent"; expression of gratitude, "I thank you for your attention"; compliment, "You were selected as jurors because you were found to be free from bias and prejudice."

A speech act may exert more than one force. The expression of gratitude just above, "I thank you for your attention", may in one instance have the force of thanking the jurors. But the speaker may also intend to use this message to persuade: "You see, I am a nice person with good manners. Therefore you should like and believe me, and be willing to do what I tell you to do."

The form in which the messages of speech acts are conveyed from lawyer to jurors is the speech event summation. The primary function of this event as understood by lawyers and judges, and often explained to the jurors just before summations are delivered, is to persuade.

However, the closing speech is not only or identical with a speech event. It is also a genre, a category or type of speech. In order to construct the notion of 'genre', I shall rely on Duranti's definition (1983): "A recognized (by its users) unit of discourse with some well-defined features such as sequential organization (viz. which part should come before what), constraints (and expectations) on (some of) its content and form, and *socially defined appropriate contexts of use*" (emphasis added).

A summation can be a speech event spoken within the context other than a courtroom. But to be considered a genre, it is always a matter of setting. If a man stands up at a party, faces a group of his friends and begins "Ladies and Gentlemen of the jury...", the persons assembled will know that he is pretending to deliver a summation, but it is not actually a closing speech for they do not find themselves in a courtroom. The function of this speech event, which is probably to amuse, and which occurs within the social setting of a party, does not meet the definition of the genre summation.

Speech Event — Speech Genre

The notions of speech event and speech genre often do coincide with one another, but according to Hymes (1972), genres "must be treated as analytically independent from them. They may occur in (or as) different events." Because we will concern ourselves with the analysis of summation as genre, it is important to separate out these two sometimes overlapping notions.

Duranti in his study referred to above, "Samoan speechmaking across social events: One genre in and out of a fono", presents the speech genre as a dynamic notion. "The same genre is bound to be performed in different ways according to the particular event in which it occurs, who the speaker is, to whom it is addressed, etc., . . . " (p. 1).

Duranti shows that the Samoan ceremonial speech, *lauga*, systematically varies along with variations of (1) purposes, (2) sequences, (3) participants, and (4) key, all components of the social event in which the *lauga* occurs.

These same notions can be applied to the speech genre summation. For example, the summation within a trial will vary according to the participants, as in Duranti's number (3) above. Each speaker (lawyer) will perform within the bounds of his or her own way of speaking, knowledge, experience, and level of self-confidence. The audience (jurors) will respond to the summation according to the life's experience of each individual juror.

The composition of the jury will differ for every trial, of course, as to the particular individuals, and will vary as to the kinds of people represented (males and females, Blacks, Whites, Protestants, Jews, Catholics, young and old, etc.) And this in turn will affect the way the summation is received by this audience as a group, for the jury functions as a group.

The summation, with its norms and rules for use, as a speech genre encompasses not only the event itself but involves preliminaries and has an aftermath. It is most often born in the mind of the lawyer well before the actual occurrence of the speech. Sometimes it is prepared as a completely detailed written document. At other times, it may be only an outline of topics the attorney wishes to discuss with the jurors, or it may be simply a mentally formulated message. However, all lawyers interviewed for this study reported some form of preparation.

The event itself occurs within the trial seemingly as a monologue addressed to the albeit silent yet responding jurors. There is an aftermath, for the effect of the summation is the impression this piece of speech makes upon the minds of the individual jurors, and how they are or are not persuaded by the arguments of the speaker. If the primary purpose of the closing speech is to persuade, and this study will explore that supposition, and if the lawyer is indeed persuasive, the jurors' actions may be the result of this discourse.

Speaking

Within the concept of an ethnographic description of language, Dell Hymes presented a heuristic guide for organizing the components of a speech situation using the mnemonic device SPEAKING (1967, 1972). The components are:

S = Setting and Scene
P = Participants
E = Ends
A = Act Sequences
K = Key
I = Instrumentalities
N = Norms of Interaction and of Interpretation
G = Genres

The summation can be analyzed within the scope of these same components:

S: Setting and Scene. The Setting refers to the physical environment of a communicative event and in the case of a summation, the setting is the austere courtroom. The Scene refers to the psychological setting having to do with cultural aspects. Many scenes can take place in one physical setting. A wedding as well as a trial may occur in an American courtroom, and that scene would be happy albeit formal. The scene for the summation is also formal, but very serious, for the result can spell personal freedom or imprisonment, and sometimes death.

P: Participants. The judge as referee and the jurors as decision-makers are the direct receivers of the summation. Other lawyers, spectators, courtroom personnel, and the press are all indirect receivers of the speech event.

E: Ends. Ends encompass two notions, Goals and Outcomes. The Goal of an event is the purpose of that event from a community standpoint. The Outcome of an event is the actual result. Often the outcome may not be what was intended by the sender of the message. The goal of the summation is to persuade an audience to the view of the addressor. But in every trial, one of the speakers can expect the outcome of the event to go against his or her closing argument.

A: Act Sequences. "A communicative event consists of a series of speech acts having both 'form' and 'content'. How something is said is of no less interest than what is said, for form constitutes content" (Danet 1980b:492).

The opening event in a trial begins when the bailiff stands at the front of the courtroom and cries, "All rise [everyone does], this court is now in session", or some variation thereof. After the judge enters and seats him or herself, often speaking words of welcome, the opening event is concluded. Other events are opening statements, presentation of evidence through the testimony of witnesses, closing speeches, the judge's charge to the jury, and the rendering of the verdict by the jurors.

K: Key. "The tone, manner or spirit in which the act is done" (Hymes 1972). The tone of the summation is serious. Sometimes a life or death situation prevails for the defendant. The manner of the speaker in the act of summing up can be persuasive, painstaking, accusatory, but always purposeful and goal directed.

I: Instrumentalities. The channel employed is spoken language, including spoken-composed, or rehearsed (Danet 1980b:471). The speakers use many styles which include formal, informal, ritualized speech, legalese, regional and social dialects, as well as dramatic emphasis.

N: Norms. This includes two dimensions. The norms of interaction govern who may speak (the lawyer who is summing up), to whom (directly — jurors; indirectly — judge, other lawyers, stenographer), in what order (the defender first in Pennsylvania state courts, the prosecutor first in federal courts), and about what (the case being tried with strictures about what may not be spoken).

Interpretative norms are those we use to 'read' the message of others. For example, rhetorical questions permit the speaker to convey his or her opinions without directly stating them because jurors know how to read these indirect messages. Silence is permitted and used for effect, for it is understood by the receivers.

G: Genre. The summation as genre is a communication form recognized by lawyers and many non-lawyers alike within American culture, and is identified by the labels of 'summation', 'closing speech', or 'closing argument'. It involves preliminary activities of preparation, occurs as a speech event within the trial courtroom setting, and has an aftereffect on the juror audience. Its stated primary function is to persuade.

How to Recognize a Summation

If one were observing a trial for the first time, how would this visitor to the courtroom know which part of the trial was a summation? The most important clue is that the lawyer will address him or herself directly to the jurors, which only happens twice in the trial. The first time is at the very beginning of the trial, and this piece of speech is called an opening statement. Being an act of summary, the closing statement will look like an opening statement, but it comes towards the end of the trial.

What the observer can see for him or herself is a change in activity in the room, for systematic physical conditions go into effect at the moment of the beginning of closing speeches. For example, in the Pennsylvania State courts, the court crier or the judge will announce that closing speeches are about to begin, that the doors of the courtroom will be locked, and no one will be permitted to enter or leave. (Some court criers even encourage those in the audience who must visit the lavatory to do so before the speeches begin.) The chairs of all jurors are turned to face the lawyers who will stand before them. (Some may have been turned toward the witness stand.) The telephones are removed from their hooks so that the lawyers will not be interrupted.

One lawyer will stand either behind a lectern or at his or her desk or some place near the jury box, but with rare exception, facing the jurors.

Although there can be and is variation in how a summation can be given, the usual form is as follows:

The summation begins with an introduction, which may take the form of a formula, or is sometimes noticeable by its absence. There may be greetings which indicate who will play what roles in the discourse (see Section 2 for examples of what can and was said for specific parts of the summation).

The witnesses and evidence are discussed, the testimony reviewed, credibility of various persons involved in the trial assessed. Law is discussed when permissible, and legal terms explained where relevant. There is an appeal to the jurors to follow the suggestions made by the speaker. Jurors are often requested to use their common sense.

The closing words may include thanking and politeness formulae, and often a request or command for the jurors to do that which the lawyer advocates. The speaker then returns to his or her seat and sits down. The first summation has concluded, and the observer may now expect at least one more to follow. The end of all summations will be obvious, for then the judge will begin his speech, called the charge to the jury.

There is nothing that a lawyer is required to say in a closing speech. All pieces of the closing speech are optional, as is the speech itself. No one observed in this study, however, forfeited their opportunity to convince the jurors of the rightness of their position.

Notice that the summation can also be referred to as the closing speech, closing argument, closing statement or final argument. All of these terms were used interchangeably by almost all the informants in the study, with the exception of one lawyer, who stated:

> I prefer to think of them as summations. I prefer to think of them as arguments — the final argument. I probably personally like 'argument' better than I do 'summation' because I probably argue more, rather than I sum up. That's my style as opposed to other people's style.

Education in Summation for the Novice Lawyer

The summation is considered by many in the legal profession to be a critical part of almost every jury trial, and certainly in every close case

(Bailey 1979, 1982; Belli 1979; Cartwright 1978; Sams 1982). Therefore, it is surprising how little formal instruction is offered to those in law school who will soon come to the bar. Until the last ten years or so, no instruction was available and even today it is but optional.

In 1949, federal judge Jerome Frank complained in his book *Courts on Trial: Myth and Reality in American Justice* about American law schools. He saw them as being virtual law libraries, and law students as being led through the analysis of Supreme Court cases by a law professor who had rarely seen the inside of a courtroom (see Chapter 10 for comments by Younger on same subject). The legal institution about which he wrote was the Harvard Law School.

> So long as teachers who know little or nothing except what they learned from books under that case-system control a law school, the actualities of the lawyer's life are there likely to be considered peripheral and of secondary importance (p. 232).

He compares law school to medical school and asks us to consider what kind of doctors would be produced in a medical school in which most of the professors had seldom seen a patient, diagnosed the complaints of a flesh-and-blood human being, or who had never actually performed surgery. He argues for the use of the Legal Aid Societies for law student exposure to what occurs in the real world of the courtroom (where summations are verbalized), just as medical students usually must participate in free clinics and dispensaries.

In 1984, the Law School of the University of Pennsylvania, one of the foremost institutions of legal education in the United States, offered only one course which specifically addressed itself to trial practice, including the preparation, delivery and value to jurors of the summation. The course, "Trial of an Issue of Fact", devoted one two-hour class of a year's course to summation. This, as most trial practice courses, is optional even for those intending to restrict their legal careers to trial work (see Chapter 10 for a detailed description of this class). Perhaps law schools are functioning according to the principle expressed by Alan M. Dershowitz, Professor of Law at Harvard Law School, who wrote, "A lawyer's education is far too important to be left entirely to law schools" (Bailey 1982).

A critical review of the literature concerning the verbal art of summation, as distinct from content and legal issues, reveals mostly instructions of the 'how to' nature in legal texts or reference books (Jeans 1975; Keeton 1973; Mauet 1980; Smith 1982, Stein 1979). For example, Jacob A. Stein in his book *Closing Argument: The Art and the Law*, after a thorough discussion of the law of closing argument, includes under the heading of The Art of Closing Argument such matters as the length of argument, use of exhibits, indecisive jurors, and objections. There is one section of two pages titled Presentation. He writes:

> The trial lawyer should begin by rising from his chair and addressing the court in a manner which indicates his respect for the dignity of the proceedings. Avoid any body movement that might be interpreted as an objection to the authority of the court (Part II-Page 4).

Several articles in legal journals pursue the same avenue (Belli 1979; Cartwright 1978; Younger 1976), and in one anecdotal article (Crawford 1983), Gerry Spence, a well-known criminal lawyer from Wyoming, reveals his secrets to success during his summation for the famous Penthouse magazine libel case. For example, "Spence knows how to alter his voice from a thunder to a whisper to get the most from his stories . . . " (p. 15).

One Ph.D. dissertation has addressed itself to the study of the summation. Hansell (1963) analyzed the written transcripts of twenty closing speeches in terms of emotional and intellectual variables in relation to the psychological principles of persuasion. No actual speech was analyzed.

This Study

This present study is unique in three respects: (1) Thirty-four lawyers who enjoy very high reputations for verbal ability in the courtroom were interviewed, and their description of summation is presented in Section 1. Those persons who were interviewed for this part of the study are among the best trial lawyers not only in Philadelphia (where most of the research was carried out), but among the best in America.

I know of no other study which has doggedly pursued the opinions of this select part of the bar on the one topic of summation. Although these lawyers have expressed their opinions on this matter many times before, e.g., on television, in books (their own and others), when asked, none of them said they had ever been interviewed solely on this topic. In some instances, this fact alone caught their attention.

(2) I observed sixty-six summations in actual trials in real courtrooms, and attempted to sort out what I heard and saw into the features which are presented in Section 2. This type of intense observation of actual summations is also a first.

(3) Postdeliberation questionnaires were completed by 223 jurors serving on 21 juries, plus 35 alternate jurors, inquiring about the effect, if any, summations had on their decisions. I know of no other jury study which has surveyed this large a sample of actual (not mock) jurors, in real (not mock) criminal trials.

Three studies which have surveyed real jurors in actual criminal trials are known to me, all with considerably smaller samples. One study (Flango 1980) inquired into the effects of note-taking by jurors and had a sample of twenty-four subjects in criminal trials (plus another twenty-four in civil trials.) "Because the sample in this study was small, it should be considered a pretest or a pilot study of a field experiment", admits Flango (p. 439).

In a second study (Report of the Committee on Juries of the Judicial Council of the Second Circuit), twenty-three jurors were asked about the same issue. A third survey (Greene 1982) involved sixty-two jurors in criminal cases in a postdeliberation questionnaire which addressed four issues: (1) note-taking, (2) receiving preliminary instructions prior to evidence, (3) having a tape recording of final instructions in the jury room during deliberations, and (4) non-disclosure of identities of alternate jurors until just prior to deliberations.

I know of no studies which have used information from alternate jurors for any purpose, other than this present one. The results of this survey are presented in Section 3.

Research Methods and Problems

As would be expected in such an excursion into unplotted research territory, there were problems. It was never easy to obtain interviews with the lawyers, and without the assistance of a well-placed telephone call or two by lawyers who knew me and found my research of interest, I would not have received the time I was given by very busy informants.

I think it is important to point out that all of the research for this study has been enhanced by the sharing of my life with a graduate of the Harvard Law School. Not only was he a source of constant enlightenment in matters concerning the workings of our legal system, but because of his success as a trial lawyer, I had entree into quarters where I might otherwise not have been welcome. I am certain that Alan M. Dershowitz, who possesses an exceptional legal mind and who keeps an extraordinarily busy schedule at Harvard, where he is a professor of law, would never have found time to allow me to pick at his brain if he and my husband were not colleagues. Nor would have Richard "Racehorse" Haynes in Houston have granted me an hour of his valuable time if he and I had not appeared in photos on the same page of People Magazine, I sitting next to my trial lawyer spouse.

I discuss this here because it was a special and significant factor in my ability to gather data, and informed the analysis of the same.

However, even with this entree into the legal community, it was often difficult to arrange interviews. For example, it took two years of telephone calls and several aborted meetings to finally interview F. Lee Bailey. I wasn't always successful. I observed a Philadelphia lawyer give an unusual and compelling closing speech (which also happened to be one of the few summations in a winning defense trial), but I was unable to gain an interview with him. There was no response to my many telephone calls and letters. (See the next chapter for further discussion concerning obtaining interviews, and Chapter 8 for a discussion of this particular closing speech.)

Since lawyers are persons of words, the thirty-four interviews which I did obtain produced almost sixty hours of taped material, which in turn produced hundreds of pages of transcription. Much of it was interesting, much of it not, and the decisions about what to include and what to delete were numerous. This process resulted in many pages of quoted material which appear in Section 1. I have sorted it according to key issues (identified in a cooperative effort between researcher and informants), so that the reader may obtain the most out of these descriptive quotes by the lawyers.

Getting into the courtrooms to observe summations was an easy matter. The courts are open to the public. However, the problems once inside were many. It is illegal to use electronic recording equipment in the courtroom in Pennsylvania, and for reasons discussed in Section 2, I did not wish to request special permission, even though I might have sometimes obtained it. Therefore, I could not tape the summations. What I could and did do was take copious and detailed notes of what I observed to be significant features of, and significant words spoken during the closing speeches.[2]

These notes, in turn, presented me with the complicated task of sorting into meaningful categories that which I heard and saw, and which I, the observer of summations, deemed significant to summation. The results of this categorization appear in Section 2.

The third part of the study, presenting questionnaires to actual jurors, was the most complicated in terms of research methods. First, I had to obtain permission from three judges to question their jurors in the jury room, or the courtroom. Some judges are comfortable with the idea of people other than trial personnel speaking with jurors after the trial, and others are not. Once again, I needed help from lawyer-friends to obtain entree into the system.

When that was obtained, I then needed cooperation from either a deputy clerk of the court (civil employee), a law clerk of the judge (novice lawyer), or the judge himself, to keep in contact with me so that I could be present at the appropriate moment. For example, one rainy Friday night, I had to wait by my telephone for the call from the judge which told me the jury had reached a decision. "Get here in ten minutes", I was told. I then found my way into a darkened and nearly deserted City Hall in Philadelphia to survey a jury which had just returned a murder verdict — and a jury which was anxious to go home.

However, once obtained, these data (although extensive) were the easiest to process. The surveys produced results which could be made meaningful with the use of statistical methods, something would could not be done with the results of my observations of closing speeches.

Many quotes contained in this study serve as descriptive examples of the text. Because it might be cumbersome for the reader to repeat quoted material every time it was relevant, related page numbers will be given throughout the text. On the designated pages, actual speech examples can be located according to appropriate topic markings. Although this requires a little effort on the part of the reader, he or she will be rewarded with informative, challenging comments from the expert informants who participated in this study.

The questions to which this study will address itself are:

(1) Is the summation important?
(2) If so, to whom and for what purpose?
(3) What counts as a good or bad summation?

Ways of Speaking

Ward Goodenough (1957) proposed that a "description of a culture — an ethnography — should properly specify what it is that a stranger to a society would have to know in order appropriately to perform any role in any scene staged by the society." Furthermore, Frake claimed that a stranger to a society needs more than a grammar and a lexicon. He needs an "ethnography of speaking" (Hymes 1962): "...a specification of what kinds of things to say in what message forms to what kinds of people in what kinds of situations" (1964: 127).

Recognizing that "no normal person, and no normal community, is limited in repertoire to a single variety of code" (Hymes 1967: 9), and that the ways of a lawyer include ways of speaking, a lawyer needs to know how to behave linguistically appropriately. When a student of the law is accepted into the legal community and becomes a participant in the courtroom scene, in the beginning he is a novice to that community and must learn the linguistic code[3] of 'speaking like a lawyer'.

When delivering a summation, he needs to know what kinds of things in which message forms he can say. He needs to know which part of his own personal repertoire is appropriate to behaving as a lawyer persuading a jury. He needs to know the ways of speaking as a courtroom lawyer while summing up.[4]

"In instructing our stranger to Subanun society how to ask for a drink, we have at the same time instructed him how to get ahead socially" (Frake 1964: 132). And perhaps in instructing our novice (the new lawyer) to the courtroom in the ways of speaking like a proper lawyer, we have at the same time instructed him or her how to get ahead in the American legal community.

Granting that there is a legal aspect of communicative competence (Hymes 1978: 58), there are yet two other dimensions of verbal behavior which are relevant. One is the concept of the cooperative principle as developed by the philosopher H.P. Grice, and the other pertains to the work of psychologists on persuasion. Observations on these two issues conclude this chapter.

The Cooperative Principle

H. P. Grice noted that our speech exchanges do not normally consist of a succession of disconnected remarks, and would not be rational if they did. "They are characteristically, to some degree at least, cooperative efforts; and each participant recognizes in them, to some extent, a common purpose or set of purposes, or at least a mutually accepted direction" (1975:45).

He called this notion the COOPERATIVE PRINCIPLE: "Make your conversational contribution such as is required, at the stage at which it occurs, by the accepted purpose or direction of the talk exchange in which you are engaged." He distinguished four categories which he named Quantity, Quality, Relation, and Manner.

Although a talk exchange doesn't literally occur during summation, as one partner is active, the other passive (the lawyer speaking to the non-speaking jurors), I explored the notion that the cooperative principle might well apply to the speech event summation.

QUANTITY:

1. Make your contribution as informative as is required (for the current purposes of the exchange).
2. Do not make your contribution more informative than is required.

* In the best of all possible summations, this is an excellent maxim — to say what is necessary and no more. But how much is necessary to be assured that you have persuaded your hearers, especially when they provide you with no verbal feedback? Also, the summation might have to be expanded in order to respond to what a speaker said in a prior summation. However, it might be shortened because many speakers will sum up if there are several defendants, and some concern must be demonstrated for the attention span of the hearers.

QUALITY:

1. Do not say what you believe to be false.
2. Do not say that for which you lack adequate evidence.

* To tell the truth should be a maxim easily obeyed, for lawyers are sworn to tell the truth in the courtroom. However, it is not the case that speakers always tell the truth in summation, which can be demonstrated in one instance by objections being immediately lodged by the other lawyer(s) in the case. Note that entertaining stories told during summation are not covered by this maxim.

RELATION:

1. Be relevant.

* If the speaker is not relevant when summing up, opposing counsel may object to what he is saying. The speaker may thereby 'lose face'. Also, if the lawyer does not speak directly to the issue at hand, the hearers may not be able to follow the course of the speaker's argument, and the force of persuasion may be lost. Furthermore, if the lawyer speaks on irrelevant issues, the jurors may believe he is being evasive because of lack of factual support for his or her argument.

MANNER:

1. Be perspicuous:
   a. Avoid obscurity of expression
   b. Avoid ambiguity
   c. Be brief (avoid unnecessary prolixity)

* If the lawyer is not clear in his or her closing speech, the jurors may not 'read' the message, and consequently not be persuaded. However, in some instances where the evidence is so clearly and so heavily against one's client, it might be productive to *flout* the maxim, i.e., blatantly fail to fulfill a maxim (p. 28), and to confuse the jurors with ambiguities. But then one might question the speaker's intention of cooperation in the discourse.

Grice's cooperative principle has not been accepted uncritically. Jacob L. Mey presents us with the notion that the maxims of Grice essentially codify a male practice, and do not reflect the female experience of language use. To agree with this view, one must accept Mey's concept of male versus female language. He writes:

Not explored further

> In our society, public communication is essentially a male affair. The men's language is tacitly accepted as the best, or even the only means of communicating in a public context . . . Men dominate the use of language all the way up from simple social conversation to the public and civil (not to forget the divine) services. If a woman wants to make it in this male-dominated society of ours, she had better acquire the men's language (Mey 1985: 29-30).

Mey, professor of linguistics in Denmark, continues with the criticism of Grice's maxims saying that they could be used repressively, "since they embody certain typically male ideas, and emphasize qualities that, in our society, traditionally and culturally are associated with males rather than females", such as being to the point, relevant and brief (1985: 30).

Another objection to the cooperative principle was raised by Stephen C. Levinson. He suggests that Grice's maxims of conversation describe a "philosopher's paradise, but no one actually speaks like that the whole time!" (1983: 102). He continues by suggesting that Grice did not mean that speakers follow these guidelines to the letter, but that speakers do orient themselves toward the principles, and that the hearers assume that the principles are being adhered to at some deeper level. Inferences arise to preserve the assumption of co-operation, and Grice dubs this kind of inference 'conversational implicature'.[5]

> So Grice's point is not that we always adhere to these maxims on a superficial level but rather that, wherever possible, people will interpret what we say as conforming to the maxims on at least some level. (Levinson 1983: 103).

Although the lawyer who is summing up may intend to engage the jurors' attention with meaningful discourse by heeding the cooperative principle, there are complications. First of all, the two or more lawyers who give closing speeches during a trial are adversaries with obviously conflicting interests. Although they may use the cooperative principle in their desire to engage in forthright communication with the jurors, can they both indeed obey the maxim of truthfulness? That leads us to the complex issues of what is truth, and 'truth versus justice in the legal system'.

If information is omitted from a discourse, is the speaker still being truthful? Is the purpose of a trial to seek truth? Or is the purpose to seek justice for those invovlved? Do they coincide? Perhaps the answers to these questions rest with the juror, the partner in the cooperative communicative event summation who is the determiner of which lawyer is obeying or flouting, for example, the maxim of Quality, i.e., do not say what you believe to be false? In fact, it is the juror who is left with this task, easier sometimes than others, of determining who is cooperating, and who is obfuscating.

One of the ways in which the task can be made more difficult for the juror is by lawyers using complex language. Complexity of legal language has been substantiated by many (Danet 1980b, Mellinkoff 1963, O'Barr 1981). While some lawyers have argued to simplify legal language (Hager 1959), others have argued not to oversimplify it (Aiken 1960).

Danet claims that there is a process, which she terms 'thickening', which occurs in legal language. She states that, for various reasons, the language of the law over time has tended to become elaborate, stylized, formalized (1980b:540).

Sherzer also addresses this notion: "It has been an assumption of research in both symbolic anthropology and the ethnography of speaking that the more ritual and ceremonial a context, the more esoteric and allusive the language and speech used . . . " (1983:214).

This implies a flouting of the maxim Manner, where a lawyer would conciously attempt not to be clear. However, the language of the sixty-six summations observed for this study was found to be virtually free of thickening and, other than a few exceptions which will be discussed later, was very similar to that used in everyday discourse. During summation, the cooperative principle did seem to be in effect. The lawyers wished to persuade through the communication of summation, and this would not be possible if the listeners did not receive the message.

The only piece of the summation which seems to fall victim to the concept of thickening is that which has to do with objections. When a speaker makes a statement to which the other lawyer objects, the judge may then ask the speaker to restate him or herself. For those of us who do not know the legal proscriptions against what may be spoken during a trial, both statements (the one objected to and the repeated one) still carry messages to the hearer. Not just a little energy and attention are spent by jurors in trying to figure out the reason one statement was unacceptable and a restatement acceptable. There is something to be lost by the objecting lawyer, and this tactic should be used sparingly for the benefit of his or her case, unless the speaker's intention is to obfuscate.

The Psychology of Persuasion

Since the speech act and speech event are marshaled by speakers as constituent factors of the genre summation for the primary function of persuasion, a detailed discussion of this topic is germane.

In a study of the psychology of opinion change through persuasion, Hovland, Janis, and Kelley (1953) stated that the major basis for accepting an opinion provided through argumentation is that the argument is in accord with the person's own thinking habits, and that it constitutes rational or logical support for the desired conclusion.

The three classes of stimuli in the communication situation that can produce shifts in incentive to adopt the new opinion are: (1) the source of the communication, (2) the setting, and (3) the arguments or appeals. Incentive is important, because change of opinion requires not only learning what the new opinion is, but being motivated to accept it.

The research evidence presented by Hovland et al. indicates that reactions to a communication are significantly affected by the intentions, expertness, and trustworthiness of the speaker. They state that if an audience perceives that a communicator has the intention of persuading them, then that communicator will be less effective in changing their opinions.

Since a jury always knows that the speaker during summation intends to persuade them to their view, one could say that the speaker is at an immediate disadvantage. However, since all the speakers have the same intention, they enjoy an equal disadvantage in this regard, which may well render it benign.

Therefore, it is the expertness and trustworthiness of the speakers which become significant dimensions, and it is these two factors which Hovland, Janis, and Kelley state are the key components of credibility.

They claim that the immediate acceptance of an opinion is greater when the the source is highly credible. "Opinion change in the direction advocated by the communication occurred significantly more often when it originated from a high credibility source than when from a low one" (p. 29). Also, "Inattentiveness will be more marked with communicators of low credibility, so that even though their message might be quite convincing it may never receive an adequate hearing" (p. 46).

Hovland, Janis, and Kelley make clear the complex issue of persuading a person to a different opinion.

> Attitudes toward the communicator and the cues which elicit them operate in interaction with many other factors of the communication situation. These other factors include such variables as initial attitudes toward the content, cues as to the source's responsibility for the content, the congruence between what is said and prior knowledge about the source's position on the issue, the complexity of the question raised in the communication, the ambiguity of the proposed answer [not usually an issue in summation], and the vividness of the source (p. 47).

And perhaps even more relevant to closing speeches:

> Shortly after being exposed to one communication, the audience is likely to be exposed to additional communications presenting completely different points of view and designed to create completely different opinions. Hence, the long-run effectiveness of a persuasive communication depends not only upon its success in inducing a momentary shift in opinion but also upon the sustained resistance it can create with respect to subsequent competing pressures (p. 17).

With all of these issues involved in opinion change, it is surprising that jurors ever changes their opinions about a case as a consequence of the summations. Perhaps few do.

A study by Mills and Aronson (1965) considered not only the intentions of the speaker, but his or her attractiveness. They suggested that under certain circumstances a communicator might be more effective in changing opinions even though the audience perceives that intention, *if* the communicator is very attractive. They performed an experiment in which they dressed a woman in two different guises. With the use of makeup, in one guise, she was made to appear very attractive, in the other guise, very unattractive.

She gave the same lecture under varying circumstances to male groups in both guises. In the attractive mode, she informed one audience of her intention to persuade them to her view. To a second group, she stated that she didn't care if she persuaded them or not. She did the same in her unattractive guise — a total of four conditions.

The result: The audience was persuaded to her view in only one of the four conditions, and that was in her attractive guise plus informing them that she did intend to persuade them. Under the other conditions, there was no difference between when she told them she wanted to persuade them and when she didn't.

Mills (1966) explored opinion change as a function of the communicator's desire to persuade the audience in relation to the speaker's liking or not liking the members of the group addressed, and making those feelings known. He found that the group (college students) agreed with the views of thc speaker more when the speaker let them know that he liked them and hoped to influence their opinions, and less if he said he liked them but didn't care if he influenced them or not.

If the speaker let it be known that he didn't like students, they agreed with the speaker *less* when he also let it be known that he intended to influence their opinions. These results achieved statistical significance even when the speaker's attractiveness was controlled.

Perhaps the most interesting finding was what happened when an audience thought that a communicator did not like them, *and* didn't care if he affected their views or not. It was then that the audience *most* agreed with his views. "The results of the experiment provide good support for the idea that the effect of the perception of a desire to persuade on opinion change depends on how much the audience thinks the communicator likes them" (Mills 1966).

Therefore, even when an audience knows the speaker does not like them, they can still be persuaded by him under the right circumstances, i.e., when the speaker lets the audience know that he doesn't care if he persuades them to his view or not. This is a circumstance that could not exist in a lawyer's closing speech to a jury.

Bettinghaus (1980) talks about the different ways that nonverbal behavior can produce different persuasive effects:

Repetition — a smile can serve as a repetition of a positive verbal message, and thus enhance the effect of the message.

Complementation — nonverbal behavior, such as a downcast face, can add weight to a verbal message.

Contradiction — people sometimes say one thing, but their nonverbal behavior says something else. Such contradictory messages may frequently account for the failure of persuasion.

Emphasis — persuasion can be enhanced by our nonverbal, emphatic clues.

Regulation — nonverbal clues can regulate the flow of communication. For example, after a verbal message, a speaker may turn to look at a different person, or a different part of the room (courtroom) and hence indicate that the next action or turn at speaking is there.

Bettinghaus speaks to the issue of emotional appeals, and since these so often find their way into closing speeches, his comments are relevant. He suggests that when an audience is well informed on a topic under discussion, such as a jury would be about a case to which they have been exposed in detail throughout a trial, the effects of an emotional appeal may be expected to be less than when the topic is new.

Furthermore, "When people agree with the conclusion, they are likely to feel that the appeal is a logical appeal, and when they disagree, they feel that the appeal is emotional" (p. 147).

"One of the differences between the message planned solely to transmit information, and the message designed to persuade, is the use of appeals", claims Bettinghaus (p. 149). However, he cautions, one should keep in mind that the response to such appeals is highly dependent on prior attitudes, and the frames of reference of the receivers of such appeals. The topics discussed were appeals to the receiver's sense of fair play, patriotism, religion, and humane concerns — all of which were used in the observed closing speeches.

One of the ways a speaker can evoke highly intense reactions is by the use of metaphor. Bettinghaus asks, "What effect does the use of metaphor have on the effects of persuasion?" He answers by quoting from J. W. Bowers (1964):

> " . . . a metaphor nearly always communicates a stronger attitude than does a conventional expression." [Bettinghaus continues] He goes on to suggest, however, that to conclude that metaphor usage will be effective in attitude change is not to conclude that such emotional language usage will

> necessarily be in a direction desired by the source. For the receiver who holds relatively moderate views about the topic, a message that uses very extreme language is likely to have a kind of boomerang effect. Attitudes may be changed less with such an extreme message than with a more moderate one. (p. 123).

Persuasion is discussed here because the lawyers who served as informants in this study claimed it to be a key issue in the enterprise of summation. In Chapter 3, in answer to the question, What is the main thing you are trying to do during summation?, 'to persuade' was the response most often given (see 3.1 C).

The Cooperative Principle is of interest because the maxims seem to be operational (although often flouted) even in a discourse which might be described as a one-way event. The functioning of this principle in summation might lend evidence to maintaining that summation can be conceived of as a two-way interaction, with jurors and lawyers cooperating. This issue is discussed again in Chapters 5 and 8.

SECTION 1: The Sender

2. A Description of the Summation According to Trial Lawyers

This ethnographic study will consider the summation from three perspectives, the main one being a description of summation according to what trial lawyers — those who use them, who produce them — conceive them to be. Borrowing a notion from anthropological studies (Frake 1964, 1972), the American courtroom trial will be considered as a tribal ritual contained within a particular culture, in this instance the legal community, and the summation as a speech genre/event embedded within that ritual.

Subjects

In selecting the population to be included in this part of the study, the 'chiefs of the tribe', the ones known to perform this ritual most effectively, were sought out and asked to share their secrets of success in the performance of this ritual speech. In fact, the sample population was self-selected for, carrying the analogy a step further, having identified one chief (trial lawyer), it was not difficult to learn from him (it was most often a male) the names of other members of the tribe (members of the bar) who are considered to be 'good at it' (delivering closing speeches). These chiefs (lawyers) were interviewed and they related how they learned this way of speaking, how they prepare for and deliver this speech, and what they believe it means to the ritual (the trial process).

The method of selecting informants was related to the issue of the difficulty in determining competence in lawyers. How competence can or cannot be measured within the legal community was discussed by Rosenthal (1976). He found that the more complex the type of practice a lawyer engages in, and the more unique the problems presented to him, the more difficult it is to evaluate performance:

> ...probably the best that can be done, even with a sophisticated evaluative instrument, is to distinguish among competence, low competence, and relatively high competence. It is unlikely that we will be able to measure precisely what makes one lawyer 'merely' very good and another superb. Lawyers refer to the genius of their craft as a matter of judgment and ingenuity. At the top of the profession, differences in degree often reduce to these illusory qualities. They can only be conveyed, imperfectly, by illustration and anecdote (p. 281).

Rosenthal stated that "Systematic peer review ... would seem to offer perhaps the most promising route for the upgrading of competence evaluations" (p. 270). Therefore, in the pursuit of similar knowledge for this research project, lawyers themselves were asked to evaluate one another. In harmony with this decision, *The Best Lawyers in America* (Naifeh and Smith 1983) was consulted. This text lists the names of lawyers selected by more than two thousand attorneys who were interviewed to determine the best criminal defense and civil litigation lawyers, as well as other non-trial attorneys.

It should be emphatically stressed that the criterion for inclusion in the sample population was *not necessarily* erudition in the law, but rather the ability to be very persuasive in performing a summation. The judgment concerning this ability was a composite of evaluations by other lawyers and judges.

Of the thirty-four lawyers interviewed in this study, only eight were women. The number of experienced, female trial lawyers is small but increasing as the number of women in lawyering in general increases. However, few have been in the trial field long enough to have gained prominence. The American College of Trial Lawyers, an organization which recognizes excellence in trial advocacy and requires fifteen years at the bar before consideration for membership, lists only four women as colleagues out of the total 1984 membership of three thousand, eight hundred and twenty seven. Two of the women lawyers 1 interviewed appear mostly in the appellate courts.[6]

Method

In order to obtain a description of the speech genre summation from those who use it, thirty-four trial lawyers were interviewed. A Question-and-Response instrument was used to elicit information from the informants (Appendix A). Both the questions and informants' answers are reported in this study acknowledging that meaningful information is obtained only when both are considered. The questions were developed in cooperation with the informants, because "the task of the ethnographer is to discover questions that seek the relationships among entities that are conceptually meaningful to the people under investigation" (Black and Metzger 1965: 144).

All interviews took place in the offices or conference rooms of the informants with the exception of two, one of which occurred in my office and a second in my home. They lasted between forty minutes and two and a half hours, and were taped by me with the lawyers' consent. All of these tapes may be made available upon request.

Fluency in the discourse of the interviewee did not necessarily co-occur with a reputation as orator in the courtroom. However, other matters might have initially intervened. Many of the lawyers who were interviewed knew me as the spouse of a trial lawyer who is a member of their legal community. It often took a few question-response pairs to establish myself as a language researcher rather than the wife of a fellow lawyer. Note that *my* husband-lawyer was included in the sample.

Having my husband serve as informant was beneficial in offering a ready source of legal information, as well as entree into other lawyers' offices. When first analyzing his interview, I thought that he might have felt more comfortable in discussing personal issues with me than might other informants. However, I found none of the informants to be reserved in offering personal views, often freely sprinkled with self-praise. I suggest that these qualities may be necessary for performing successfully in a public arena such as the courtroom. (See 3.2 C: 'The matter of ego in closing speeches' in Chapter 3.)

All of the informants seemed genuinely interested in the topic, and willingly participated in the study. They were extremely generous with their precious and limited time, once the interview was gained. The only attorneys who were reluctant to grant interviews were several women lawyers to whom the ethnographer was unknown. It was often necessary preliminarily to convince them that there was value to linguistic-legal research.

"Whenever a larger system is dependent upon communication among persons, then the point of departure is persons" (Hymes 1967: 15). The larger system is the system of justice, and the persons who are the focus of this study are lawyers. They shared with me their beliefs concerning how they achieved communicative competence in the verbal art of summation, and how they believe that competence can be transferred to the next generation within the cultural community of trial lawyers.

However, one of the major considerations in evaluating the information which was obtained from the lawyer-informant interviews was the knowledge that the informants were evaluating their own behavior. How reliable is self-report? To what degree are people adequate reporters of their own behavior?

Saville-Troike (1982) wrote about "the significance of differences between answers which reflect cultural 'ideals' or norms, and the 'real', or what actually occurs. This distinction between the *ideal* and the *real* . . . is not a matter of truth and falsehood, and should not be put in a negative light. Rather it is a recognition of specific behaviors" (p. 120).

Acknowledging this fact, the descriptions of the summation presented in this section of the study will be examined along side of actual behavior of observed lawyers in Chapter 8.

Instrument

Each of the interview sessions was based on questions which can be grouped around the following notions: (See Appendix A for the complete questionnaire.)

1. The value of the summation to the trial process.
2. The primary purpose of closing speech.
3. Delivery: way of speaking, memorization, reaction to audience (jury and judge), length of speech, use of poetry, metaphor, or bible quotes, etc.
4. Self-evaluation, i.e., are you good at it?
(If yes, why? How?)
5. Juror quality in general and preference for selection.
6. Standard openings and closings of summation, and any particular topics or definitions usually included.
7. Emotional versus intellectual arguments.
8. How, when and with whom is the summation prepared.
9. Use of physical evidence, notes, lectern, etc.
10. How and where one learns this way of speaking.
11. How one would teach a student of the law to deliver a summation; what to do, what to avoid doing?
12. The relationship between liking someone and belief.

How the questions came into being is of interest because it reflects both my views as observer of summation, and the values of the lawyers as users of summation. I began creating the list with questions that I thought would touch areas relevant to summation. These included questions such as:

What is the value of the summation to the trial process?
How did you learn to make a closing speech?
Do you aim for the head or the heart? The intellectual or emotional side of the jurors.
What makes a summation good? What weakens it?

The questions were aimed at learning what the lawyers thought they were doing in summation, what they thought its value was to the legal process, and what is considered to be a good summation. A key issue for me was how they learned to do it, and how they would teach a novice lawyer how to do it (see Chapter 4).

All of the first eighteen questions (see Appendix A) were researcher generated. But as the interviews continued, the informants introduced issues that were important to them in defining summation, such as the use of humor, disparaging opposing counsel, female trial lawyers in summation, and the manner in which they thought it important to dress when summing up. These became topics for future interviews.

The development of the questions for the interview was a cooperative venture between interviewee and interviewer. There were researcher generated questions and informant generated questions. Each reflected what was important to whom. The list of questions was, in reality, only a format for the interview, because we often drifted into areas of discussion not provided for, but relevant.

The questions were rarely asked in consecutive order, but fell into the discourse where appropriate. I never considered the list of questions a set instrument, but rather a malleable outline for issues of discussion, always willing and wanting to go wherever the questions led us — the interview creating the instrument. After every interview, the list of questions was reevaluated.

As demonstrated by Wolfson (1976), the researcher must be alert to the fact that during informant interviews the speech event 'interview' can itself become the object of study rather then a research tool being used to explore a linguistic event. I was aware of and remained sensitive to this issue throughout interview sessions.

The initial discourse of the interview usually related to the educational background of the lawyer. Age was never directly requested, but was approximated by the dates of graduation from undergraduate and law schools. Special efforts were made to engage the lawyer in conversation about legal issues in general and not specifically about summation. When we finally moved towards the topic of the interview, the first question was almost always, 'What do you think the value of the summation is to the trial process?' Other questions were inserted into the interview according to the flow of discourse.

The lawyers knew what the topic of the interview was to be. In order to gain the interview, I had to tell them what we were to discuss. Therefore, when the first question (mentioned just above) found its way into the interview, the lawyers always had an immediate and well formulated response. I could not be certain if this reflected some preparation for our interview, or if they had been asked this question — or lectured about it — so many times in the course of their careers, that they had at the ready a 'canned' rather than a candid response. Or were they saying what they thought the interviewer wanted to hear?

The 'canned' response would be formal, with grammatical forms and vocabulary which might be more appropriate in a written context. For example, Herald Price Fahringer began his interview with:

> It's the one time in a trial when almost without restraint a lawyer can stand in front of a group of people and literally argue his case . . . His summation . . . brings to bear on the litigation all of the lawyer's skills: his imagination, his use of language . . . .

Perhaps the framing of the question encouraged a 'canned' response, or the newness of the interview situation, for later in the interview, as we became more comfortable with one another, more candid information was forthcoming. For example, far into the interview with Eugene F. Toro, the following candid remark was made:

> The lawyer is gearing the whole trial to that hour he can stand up before the jury and *go! He can do his thing.*

I note that the phrasing of some questions was altered depending on whether a defense attorney or prosecutor was the interviewee.

Data Analysis

The analysis of the interviews, and hence the description of the speech genre summation, was organized around the responses to the interview questions. Some of the responses were evaluated in terms of the degree of presence or absence of some particular quality of summation, and responses were placed along a spectrum with strong evidence of the quality at one end, and absence of same at the other. For example:
Question: Do you make use of metaphor in your summation?

1. Always 2. Sometimes 3. Never

Other questions offered the informant several degrees of response to a feature of summation. For example:
Question: To whom do you generally address your summation?

1. All of them
2. Most of them
3. One or two particular jurors
4. To those who seem to agree with my position
5. To those who seem to need convincing

Other questions offered the informant a yes/no option:
Question: Do you like to use a lectern when giving your closing speech?

Other questions were open ended.
Question: What are you trying to do during your closing speech?

Whatever the form of the question, the response was almost always followed by a discourse of at least more than one sentence, and usually far more. Only one lawyer responded to yes/no questions literally, with a one-word or one-sentence response, and this was the shortest interview (40 minutes).

Lawyers are people of words, and the researcher found them to be persons who like to talk about what they do. Almost all of the interviews which took place in the lawyer's office were scheduled for late in the day, after court or office appointment hours. Only the one interview mentioned above ended in less than an hour's time, most lasting an hour, many closer to two hours.

The interview was usually terminated by mutual consent when the questions and/or the topic had been exhausted, which was signaled by the discourse drifting into and remaining focused on new topics. In one case, however, a lawyer talked for two and a half hours with no sign of concluding, and since he had strayed far from the topic, the interviewer terminated the discourse, or tried to, by physically leaving the office. This lawyer followed and continued speaking up to the door of the elevator.

The answers to the questions were categorized and counted in order to make some sense out of the many words that the lawyers used to describe summation. For instance, which features were common to the closing speeches of all or most of the informants, and which seemed to be idiosyncratic?

After the quantitative organization of lawyer responses, qualitative data follow in the form of direct quotes from the lawyers. In this way, the speech event summation is described by the users in their own words.

The reader can expect to find the following descriptions which were conveyed by the lawyers in the next three chapters:

Chapter 3: An overview of the summation
Chapter 4: Learning and teaching the ways of speaking in summation
Chapter 5: Significant other issues, e.g., use of metaphors, rhetorical questions, style, truth versus justice in the courtroom

3. Summation: In the Words of the Senders

"It is the ethnographer's duty to report the significant dimensions as perceived and reacted to by participants in the culture" (Black and Metzger 1965). In an effort to define the speech genre 'summation' in terms of pattern and function as it is perceived of by trial lawyers, the words of the users will be quoted in this chapter, organized around the issues presented below.

All quoted material is verbatim. Where material is not included in quotation marks, the uttered words may have differed somewhat but the semantic content is held constant.

During the almost sixty hours spent with the lawyer-informants, many interesting words were spoken. The decision as to which utterances to include in this text was difficult. The ultimate choice was related to the utterance being descriptive of the event, revealing of attitudes toward the event, uniqueness, and if it would be of interest to the reader who wishes to learn what these particular speakers in the legal domain conceive the speech genre summation to be.

All lawyers interviewed gave permission to be quoted. However, the decision to give name credit or not was based on two factors: (1) Whether the quote might prove embarrassing for the interviewee, and (2) Whether it would be instructive to know how a certain informant felt about a particular issue. All responsibility for the decision to give or not give name credit rests entirely with me. In the interest of brevity, complete names are usually given only the first time the informant is quoted.

Often when names are not given, it is still pertinent to know from which direction a comment came. Therefore, anonymous speakers may be identified by one of the following: *Prosecutor* (could be state or federal), *Criminal Defense*, or *Civil*. Some lawyers have served the law in more than one capacity, and that too is indicated.

Written and spoken forms of language differ, "because most speakers constantly simplify words phonetically in the stream of speech . . . . If the analyst normalises to the conventional written form, the words take on a formality and specificity which necessarily misrepresent the spoken form" (Brown and Yule 1983). In the effort to preserve as far as possible the true flavor of an utterance as it was verbalized, sometimes contracted forms are given as they were spoken, i.e., 'gonna' for 'going to', 'oughta' for 'ought to', and similar elided forms. The decision to contract or not rested upon how obvious it was in the speech of the informant. Also, to remain coherent for the reader, occasionally words are added or deleted. All additions and deletions are indicated in the traditional fashion.

Although thirty-four lawyers served as informants in this study, the number of respondents to any one question may be fewer. This is a result of questions evolving throughout the interview process as the informants made explicit to me what were important issues for them in regard to the speech event summation. Also, sometimes lawyers did not respond to a question, or the response was unrelated to the question. Some information provided by the lawyers was relevant to more than one issue. Therefore, some quotes appear in more than one place.

No evaluation of the comments of the attorneys is given in this chapter. These are their words; these are their descriptions and opinions of summation. They appear here as in the words of one of the informants, Richard Haynes: ". . . if my case has warts and pimples, I am very quickly the first one to say, 'we have warts and pimples' . . . because the issue may not *be* whether or not we have warts and pimples."

However, a summary of the data indicating what was significant to these users of summation can be found at the end of Chapter 5. The evaluation of what the researcher believes is the essence of these descriptions will be discussed in the final chapter.

Physical Context of Interviews

The physical environments in which the thirty-four lawyers were interviewed were often as distinct as were the informants themselves. Some offices were dignified and luxurious with handsome traditional furnishings. Others were spanking clean, modern, with huge glass windows offering spectacular views of New York City or Philadelphia. Almost all were virtual containers of hundreds of legal texts and publications, and stacks of files.

One of the interviewees held forth in his very own, newly built office building, with a white Rolls Royce parked in spot number one. To the other extreme, prosecutors and public defenders enjoyed little or no office space appropriate for an interview, and we would usually talk in a windowless, dreary room, outfitted with only half-way decent and sometimes broken furniture. I had no notion that tax-payer monies were being squandered on creature comforts for our public servants.

One interview took place in the midst of packing cartons when a lawyer took time off from his office-moving to share his views on closing speeches. Another took place in a restaurant in an airport hotel while that attorney was engaged in an air pilots' strike. A third interview began in a hotel room in the presence of a law student who was also awaiting his turn for an interview with a lawyer who had just presented at a seminar.

A person's world view is expressed in many ways. The spaces which the informants in this study carved out for their working selves, or had carved out for them, reflected those views as clearly as did their words. I was persuaded that there was a connectedness. Both were informative and interesting to behold.

Directions for Use of Following Data

Lawyers, being men and women of words, provided me with many interesting quotes. In order to make these valuable data more assessable for the reader, the quoted material has been divided according to topics relevant to summation, as determined through cooperative exploration of the speech event by interviewees and interviewer. Each topic is separated into the questions which were used to probe this area of concern.

In order to focus and make readily assessable the quoted material, I include here a chapter index. For example, a reader who is especially interested in the issue of disparaging opposing lawyers in summation may refer to the index below where they will find the question:

3.2, F. Do you ever disparage the opposing lawyer? (50)

That question (sometimes a statement) is followed by a number in parenthesis (in this example 50), which is the page on which the reader will learn that two-thirds of the informants said they do not disparage opponents, and that one-third said they do. The reasons for doing or not doing so are explained in the quoted material which follows the quantitative analysis.

This same treatment of the data will be used in Chapters 4 and 5.

Index for Chapter 3

D. Do you believe in using social scientists for selecting jurors? (62)
E. Do you think that jurors should be allowed to take notes? (63)

3.5 Content of closing speeches

A. The topics which were mentioned most often as being included in the closing speech, influenced by the side of the case on which the lawyer argues. (64)
B. Do you have a usual way of opening or closing your final argument? (65)
C. Do you thank the jurors for their jury service? (66)
D. Do you like to use metaphors, stories, poetry, biblical or literary quotes? (67)

3.6 Methods employed

A. When do you begin working on the summation? (68)
B. Do you include the client in the preparation of the summation? (Or for prosecutors, do you consult with other lawyers?) (70)
C. Do you memorize any portion of your closing speech? (71)
D. If there are several defense attorneys representing several clients, when do you prefer to give your summation: first, middle, last, doesn't matter? (72)
E. Do you address your summation to one particular juror, all of them, or a few? (73)
F. Do you like to use a lectern? (76)
G. Do you use notes during the summation? (77)
H. Do you like to use blackboards, large charts, overhead projector, props during the summation? (78)
I. How long do you like to talk? (79)
J. What is your reaction to lawyers 'objecting' during summation? (80)

3.7 Statistical information

A. How many closing speeches do you make in the course of one year? (81)
B. Number of lawyer-informants in study. (81)
C. Lawyer-informants by usual type of law practiced. (81)

3.1 The value of the summation to the trial process:

A. What is the value of the summation to the trial process? (N=34)

a)	*Extremely important*	26	.76
b)	*Important*	8	.24
c)	*Not important*	0	.00

a) *Extremely important*

1. "If a case can still be won or lost at the summation stage, then it is clearly the most important part of the trial." S. Gerald Litvin

2. "I regard the trial as only a device to enable you to sum up to a jury." A. Charles Peruto

3. "I think it's probably the single most important factor that determines the guilt or innocence of the defendant. It's that important."

"To me the entire trial is a preface to a summation. It's all leading up to that. The lawyer is gearing the whole trial to that hour he can stand up before the jury and GO! He can do his thing." Eugene F. Toro

4. "I think it's probably the most important part of the trial because it's the only part of the case that represents pure advocacy. It's the one time in a trial when almost without restraint a lawyer can stand in front of a group of people and literally argue his case. It's the most persuasive part of the case. He tries to explain away some of the calamities and exploit some of the good fortune he's experienced."

"His summation . . . brings to bear on the litigation all of the lawyer's skills: his imagination, his use of language . . ."

"Those of us who defend criminal cases are concerned with that perhaps 20% in the middle where the lawyer's skill can make the difference. And in that category of cases, I think the summation is probably the most influential part of the trial." Herald Price Fahringer

5. "It's the most important thing I can contribute." Donald J. Goldberg

6. "I think a proper summation can make a difference in a case that's *not* even close." Raymond A. Brown

7. "From a defense lawyer's standpoint, it's the critical stage of the trial. Particularly in fairly lengthy cases involving complicated factual patterns, where it's not going to be clear to the jury what the case is really about until they hear it summarized and put together and related to one theory or another. I think it's probably, from the defense

standpoint, the single most important phase of the trial." Thomas Colas Carroll

8. "It's priceless — if properly used. Communicating is *the* key point. By communicating you persuade." John Rogers Carroll

9. "It's of real significant value primarily because you have an opportunity for the first time — and actually for the last — to have direct contact with the jury."
Joseph J. McGill

b) *Important — but not the most important phase of the trial*

1. "Summations aren't as valuable a tool as a lot of lawyers think they are. Summations are important, but far too many lawyers think if they make a great speech, and do nothing else, they're going to win the case. I don't think that's true at all."
F. Emmett Fitzpatrick

2. "They are not the crowning glory of the trial [which she believed them to be in law school.] They are not the most significant moment in this magic time. But they are very important." Holly Maguigan

3. "I like to think that it is the most important part of the case, but I'm not convinced that it is . . . I think it's only important in certain cases." Thomas A. Bergstrom

4. "I've heard so many awful summations — by the government, for example — and then they routinely win their cases. So I'm just not convinced that a summation is the end-all and be-all." Criminal Defense

5. "Closing speeches don't make a damn bit of difference. It's part of the show. But the jurors expect it." Criminal Defense

6. "It can be everything, or it can be nothing." Stephen P. Meyer

7. "I think it's important — extremely important. But I think it's only one important phase of a multitude of important phases of the case. I think your opening is just as important. Much, much shorter, but just as important." Barbara L. Christie

8. "The jury is entitled to it. The jury wants to know how you really feel. They need to know you more. They need to hear from you. They need to know what it is that you think about the case, what you think about the witnesses . . ." Richard Haynes

B. Would the outcome of the trial be different without the summation? (N=25)

a) *Yes*	17	.68
b) *Maybe*	8	.32

a) *Yes*

1. "Undoubtedly. I can't imagine a case where the final argument would not have made any difference." Toro

2. "Oh, I think so. And more importantly, not only would there be different verdicts, I think the quality of litigated justice would be severely compromised." Litvin

3. "If there were no summations, I'm not sure I'd be a trial lawyer. So I'm convinced that in a lot of situations without closing arguments, you would get different verdicts." Criminal Defense

4. "Indeed, I think they often would be, particularly in the federal courts where the U.S. brackets you. He sums up, you sum up, and then he follows. That's deadly." Criminal Defense

5. "I think there's much more opportunity for confusion on the jury's part if there's nobody there to give them a summary." Elwood S. Levy

b) *Maybe*

1. "Cases can be won that are teetering, in closing argument — and sometimes are. There are some cases that are hopelessly tilted before you get to [that] point, and you are merely doing a necessary service for your client, but there is hardly any expectation that you're going to persuade anyone." F. Lee Bailey

2. "I don't know. It might or might not be. It depends on the case. If you have a case in which the facts are fairly evenly balanced, the summation is going to become very, very important. Sometimes critical. If you have a case in which the facts are all weighted against you, probably nothing is gonna matter — including the summation." Donald J. Goldberg

3. "I'm not sure. Summations are not as important as they're made out to be. But I do think they're important. Probably taken on a long scale — a year's period of time — in comparing trials, I don't think you're gonna find many more not-guilties or guilties than you would in a different environment if you didn't have speeches." F. Emmett Fitzpatrick

C. What is the main thing you are trying to do during the summation?

Below are listed the core ideas offered in response to this question. Some notions were repeated, and this fact is noted. Some of the more interesting statements are then quoted.

SPEAKER ATTEMPTING TO:	INFORMANTS
Persuade	15
Clarify or explain your theory of the case	7
Focus the jurors attention on the issues in the case	3
Emphasize points favorable to your side (Defense Attorneys)	3
Tie the whole trial together	3
Paint a picture	3
Perform	3
Develop a rapprochement with the jurors	3
Justify 'reasonable doubt'	2
Trying to raise doubts	2
Sum up	2
NOT to persuade	2
Convince the jury that I (the lawyer) believe in the defendant	2
Evoke sympathy and/or concern for the client	2
Attack the other side's case	2
Place in the trial where the size of the verdict is determined	2
Win the case	2
Solve the puzzle	1
Argue the law	1
Put the facts on a framework of the law	1
Develop a theme for the case	1
Establish a motto for the case	1
Get their attention and then do something useful with it	1
Explain away the evidence	1
Communicate	1
Create a miasma	1
Make 'love' to them	1
Answer the questions you have guessed to be in their minds	1
Arm the jurors for the jury room	1
Become a part of the jury	1

Quotes:

1. "I've heard it called summation, final argument, final address to the jury. I don't think it's any of those things. I think it's just your last chance to make love to 'em."

"The trial is like a jigsaw puzzle. It has a bunch of tiny little pieces of evidence, all coming in at different times — and really meaningless to a jury. And when you put it together in the summation, it becomes a great big painting. A beautiful painting is what you want them to see." Stanley E. Preiser

2. " To try to put it together for them in a persuasive package — to raise a doubt in their minds." T. C. Carroll

3. "Much of the time I am trying to raise doubts. Unpersuade. To create growing feelings that make the trier of fact uncomfortable."

"It's very important to make them address only one question: not 'guilty' or 'innocent', or anything else. [Just], did the proof presented by the government eliminate every reasonable doubt, or didn't it? That's all the verdict required. 'The minute you find that it didn't, your job is over.'" Bailey

4. "Most times people can't understand what they've heard over a period of a week and a half, until you tell them at the end." Criminal Defense

5. "'Come let us reason together' should be the title of the summation."
Frank E. DeSimone

6. "The real secret of closing argument . . . is trying to put yourself in their position. Not trying to tell them what they should think, but trying to see what they are probably thinking — if you were sitting where they are sitting. And then come from them, and answer their questions. Don't try to tell them what is right — or what they should do — but give them the answers to the questions they most likely have. And give it to them in a way that's going to make them *believe* in your story." Gregory T. Magarity

7. "As a criminal defense lawyer, the point of my summation is to point out the holes in my opponent's case." Maguigan

8. "My mission is to persuade the jury of the equity of my client's cause. So I'm gonna use the facts that support me. I'm gonna use, if I'm on the plaintiff's side, whatever developed in the trial that impales the defendant — if I'm lucky enough to get something like that. And I'm gonna try to do all that . . . with rapprochement with the jurors, creating, hopefully, the feeling that we are a team, the court, the jury, and me as a lawyer. 'We are part of a team that's here to find out what the truth is.'" Levy

9. "Sell a pathetic kind of creature caught up in society's ills." Criminal Defense

10. "Jurors like to be entertained. 'OK, smart, bigtime, well paid lawyer. Entertain us a little.' And they expect to hear just a tad of oratory. To the extent that we all try to dress well, and not use bad language before them, and try not to show our worst side to them, we are catering to that fact." Criminal Defense

11. "What your job is . . . touch their feelings and give them a series of mini-arguments that they can use for your side in the jury room." Meyer

3.2 Style of presentation of the speech event

A. Can you describe your style?
(N=26)

a)	*Yes*	21	.81
b)	*No*	5	.19

a) *Yes*

1. "Preachin' and screamin' . . . it's neither learned or pretty." Raymond A. Brown

2. "Formal — flamboyant — tough . . . I describe myself to others as the meanest, toughest son-of-a-bitch that ever lived — and very proud of it." Preiser

3. "Sincere, intellectual, emotional. Really straightforward. You won't catch me saying something to a jury that doesn't make any sense. You'll rarely catch me talking to a jury in a way I would talk to anyone else. To be sure, it is a speech . . . I'm paying a lot of attention to almost the beat of what I'm saying . . . and you'll find me going loud and soft." Criminal Defense

4. "I think I'm humble. I try to get across the impression that this is a very serious matter . . . I'm more dignified than not." Civil

5. "Informal, but not homey. I move around a lot. A lot of gestures. A little 'Iowa', but not corny." Criminal Defense

6. "Other guys shout and scream. I just try to talk to the juries; I don't try to make speeches. I try to adopt a conversational sort of approach." Criminal Defense

7. "I like to get mad. It makes me feel good to raise hell . . . it gives me a real big charge. I'm bored waiting for it. It's like a cheap high. You get ecstatic with emotion. That's part of your pay — your non-reportable income. This is not everybody's style. This is just what I like to do. I know there are other styles, but I know that I could not be anywhere near as effective using anybody else's style." Civil

8. "I am clear; I am loud enough; I am not boring! And my delivery conveys conviction in my . . . belief in my position . . . I am sincere." Prosecutor

9. "There are two types of lawyers, in my experience. The 'personality lawyer'. The lawyer who may not be very prepared, but tries the case basically on his personality. He relates well to people, relates well to juries, and if they're with him, he wins. And if they're not with him, he loses.

And then there's the other kind of lawyer — and I'm in that category. I prepare a lot. I'm knowledgeable in the law, and in the technicalities. And my jury speeches are very, very tightly prepared, very tightly structured. I don't practice them, but I'm very, very aware of their content and structure. And I deliver them as though I'm extemporizing." Carolyn E. Temin

10. "In final argument, I have a very serious, heavy, didactic rhetoric — to wake the jurors up to where they're gonna be the minute we all sit down and say, 'Go decide'."

He said that others have said about his style: "Some people speak in phrases, some in sentences. You speak in paragraphs. The whole thought works . . . It comes close to being acceptable prose . . . That's just a refined way of speaking without giving up any of the nuances of an oral delivery; which is continually taking the temperature of the recipient to see if you're getting through, and shifting as often as you have to. And a thought phrased in fashion A to persuade you, may have to be warped into B to get to this guy."

"In public speaking and summing up, all of which is done without any resort to reminders, unlike most good speeches, what I say looks good if you were reading. Because the oral word and the written word are different structures totally . . . To hedge that bet, we'll say everything twice, but not in the same language. But apart from that, the sentence structure, the grammar, and the placement of words [in my public speaking] is almost acceptable in written form." Bailey

B. Are you good at it (giving closing speeches)? (N=33)

a)	*Great*	17	.52
b)	*Yes — Okay*	12	.36
c)	*No (or Getting Better)*	4	.12

a) *Great*

1. "I am the best lawyer in the city in terms of making a summation. I do this better than anyone else. I really have given a great deal of study to it — I've perfected it. I'm the best in the city. Just a feeling of great confidence." Criminal Defense

2. "I know I am . . . because jurors have told me so." A juror told him: "Oh, Mr. X — you should have been an actor." Mr. X: "What do you mean — *should* have been?" Criminal Defense

3. "Yes! I'm good at it because I work at it. I think I understand the process of persuasion. I have always been aware of my ability to sell myself . . . Closing argument is not unlike a lot of things we do in life when we're not lawyers. We're always trying to persuade people to do certain things for certain reasons." Criminal Defense

4. "I think all trial lawyers secretly think they're always the best." Criminal Defense

5. "To be blunt about it, the answer is 'Yes'." Criminal Defense

b) *Yes — Okay*

1. "I like doing it. Sometimes I'm good — sometimes I'm not so good. At this particular trial, I didn't make the Mona Lisa when I painted. Sometimes I paint the Mona Lisa. Sometimes not." Frank E. DeSimone

2. "I don't know. I think sometimes I am, and sometimes I'm not. Because I have an almost irresistible tendency to preach . . . which is the Black tradition of Jesse Jackson preacher type."

"I've won quite a few cases. I guess my percentage is pretty high."
Raymond A. Brown

3. "Who can tell? I feel comfortable doing it. I don't have any trouble talking to juries. After thirty years it gets to be like an old shoe . . . I feel sufficiently at ease with what I'm doing that I don't worry about it. I don't have to be concerned about whether I'm going to trespass over the boundaries, or make the judge mad, or provoke the other guy to shout and scream." J.R. Carroll

4. "I don't know if I'm good at it or not. I do not judge how well I do in closing by the verdict . . . maybe I [gave] a great show, but I didn't have the substance — and they knew it. I just did not have the case." Stephen P. Meyer

5. "Fairly good. Some days are good days; some days are not so good. I am not as good as I would like to be. When I say I'm fairly good, I think I'm fairly good because others, in general, are that poor. If you ask me — am I a good lawyer? — I don't even think I'm particularly a good lawyer. I appear to be a good lawyer only because the general level of lawyering is that low. I'm not as good as I would like to be."
Criminal Defense

c) *No (or Getting Better)*

1. "It's not my favorite part of the trial. I don't consider myself an actress. I'm very happy when it's over. I've never loved being on my feet. I'm better on a one-to-one. [However], I guess I'm successful at it because I've won all but four homicide juries in ten years." Prosecutor

C. The matter of Ego in closing speeches.

1. "I've heard some summations that are just walking disasters . . . and I then ask the lawyer, 'How do you think you did?'. 'Oh, great. Wasn't I wonderful?'"
Alan M. Dershowitz

2. "I think I have a talent for it. And I think that having developed my own style from

the very beginning, only with me and my own personality, and the material that I have, has been a strength for me. It's grandiose to make the comparison, but I would think of — was it Irving Berlin saying to Ethel Merman? — that she never take a voice lesson; that it would interfere with the assets that I think I have —which I think are primarily based on my common sense and sincerity." Prosecutor

3. "Most trial lawyers are egotists to a degree — and actors." Prosecutor

4. "Most criminal defense lawyers whom I know are such egotists that they think that by their cross-examining ability, and by their eloquence alone, they will win. And that's the majority." Criminal Defense

5. About having a sense of power as you deliver the summation: "Oh, yes. Absolute [power] . . . because you're on stage. This is my time. If somebody interrupts me, they do it at their peril . . . All eyes are on you . . . I mean it's that being an actor again, being an egotist, and enjoying the attention. Anybody who denies that they don't like all that attention, when you get up to give an argument, is not being truthful. I love it. I *love* it. And the more people in the room, the better. It's a cheap high!" Prosecutor

6. "All lawyers are eloquent; they can speak well. All the trial lawyers. But the difference between the greats and the average is the thought process of using the various types of psychological principles of persuasion, such as primacy — lastness." Preiser

7. About keeping the client out of the courtroom during closing argument: "I hate to do that . . . I enjoy the closing so much, and I hate to deprive my client of listening to it." Civil

8. "I'm convinced that I have the ability instantly to put a thought into good shape in the spoken word — and I don't worry about it." Bailey

9. "On those few occasions where I've settled a case during the trial, I'm always saddened by the fact that I've missed listening to my closing." Civil

10. As a prosecutor, "it's a little scarey when they [jurors] come back 'first degree', and you're surprised because you thought it would come back 'third degree' — and you think, maybe, just because of your skill they came back 'first degree' — and it's not supposed to work that way."

As a defender, "to *free* someone because of your skill is a little more comforting than to stick 'em away just because you were clever. But it's always fun when the guy walks, and you have the feeling that if you hadn't been in the courtroom, the result might have been a little bit different." Temin

D. Do you prefer to give an intellectual or emotional closing?
Do you aim for the head or the heart?
(N=25)

a)	*Intellectual*	13	.52
b)	*Emotional*	3	.12
c)	*Combination of both*	9	.36
d)	*Depends on case, but prefers a) or b)* (N=14)		

a) *Intellectual*

1. "Always the head. We have to be so careful as prosecutors in our closing arguments not to appeal too much to the passions because we can get into legal trouble with the court of appeals if we do."

"During the rebuttal more is forgiven us on the appeal. And for that matter, we are more likely to have the jury with us if we engage in passion. So that if the defense lawyer has, God forgive him, engaged in some sort of unfair tactic in the closing argument himself, then they [jurors] expect and relish a certain amount of righteous indignation."
Prosecutor

2. "It's an intellectual approach . . . I don't think I've ever made an argument in a courtroom that I don't believe is right. I don't think I'm capable of looking into a jury's eyes and making an argument effectively that I'm not convinced of myself . . . I don't try to razzle, dazzle a jury. I represent people who are catastrophically injured, quadriplegics, brain damaged people . . . I tell the jury in my closing argument, I don't want their sympathy. That if all they're impressed by is the sympathy of the situation, the nature of the injuries, then I agree with my opponents. That's no basis on which to return a verdict."
Litvin

3. "If you can grab them by the brain, the heart and everything else will follow."
Thomas B. Rutter

b) *Emotional*

1. "I aim for the heart. I'll give you a little tears if I can. If you ask me how I do it, sometimes I think about my father's death . . . It's an emotional appeal. I usually end as close as I can to that. The judge hates me when I do that, because the last thing he ever wants to see is a hung jury and the case to be re-tried."
Criminal Defense

2. "I pull out anything I can to touch emotions. I have a 'Red, White and Blue with God' [speech]. I always use God. Most people on juries today believe in God. It's not all the sophisticates like myself — the agnostics. They really believe in that . . . I happen to think the less education the more emotion. That's why I go for emotion. You can't really have intellectual arguments."
Criminal Defense

3. "If you're defending a case where the evidence is really pretty powerful against you, and yet you have a very sympathetic client, in that kind of case the appeal will be a much more emotional one, and you're looking for jury nullification."

"I'm comfortable with both, but I think I like the emotional appeal more . . . It lends itself to the most extravagant language and appeals." Criminal Defense

4. "Emotional. And I go for the jugular . . . It's a passion play [and in the end] they're gonna do something emotionally significant." Civil

c) *Combination of both*

1. "A masterful summation is a combination of both. In most cases you really have to combine them." Brown

2. "I am totally convinced that you cannot persuade or convince anyone emotionally or intellectually until you can move then first physically. If I can make you move physically in a summation, respond to me, . . . then I can talk to you intellectually and emotionally; then I mold it together." Preiser

3. "I think it's a combination of both . . . I believe that a closing *includes* emotion. Includes emotion on the part of the closer. But to make a blatant appeal to the jury's emotions? No. I don't think you *can* do that, and you shouldn't do that. I'm talking about legally speaking." Prosecutor

4. "Both . . . When the case is overly brutal and you can't do anything else, then you aim for the heart . . . Depends on the jurors. Some jurors don't have any heart. They all have heads." Criminal Defense

5. "Both . . . in order to get the courage to stand up and look at someone in the eye — or even look up and say, 'Convict this man of first degree murder', and possibly go on to the death penalty — you have to reach the heart . . . The head will justify what the heart wants to do. The head through the heart!" Joseph J. McGill

d) *Depends on case, but prefers a) or b)*

1. "Definitely the intellectual on a case where I think that the evidence should be viewed in that fashion. When I have something that is pretty cold against me, then — pluck on the harp strings, bring in the priests, the rabbis and the character witnesses, and tell the jury that they've got to believe that *they're* liars in order to convict." Criminal Defense

2. "No matter how many trials you've done, there is an emotional element. There are points that cause you to feel a bit more. A particularly gruesome, a particularly savage killing still gets to me. There are times it creeps into a closing." Prosecutor

3. "It depends on the kind of a case. I prefer . . . the intellectual appeal as to the emotional appeal. I don't think I've really ever had a case where I've had to go purely on emotions . . . If I deal anything with emotion in a closing argument, it's towards the system of government, and the pride in country, and a pride that this is the kind of system that we have . . . this is really something beautiful about the country! Then they take their responsibility that much more seriously, because they really feel they're protecting something, and not [just] going along with all the liberals, or helping out the criminals."
Criminal Defense

E. Do you ever use humor
(N=16)

a) *Often*	1	.06
b) *Sometimes*	8	.50
c) *Almost Never*	7	.44

b) *Sometimes*

1. "It's the hardest thing to do . . . Yes, I will try. All through the trial, I'm watching for a place; something a witness said, or something that happened where no one is being hurt, that you can make fun of."

"If you can make a jury smile or laugh a little, why — I think that's an asset."
Fahringer

2. "It depends on the nature of the case. Never, never, never do it in a rape case if you're a male, for example . . . You can't do it if you're of a different background then the victim. You have to show great sympathy for the victim, particularly in a criminal case."
Dershowitz

3. "I like to get them to laugh . . . I want to put them at ease." Lytton

4. "Even though I'm representing people who are tragically injured, I try to take advantage of an opportunity to be funny — which is to be human. It's gotta arise out of the situation. It's gotta be natural. Otherwise I don't want it." Litvin

c) *Almost Never*

1. "I don't consider it a humorous undertaking. There's no humor about a murder."
King

2. "I have stood up in opening statements, and come up with a big laugh. And then I tell them: 'This is the last time you will laugh during the course of this trial, for everything else that will happen is *deadly* serious. We gotta body here.'"

"In the closing speech: 'There is a time for laughter, and a time to be done with laughter. I submit to you, ladies and gentlemen, now is the time. This is not a laughing matter.'" Prosecutor

F. Do you ever disparage the opposing lawyer? (N=12)

a)	*Yes*	4	.33
b)	*No*	8	.67

a) *Yes*

1. "I do not exchange in sidebar with the counsel — unless he slaps my face twice, just on the theory that American juries don't like dirty pool . . . Juries that *I* pick don't like dirty pool. On the other hand, juries *I* pick, if they [other lawyers] slap your face and you turn the other cheek, and they slap *it*, they [the jurors] don't mind if you get back. So they get two slaps on me, and then it's World War III."

"Sometimes I challenge them. I take exception to their failures." Richard Haynes

2. "Yes, if he deserves it . . . You're damn right I'll insult him. But only in a nice way." Criminal Defense

3. "If I've got good solid grounds . . . If you have to land on the other lawyer, do it reluctantly but courageously, or they'll penalize you for it. Jurors don't like that unless there's good warrant." Bailey

b) *No*

1. "No. I don't wanna make that jury think that there's a contest — that if they return a verdict of not-guilty, they're saying the prosecutor was a rotten guy. I really like the jury to recognize that this is a lawyer who has presented a case, and has done the best he can; he just didn't have the facts to go with it. I don't want to make it a personality contest — because I'm liable to lose." Donald J. Goldberg

2. "No. Particularly at this stage in my life, where now I'm no longer the young lawyer in the courtroom. More frequently now, I'm the older lawyer in the courtroom. It was a lot easier, I think, when I was a young kid with a crew cut, and my opponents were old men. Now I'm the old guy, and many of the lawyers are young people, and sometimes their inexperience shows. And I personally would like to help them, because I know many of them and I'm very friendly with them." S. Gerald Litvin

3. "Never. I don't think you gain anything, because you're up there to present your case . . . The case is not about personalities. The case is about evidence, and witnesses, and their demeanor — and you're just a mechanism for presenting evidence in the courtroom." Barbara L. Christie

4. "Never would we, down here, insult the other lawyer. It may be cultural — peculiar to the southern West Virginian community . . . If a lawyer is ugly, and he's rude — that's his problem. And the jury will punish [him]." Stephen P. Meyer

G. Do you experience stage fright or nervousness before summation? (N=33)

a)	*Yes*	13	.39
b)	*Some anticipation*	9	.27
c)	*No*	11	.34

a) *Yes*

1. "Any lawyer who tells you that he doesn't feel anything when he enters into the courtroom is lying to you . . . If my fly wheel is spinning at 6,000 rpms when I open, it's got to be at 6 or above when I sum up." Levy

2. "Do you feel anxiety? Absolutely. Do you feel tension? Yes. Do you feel apprehension? Yes. You try like mad not to show it. It's death to your case in front of a jury to show that." Civil

3. "The lump always comes up . . . It disappears very, very quickly — and I suppose it's proportional to the confidence that I have in my ability in what I'm saying." Criminal Defense

4. "I'm nervous three times during a case. Before giving the opening statement, before giving the closing argument, and right before the verdict . . . Right before the verdict, you're helpless. Right before the giving of the closing speech, the whole trial runs before your eyes, and I would say at least 75% of what I will say, although I have prepared the night before, is centered on what in fact the defense attorney said." Roger King

5. "Yes. Attitudinal and physical pumping up that occurs prior to the final argument . . . it's like somebody getting ready for a fight. The best thing to do if you're gonna fight somebody is stretch." Bailey

b) *Some anticipation*

1. "I'm excited before — but not nervous. I get intense. I get hyperactive — like my adrenalin builds up. I kinda pump myself up, so that when I go in, I will be keyed up and ready to go." Lytton

2. "You always get that twinge in your stomach. And if you don't have the twinge in your stomach, you're not going to give a good speech, because it's gonna come over flat." Frank E. DeSimone

3. "I look forward to doing it." It's anxiety, not stage fright. "The fear is that you will leave something out. Something that you should have mentioned that will convince one juror who will then go the other way." Criminal Defense

c) *No*

1. "Oh no. I love it. I wait the whole trial to get up there . . . I can't get up there fast enough. That's the most important part of the trial." Toro

2. "I used to. It diminishes over the years." Brown

3. "Used to. I'm not so sure nervousness is an asset . . . Jurors pick it up. It's a barrier to communication." The jurors might think: "A nervous lawyer. That s.o.b. has a guilty client." J.R. Carroll

4. "I'm charged up. Not for a summation, but for a trial. I don't feel different for a summation." Richard A. Sprague

H. Are you attentive to the way you dress on the day you sum up? (N=20)

a)	*Yes*	14	.70
b)	*No*	6	.30

a) *Yes*

1. "Conservatively; 'Sincere Blue' . . . Yellow [informant points to yellow shirt he is wearing] is a little too happy for that somber responsibility." Bailey

2. "I'm the kinda person — and I guess all trial lawyers are — I'm always conscious of my image. I'm always very aware of what I look like, and what other people are thinking about it — or what I *want* them to think about it, and using it to manipulate. . ."

"I usually, for a closing, dress a little more formally. I usually dress in all black and white, or something like that . . . It seems like the jury is entitled to connect you up a little bit with those people on television." Criminal Defense and Prosecutor

3. "I have a reaction against the sling of blue suits that arise on opening day of the trial; on closing day of the trial . . . you can walk into a courtroom where you've got six lawyers, and everyone of them is in a blue suit." Goldberg

4. "I think dressing is extremely important. I think the way that you look is very, very important . . . and especially as a woman. You have to dress in a manner that they're gonna have confidence in you." Criminal Defense

5. "All I really want to do is continue a pattern which I hoped I've established of being

well dressed in a clean, well-pressed suit, with a clean shirt and a clean tie, and something which is a little different from that which I wore the day before." Rutter

3.3 Women in the act of summing-up:

A. Are women different from men in effect in the courtroom? (N=12)

a) *No, or yes — but in a positive way*	8	.67
b) *Yes — and in a negative way*	4	.33

a) *No, or yes — but in a positive way*

1. "The ones that are good are very good. There's a difference between being good and being effective. One of the best trial lawyers in the office is (Ms. X). One of the most effective trial lawyers in the office is (Ms. Y). But you can't compare Y to X as trial lawyers. What you have to look at is the end result. They both win cases — in their own fashion."

"It does matter if you're male or female . . . I think one of the most effective methods a female lawyer has is her femininity, her softness, and her approach to the subject matter. However, with the new thought of liberation . . . some people mistake being obnoxious to being tough, and I don't particularly care for the 'macho', 'one of the guys' approach. And a very subtle thing about Ms. X — she is completely business-like, and cool. She has a chilling effect, but she's extremely feminine in her own way." Prosecutor

2. "There are differences, particularly with the jury. Women are expected to argue somewhat differently than men." Dershowitz

3. "They're great. Equal for equal, they're so damn much better!" Preiser

4. "I think a closing is genderless. Or it should be . . . I don't perceive any difference." Ms. X

5. "I can't think of a reason why women can't try cases, or do anything else as well as or better than men." Litvin

6. "I would want to simply be professional; to then hopefully forget the fact that I am a woman, or I'm black or white, or anything. 'I'm a lawyer, and I have a client, and that's the most important thing to me right now, and it ought to be the most important thing to you.'"

"Of the women that I've seen in a courtroom, the worst mistake that women make is being too masculine, or over-aggressive. I'm not saying that all women do that, but of those that I think really handle themselves poorly in front of a jury, it was to come off too tough. And that can turn almost anybody off." Woman Criminal Defense

b) *Yes — and in a negative way*

1. "There are very few women at the criminal bar, and I haven't got a lot of regard for most of them that I'm familiar with. Some of them have, to be sure, decent reputations. Whether they're deserved or not, I can't tell you." Criminal Defense

2. "There isn't a top trial lawyer whose a female that I know of. . . Some of the young ladies who are trying to be trial lawyers are trying to be too masculine."
Defense Attorney

3. "I frankly don't think much of them. I don't like women lawyers, except in a very limited sense. First of all, they're too good . . . and too detailed . . . They'll take the time to do the details . . . I don't think they give a better closing argument. I don't think they can go for the jugular. The jury wants to see reality." Defense Attorney

4. "Women have an innate talent that's peculiar and particular to the feminine species in that they have tunnel vision — concentration — and they're not as easily distracted as their male counterparts."

"In closing, they're not as evangelical, they're not as likely to get off on the histrionics, they're not as likely to utilize the full range of the voice, the full range of the body in the closing argument. I think the man is freer to wave arms, to pound on tables . . . I think the woman is constrained to some extent. If she gets too rambunctious, she might lose her most prized audience — that being a jury. She has to be more lady-like than a man has to be a gentleman."

"They have their material totally prepared; outlined. And it's almost as though it's memorized. They can get off into it — but without the same kind of fervor, and zeal, and gyration that a male can. You can't get a woman to be an effective communicator in the same way — cause it just doesn't come across in the same way."
Defense Attorney

B. Does being female in a traditionally male arena make a difference to you?

Seven of the eight women informants responded 'Yes'

1. "Of course. Once you get to the point where you know you can do it, being a woman can be a real advantage, because it's startling to people still. They're not enough of us, and if you agree with me that your main job is to get their attention and then do something useful with it, if you're startling and then you're engaging, you're way up on somebody who is neither startling or engaging."

2. "I think women *cannot* forget that they're women when they're talking to a jury . . . because the jury never forgets it."

"Women have to careful about voice modulation . . . I think a high voice is very irritating. You don't want to be squeaking at the jury. You want to be very careful that your movements don't distract from what you're saying . . . I think they expect women to be graceful."
"I think that expectations of women is higher — period! Including from a jury, from a judge, from a boss, from an everything. Because I think they're more closely scrutinized."

3. "I don't think you should try to out-man a man. I don't think you should go in there and downplay the fact that you're a woman."

4. "Sometimes I try and use it [being a woman]. Common sense would tell us that if the victim in a murder case was a woman, and you're the prosecutor and you're a woman, you should get as many women as possible on the jury, and get some subliminal message going: 'We're gonna get this bastard by the balls and put him away forever.' But it doesn't always work!"

C. Are you attentive to the way you dress in the courtroom — with an awareness of being a woman?
(N=8 Women)

a)	*Yes*	7	.875
b)	*No*	1	.125

a) *Yes*

1. "I want to look 'business like', but I'll be damned if I want to look like every one of those — we're turning out all those little women lawyers that all look alike now."

"I'm the kinda person — and I guess all trial lawyers are — I'm always conscious of my image. I'm always very aware of what I look like, and what other people are thinking about it — or what I *want* them to think about it, and using it to manipulate . . . "

2. "You have to be mindful of how you dress . . . I still think there's resistance to some extent — maybe not conscious resistance — they're not expecting to see a woman trying a case."

"I'm not even sure that women should wear suits when trying a case. Women should wear dresses . . . very graceful, very becoming, and doesn't look like she's trying to look like a man; the jury doesn't want to see these women in there who dress up like men. I would never wear sling-back heels, or high heels, or poorly groomed heels. They notice everything. I think you have to be very, very discreet with your jewelry."

3. "I think dressing is extremely important. I think the way that you look is very, very important — and especially as a woman . . . You have to dress in a manner that they're gonna have confidence in you. I don't think women should go in there — well, I don't have this problem! — trying to be some kinda sex symbol."

4. "It's extremely boring to have women showing up in court looking exactly like the men lawyers."

5. "I always try to be a lady. But that's the way I was raised . . . Be tailored — not frilly."

6. "I usually, for a closing, dress a little more formally. I usually dress in all black and white, or something like that . . . I don't wear suits. I used to wear pantsuits. But not now."

3.4 Lawyers' views of the receivers (jurors) of the closing speech:

A. Do you have a high or low regard for jurors and the jury system? (N=34)

a)	*Very high*	22	.65
b)	*Ambivalent*	7	.20
c)	*Low*	5	.15

a) *Very high regard*

1. "They're like an insurance policy; it's like paying premiums. It's a pain in the neck to pay the premiums, but they sure as hell protect you against terrible disasters."

"I think the jury is essential in a heterogeneous society. It's no accident that the jury has received its highest status in the most heterogeneous country in the history of the world. Because we don't have a common goal in our legal system that can be achieved by judges just sitting there and applying the common morality. We don't have a common morality."

When asked about studies that imply jurors are not bright enough to handle the facts in civil cases: "I think that's right for the most part. And I think that's a great protection [against] judges who aren't bright enough to handle the facts . . . if you're going to have a weakness, it's better to have it in the jury than on the bench."

Alan M. Dershowitz

2. "I have an absolute, 100% regard in the perfection of the jury system . . . there is absolutely nothing that a jury can do that is wrong. Nothing. Cause whatever they do, it is the verdict — it is the law. It doesn't matter how right you are — how good you are. If it doesn't happen in the jury box, it doesn't happen in the courtroom. It just doesn't exist. If they don't agree that you win, you don't win. No matter what." Magarity

3. "It's a very unique, very special entity that is not duplicated anywhere else . . . They want to do the right thing. They want to base their decision on truth." Litvin

4. "I don't know of anybody who says it's perfect — the system. I don't know of anybody who says the way we get jurors is perfect. I don't know of anybody who says the jurors themselves are perfect. But I do know this: it's the best goddamned system human wisdom has been able, thus far, to devise." Levy

5. "Absolutely! I think they're right 99 times out of 100 . . . maybe more! I really think they're conscientious. Their conscientiousness never ceases to astound me . . . I think the jurors really listen to the facts. They really pay attention." Thomas A. Bergstrom

6. "They probably reach the right decision in 90% of the cases. I think they seldom if ever convict an innocent person . . . and sometimes a guilty person will be acquitted." Ronald F. Kidd

7. "In a jury trial, the most important thing is the jury. The jury is first, evidence is second — and everything else is conversation." McGill

8. "You're going to get a much fairer trial if you're gonna get a jury trial. And I think a defendant has a much better chance of getting acquitted before a jury than before a judge, because juries — they really take that seriously . . . For the most part, they want to believe that the person didn't do it, so they really, really try to acquit. That's what they want to do. It makes them happier if they can do something like that. I don't think anyone wants to send anybody to jail, or find anybody guilty of anything." Jean Purnell

9. "I'm always amazed that in the most highly publicized cases, where there's so much pressure on the jury to return a verdict of guilty, they often will not . . . That seems to me to be a sign that the jury system works." Carolyn E. Temin

10. "We don't have, generally, intellectual jurors [in West Virginia]. What we do have are people who are hard-working, middle-class people — who have worked all their lives. And they sense when somebody's lying to them; they sense when somebody's really injured; they sense when somebody deserves something. And if they can give it to them, they will." Meyer

11. "The jury is an absolute, fool-proof detector of B.S." Haynes

b) *Ambivalent*

1. "For the most part, they're capable. But I think that they do bring into the jury box an awful lot more bias and prejudice than they admit. I think that many of them try, through their jury service, to do what they can about cleaning up crime. I think all too often this puts them on the side of law enforcement — and that's not their job." Fitzpatrick

2. "Today, with the complex litigation, I wonder if the complexity of the litigation is not beginning to outrun the intellectual capacity of some jurors." Criminal Defense

3. "The thing that can be disheartening at times is when you're a language enthusiast and then you find yourself deliberately composing a summation that is almost like writing a newspaper article, in the simplest of language, so that a twelve year old will understand it — and that seems to me to be a waste of skills." Criminal Defense

4. "I think that the jury system is the worst possible, conceivable system. But I don't know of a better one . . . it's amazing that they usually discern the issues." Peruto

5. I have an "uneven" opinion of jurors. "Sometimes they see things; sometimes they don't understand what's going on . . . and jurors don't tell the truth on voir dire." David Rudovsky

6. ". . . I have a hand in selecting them, so I usually have a fair opinion of them . . . Jurors chronically deny having an opinion when they have one, because they're embarrassed to admit they're small enough to pre-judge an issue. Those that honestly deny it may have a subconscious opinion, which very rarely is in favor of the defendant." Bailey

c) *Low regard*

1. "I have a very poor opinion of juries. I think it's probably a terrible system that we're straddled with — but I can't think of a better one . . . Jurors lie; they lie constantly. And then they're expected to pass upon the credibility of witnesses. How much more hypocritical could you be?" Criminal Defense

2. "I'm not that impressed with the general population of citizens. I think they are generally uninformed and uneducated . . . and amazingly so." Prosecutor

3. "I used to, incorrectly, assume a certain amount of intellectual integrity on the part of jurors. And they used to disappoint me, because their reactions were emotional. [Now] I don't assume they can put two and two together and get four. I spell it out." Criminal Defense

4. "In general, the quality of jurors is a poor quality, and the level of performance is at a lower level that the law would like to concede." Criminal Defense

B. What kinds of persons do you prefer as jurors?

Below are listed some of the more salient responses:

Younger
Sane
Depends on the case
Intelligent
Women

Non-authoritative
Those who will listen
Doesn't think you can predict effective jurors
Has no feel for selecting jurors

Comments:

1. "You almost could find a case where any kind of person could be, for that particular case, a good juror." Richard A. Sprague

2. "In most cases, I want a jury that's going to understand the law, because the facts — they can probably all understand." Judith Rubino

3. "I'm looking for people who will not try to think themselves out of a decision . . . the private detective group . . . [but] be willing to accept the law, and [have] the courage to apply it."

"People who have a stake in the community." Joseph J. McGill

4. "I try to pick intelligent jurors because I think I relate better with them, and because I think for the most part intelligent people are happier with their station in life, and the cards that have been dealt them by fate, [and] are not as likely to visit their own problems on the poor soul in the dock." Richard Haynes

5. "Most of my clients are men, and I think women tend to be better listeners, tend to be more sympathetic, tend to be more deliberate." Thomas A. Bergstrom

6. "I don't particularly like men jurors . . . They're not as fair as women. Women are much better jurors in any kind of case, with one exception. Self-defense cases. I think that men understand the law of self-defense. As far as they're concerned, if somebody does something to you, you have a right to hit 'em back. That's the way men were trained from the day they were raised. And older people are usually good jurors too, because they've lived a good life and don't wanna see anybody else get hurt."

Criminal Defense

7. "I'm looking for liberal, non-authoritarian personalities. People with some kind of sympathy for other people's problems. People who are not rigid; people who are not going to accept — just accept the word of a cop. I want the opposite."

Criminal Defense

8. "If you take twelve people off the streets, just give me [ones with] an open mind. As my father said, 'Just listen. If you're willing to listen, I'll convince you.'"

Roger E. King

9. "I don't think you can say 'this type of juror', or a juror from this background, or a juror who's in this profession is an 'absolute no-no', or a 'gotta-have-em' type juror."

Christie

10. "The kinds of people I can sense I wouldn't mind sitting down and having a drink with. Now I'm never going to find more than three or four on any jury who meet those criteria; but those three or four will always swing the verdict. It's a minority of the jury that controls the verdict. If you win them, you've won the case."

"If I have a good case . . . I would prefer bright people. If I have anything to argue about, they'll sell the best; they'll discipline the best. If I get a bad case, you want the dumbest jury in the world." Bailey

C. Do you think there is a relationship between liking someone and believing them? Do you try to get the jurors to like you?
(N=32)

a)	*Absolutely*	20	.62
b)	*Yes (with reservation)*	6	.19
c)	*no*	6	.19

a) *Absolutely*

1. "Absolutely. It's probably the single most important factor of a lawyer's responsibility in a jury trial . . . If that jury doesn't like you, you are going to lose. They are going to find a way to rule against you."

"'Liking' is the single most important factor. The second factor is the facts." Toro

2. "Absolutely. If they don't like you, they're less likely to have any confidence in you, or listen to what you're saying. You have to try and make them like you. You just have to. I suppose they could find someone guilty or not guilty depending on what side you're on if they didn't like you. It's gonna make your job much harder. So whatever way you can get the jury to like you, I think it's important. And if they don't like you, if there's something about you that you think the jury might hold against you, whatever it is, I think you should bring it to their attention and put them on the defensive. You know — like, 'Say, hey, I'm fat. And maybe you don't like fat people. But don't base your case on the fact that you don't like fat people. Base it on evidence.'" Criminal Defense

3. "In so many cases, a juror never really gets to hear the defendant . . . so they have no vehicle to relate to that guy with, except his lawyer. And if they like his lawyer, they might like him, even though they've never heard a word from him . . . I've gotta hope that there is some association." Bergstrom

4. "You improve your chances of success if the jury likes you, finds you pleasant and appealing. So that my conduct in the courtroom, to a great extent, is designed to try and encourage that kind of affection." Fahringer

5. "'Courting' is an important part of being a lawyer." Dershowitz

6. "Absolutely, they must like you. Because how can you be persuaded by someone you don't like? . . . I like to make love to a jury." Preiser

7. "A lawyer has to 'lock on' to a jury, eyeball to eyeball. Maybe a juror at a time. And I think that the lawyer who doesn't do that is deficient. I don't think that's prostituting. I don't think the guy's whoring when he does that. His purpose is to persuade a jury of the validity of his position. You can't make friends with somebody by calling them names." Civil

8. "It's my considered opinion that juries react more in line with whether they favor the lawyer rather than the client. And if they trust and like the lawyer, and are entertained in a proper sense, that they will . . . give the verdict to the lawyer, rather than the individual . . . I've never seen a jury do anything for anybody where they hated his lawyer." Peruto

9. "The whole bit about coaching, dressing — it still comes down to, 'Do they like you? Do they like the side that you are representing?' And you can spend thousands on research, and if they answer the question [that] they don't like you — they don't like your side, you're not gonna win!" King

10. "A lawyer who contends that he or she does not put their best foot forward is not being totally honest . . . Your obligation is to be professional, and to advance the cause of your client in the best light that the parameters of the law permit." Haynes

b) *Yes (with reservation)*

1. "I think that's a plus. But what I try to do is avoid the negative. What I try to do is not have the jury dislike me . . . It's important that they respect what you're trying to do . . . respect the sincerity, and the image of what you're trying to do." McGill

2. "Yes. But they could decide in your favor even if they didn't like you."
Diane M. Nast

3. "I believe that jurors sitting in a jury box today compare us either consciously or unconsciously with the lawyers they see on television. Therefore, they expect us to be reasonably well-dressed; they expect us to be able to speak in complete sentences; they expect us to know, sort of, what we're doing in the courtroom, and not be fumblers and stumble bums . . . It's a negative correlation: if they don't like you, it's much harder for them to vote in favor of your client. If they do like you, it doesn't mean that they're necessarily going to vote in favor of your client." Thomas B. Rutter

c) *No*

1. "I don't really want them [the jurors] to be my friend, or like me. I don't care what they think about me as far as being a decent guy or a bad guy — as long as they have respect for what I do in the courtroom, and my client's rights."

"It is not an aim of mine to make them like me so they will therefore believe me. I would like to make them believe me because my story has the ring of truth, and I'm able to put it across well to them. Respect is far more important to me than liking."

Fitzpatrick

2. "I hope juries really don't worry about personalities of the attorneys. The judges tell them, you know, that they shouldn't, and I hope that they're smart enough not to. There's too much at stake . . . If they like me, that's great. But that's not what I'm gearing in for."

Rubino

3. "You want them to respect you. Affection doesn't win verdicts. Respect does."

Bailey

D. Do you believe in using social scientists for selecting jurors? (N=12)

a) *Yes*	6	.50
b) *No*	6	.50

a) *Yes*

1. "I believe in buying those brains, if I can afford them, and if my client can afford them, and if the case warrants it."

"I believe it's absolutely essential, and damn near malpractice [if you don't use them] . . . I would be willing to testify that in most major cases, if the lawyer has it available to him, and doesn't use it, I would consider that a deviation from the required standard of care of a lawyer."

Preiser

2. "I think they're very helpful . . . This is another tool, a recently developed tool, a psychological tool, and it seems to me that the lawyer's under an obligation to use every tool that will help his client, just as much as he's under an obligation to research what the law is."

Levy

b) *No*

1. "Bull feathers! You tell me when you're gonna have another person be able to fathom anybody else's mind to determine how they're gonna react — even how they felt about a past situation — let alone how they're gonna react to a future situation. I'll take good old horse sense from an experienced trial attorney over a 'jury picker' any day!"

Christie

2. "In the federal court system, it really doesn't work very well, because you [the lawyer] are not permitted to voir dire the jury. The judge asks the questions."

"Some people have sat there with a psychologist or psychiatrist at their side, looking at the jurors. I don't like the appearance of that. I think that if I were a juror, I might resent it. And I don't have an awful lot of confidence in their ability to pick a jury any better than I can . . . I think that given that body [32 jurors in a pool] to pick from, I think I'll make as good a selection as I would with ten experts." Goldberg

3. "No, I don't have any confidence in that . . . In civil cases, we don't even select a jury. We say we're selecting a jury, but there is no selectivity involved . . . All I'm able to do is strike out three or four names, to eliminate three or four people that I'm least comfortable with, or who may worry me most. I don't call that selection . . . it's elimination."

"The striking of several jurors, which is all I get to do in this process, is the one single aspect of jury trials in which I have absolute humility. I've never believed that I really have any insight into what I'm doing . . . But I would not surrender that judgment to anyone else. I wouldn't surrender it to a psychologist; I wouldn't surrender it to my client; I wouldn't surrender it to co-counsel." Litvin

4. "I'm unpersuaded . . . An off-the-cuff public opinion which a poll will pick up does not survive once the juror finds out the enormity of the responsibility that's been dumped on him. The jurors' attitudes change during the trial, and we wipe out those superficial, knee-jerk responses . . . We turn you into a different person . . . If a client wants to pay for it, I won't resist it." Bailey

E. Do you think that jurors should be allowed to take notes? (N=16)

a) *Yes*	10	.63
b) *No*	5	.31
c) *Not certain*	1	.06

a) *Yes*

1. "I like it when a juror takes notes, because then I know what they're thinking about. I get some kind of feedback." Meyer

2. "Why shouldn't they be allowed to take notes? As long as they understand the note-taking process is not the gospel, and they sometimes make mistakes on what they hear and what they write. And as long as they're instructed by the court in the true use and meaning of the notes. The judge takes notes!" Preiser

3. "Very much in favor of it. The nonsense that a juror can remember all this evidence while the judge and all the lawyers have to write it down is just — nonsense. Good judges will let jurors take notes." Bailey

b) *No*

1. "I don't like it at all. Most often they don't know what's important, and they can get

so caught up in taking notes, that they're not listening; they're not watching. Observing someone as they speak is very important, and if you're taking notes . . . you're not watching [the speaker]." Pamela W. Higgins

2. "For the speaker, it's distracting . . . You loose your eye contact. I prefer they not take notes." Fahringer

3.5 Content of the closing speech:

A. The topics which were mentioned most often as being included in the closing speech, influenced by the side of the case on which the lawyer argues.

Reasonable doubt (Criminal Defense)
Using your 'good common sense'
Pain and suffering (Civil)
Discussion of what witnesses said
Patriotism
God
Presumption of innocence (Criminal Defense)
Burden of proof (Criminal Defense)
Defender reminds jurors that the prosecution has the last word (speech)
Quoting information which the lawyer knows will be conveyed by the judge in his or her charge to the jury which will follow
A discussion centered around what the speaker guesses the opposing lawyer will discuss
About a witness who did not testify (Criminal Defense)
Discussion of 'type of witness' one had to call to witness stand
"If you don't like me, don't hold it against my client." (Defense)

Comments:

1. "The whole reasonable doubt speech is basically the same every time I give it. I like it. I think it's effective. I've improved upon it over the years." Defense Attorney

2. What I say about my witnesses: "'A witness is a witness is a witness . . . I can't apologize for *what* I call. I don't choose my witnesses. The circumstance dictates who I will call; what they will say.'" King

3. "I always pitch the American system, the bible, God . . . I always talk about the history of the jury system, and tell them that they're performing a God-given function. That this is the greatest duty a citizen can perform — to sit in judgment of his fellow man; and that 'you have the liberty of a person at stake, and that the only other person who does this is God on judgment day.'" Defense Attorney

4. "I try to quote from the judge's charge . . . Then I will read exactly what that charge is, knowing that the judge, when he gives the charge, will repeat the exact same lan-

guage. It's a reinforcement principle." Kidd

5. "I try, in closing argument, to anticipate the closing argument of the prosecutor — because they're gonna have the last word — and I wanna take some of the sting from what I can anticipate they're gonna say." Haynes

6. I open with a discussion on how they perform their function as jurors, "that they are entitled to say that the defendant had been represented by a bad lawyer, or by a lawyer who had done bad things, but they should put that out of their minds. 'That has no bearing on the guilt or innocence of Mr. X.'" Rutter

7. "If a defendant is not on the stand, I say the same thing to them every time; about why he's not on the stand, and that they should not consider that, and that it would be a violation of their oaths if they think about it or even mention it in the jury room — and that the judge will tell them that." Goldberg

B. Do you have a usual way of opening or closing your final argument? (N=21)

a) *Yes*	17	.81
b) *No*	4	.19

a) *Yes — Opening the closing*

1. "'This is reality. This is not fantasy. This is not a play. This is not a television show. There's no director telling you to cut. They're no re-takes. You see all of the warts here. We can't solve crimes in a half hour with time out for commercials.'" King

2. "I always say, 'May it please the court; counsel for the defense'; If I have a co-counsel I acknowledge him; 'Ladies and Gentlemen of the jury.' I do that for two reasons. Number one, it shows to me that I'm not going to fall over in a dead fright, and I can actually speak, and words are coming out of my mouth. And it's a way to just start talking. And number two is, I think it plays on the anticipation of the jury that this is an important event." Lytton

3. "'Ladies and Gentlemen of the jury, it's my pleasure to talk with you. I wish you could talk back with me. So let's have a one-sided conversation, and when you get back in that jury room, you talk for me.'" Preiser

4. "I like to start serious and end serious — with the frivolous, funny, snotty or snide in the middle." Criminal Defense

5. "Before I start any statement to any jury; 'You just listened to the biggest bunch of garbage for a month that one could imagine.'" Criminal Defense

Yes — Closing the closing

1. "'You have the last word here. You have the last two words.'" Criminal Defense

2. "One thing I believe very deeply is when you get to the end of your summation, I think it should be uplifting. The end of the summation should be inspiring." Fahringer

3. Talked about 'staging' the last thing he says to the jury: "Oh, I almost forgot . . ." Criminal Defense

4. "I know that most of the good defense closings have been based on reasonable doubt, and what I would like to do is make some kind of reference to that at the end of my closing that will make it somewhat more difficult for them to come back and wrap themselves in reasonable doubt." Prosecutor

5. "I usually close by telling them that it's a very difficult thing to represent someone. And I ask for forgiveness for my own inadequacies — if I've forgotten something — and I ask them to be *my* lawyer, collectively — 'that if I've forgotten to bring something out that you remember, please tell your fellow jurors.'" Peruto

6. "At the end of the speech you have to reach a crescendo . . . As a prosecutor in a first degree murder case, you're going to ask them to put the man to death, or you're going to ask them to come back with the verdict of murder in the first degree . . . You have to give them courage." DeSimone

7. "I usually try and tie it somehow into God . . . May God aid them in their deliberations. Or, 'It's now in the hands of God.'" Criminal Defense

b) *No*

1. "I may start off with some attention getting thing. I frequently sympathize with the way jurors get pushed around . . . I like to try and let 'em know that I think of them as intelligent human beings who have an important role to play." J. R. Carroll

2. "No. For example, in closing in Abscam, my opening was 'Bullshit!'" Brown

C. Do you thank the jurors for their jury service? (N=13)

a) *Yes*	6	.46
b) *No*	7	.54

a) *Yes*

1. "I always start out by thanking them for their kind attention — even if they fell asleep in the middle of the trial and stayed asleep." Peruto

2. "I thank the jurors — very quickly and courteously. I do not slaver over them as some lawyers do . . . I don't thank them for their attention during the trial because they're required to give their attention. And I think, to an intelligent person, that looks a little phoney." Bailey

b) *No*

1. No, but might say something like, "'Sure — it's been an ordeal. Sure — we're not asking you to do something easy . . . you're deciding on a life and death situation.'" King

2. "I think that's bullshit." Criminal Defense

D. Do you like to use metaphors, stories, poetry, biblical or literary quotations? (N=34)

a)	*Yes — at least occasionally*	17	.50
b)	*No*	17	.50

a) *Yes*

1. "When that jury is selected, then I understand whether I'm going to quote Shakespeare, or I'm going to talk about 'Dallas'. And I can't talk about 'Dallas' to the college professors, nor can I talk about Shakespeare to the butchers. And if I do, I'm wasting an hour up there." DeSimone

2. "Oh, yes . . . For example, 'It was Carl Sandburg who said the best witness is a written piece of paper' . . . I think you can reinforce arguments with quotations from great men." Fahringer

3. "I use some quotes in summation in criminal cases because I think it is necessary to give the jury some courage. A jury needs courage to do the job." Preiser

4. "When you use quotes, the jury starts paying a little more attention." David Rudovsky

Yes — Metaphors

1. "Metaphors, analogies, examples . . . that can make all these rules more meaningful for them. I think a lawyer's skill has to be devoted to . . . the effective use of language . . . Language is still the most powerful of all human forces, and we make our living working with words." Fahringer

2. "Metaphors; that's one of the King trademarks. I like to use appropriate metaphors that relate to people — that people can relate to." King

3. A standard metaphor I use: "I have often said to the jury that if they believe a certain piece of evidence to be true, or for a witness to have testified truthfully, then I suggest to them that they also oughta go back to believing in the Easter Bunny . . . or Santa Claus." Rutter

Yes — Biblical quotes

1. "I have been guilty of quoting the bible to jurors . . . I've never felt totally comfortable doing it, because for each quote the defense can give, the prosecution can go to the Old Testament and get you some dandies . . . so that's a two way street."

"The jurors take an oath to God. I don't see anything, per se, reprehensible about a reference to the deity in so solemn a proceeding as a trial in a criminal case." Haynes

2. "I have been known to quote biblical phrases to make a point!" King

3. Yes, "I believe what I'm saying." Rutter

b) *No*

1. "I rarely quote anything. I might plagiarize. I mean, I might say what someone else has said as if it were my own." Criminal Defense

2. "I don't normally do it . . . it tends to be hokey if you don't do it right — and I'm not sure I could do it without being hokey. So I don't." Lytton

3. "I don't want to read from the bible because I don't particularly believe in the bible, and I think it's hypocritical. And I don't think it's proper to make references to something that you don't believe in because — it's just wrong!" Criminal Defense

3.6 Methods employed for the speech event summation:

A. When do you begin working on the summation? (N=34)

a)	*When I take the case*	23	.68
b)	*Just before*	8	.23
c)	*Other*	3	.09

a) *When I take the case*

1. "Usually the whole case is geared into my jury speech . . . It's like a Bach fugue. There is a theory about Bach fugues. That Bach wrote all the stretti first, and worked backwards. In a Bach fugue, a stretto is when all the voices come together. And the Bach stretti just work; they just always work; and people marvel at them . . . and in a

way, I compose my case backwards." Temin

2. "The day the client walks in the office, I open up a file called Argument, and I start throwing 3 x 5 cards in it . . . Because I really see the importance of the closing and the importance of early preparation to a good closing. And it's a simple thing to do; just start jotting your closing thoughts down as you go along." Goldberg

3. "I begin working on summation when the referral lawyer calls me and brings a client in with potential claim . . . In that process of interviewing a client to make judgments as to whether that case turns me on, whether I subjectively believe what my client says — which in civil litigation is very important to me — I don't accept a case if I don't believe the client. In making all those assessments as to the merits of the case, whether it's exciting, what the potential value is, that's when I start making my preparations for my closing. And I mean that very literally. I could taste the closing argument by the time I finish interviewing the client . . . However, it's the trial itself which gives the final substance to the closing argument." Litvin

4. "At the interview, [when] the client comes in for the first time, I listen to the problem, analyze the case, and prepare the summation — and then try to steer the case to fit the summation — or discount that which won't fit into my theory of summation. Highlight that which will. Because, as I said in the beginning, I view the trial as merely an excuse to make a summation." Peruto

5. Before you pick the first juror: "You have to know where you're headed, so you know who you want to take with you." Maguigan

6. "You've got to have a theory of the case. Ergo, you start to think about the closing, i.e., the theory, how it all organizes, almost from the very beginning." Rutter

7. "If you don't tone the trial effectively in your opening to the jury, so that your summation is a continuation of that specific address, then you're making a terrible mistake."
James M. La Rossa

b) *Just before*

1. "There is no time when that happens, because the whole trial is a series of events leading to a closing argument, and it's constantly being molded and adjusted. But I don't decide on what it is 'til the prosecutor sits down. Because I must do two things. I must give my position, and rip his apart." Bailey

2. "I don't write mine out. I make notes . . . The night before. It would be difficult to do it before that because usually you don't know what the defense is presenting until the day before." Prosecutor — Rubino

c) *Other*

1. "Just before the trial." Kidd

2. Two minutes before he makes it, he couldn't tell you what he was going to say. "I make my summation . . . as I speak." He has parameters of where he's going "that give me the flexibility to decide, when I'm following my opponent's speech, what I think has been the effect of his speech, what is the best way to counter what he said. Should I do it immediately? Should I do it later? How?" Sprague

3. "I may have given it some thought the night before, but I'm really putting it together while I'm doing it." Levy

B. Do you include the client in the preparation of the summation? (Or for prosecutors, do you consult with other lawyers?) (N=29)

a)	*Yes*	5	.17
b)	*Depends on the case*	3	.10
c)	*No*	21	.73

a) *Yes*

1. "I will always ask a client if there's anything special, from their perception, that needs to be said; that they want said by me. I am the spokesperson for the team. I am the guy doin' the talkin'. I'm the mouthpiece. And if you're the client and you want something said, you are at least entitled to tell me about it. I may reject it if I think it's off the wall and out of hand. But it's amazing; many times clients have things that they know need to be said — and you do . . . They are in the dock; It's their life." Haynes

2. "Yes, I often ask them. When I have bright clients, whether they're lawyers or not, I always ask them to give me their thoughts as to what ought to be said to the jury. There's nothing lost by it. Because many of the people I represent have been lawyers, it comes easily to them. Whether they're lawyers or not, in recent years they've been very, very bright. I've never failed to at least get some idea from a client, and it helps the client to know that he's participating in the trial, and that he's doing something other than sitting there like a bump on a log." Goldberg

3. "Yes, the vast majority of my criminal cases are for lawyers — prosecutors, [criminal] lawyers and judges. I usually have that lawyer, or the judge, sit down and write what they would say to the jury. Not that I necessarily pay very much attention to it, but one, it gives them some participation in the trial; keeps them busy; makes them think they're helping . . . I don't think I have ever used anything a client has ever written. And I have never had a non-lawyer participate in the summation . . . I don't ask in civil cases." Preiser

4. "You have to. Who else is looking with that same kind of rigid concern at the jury the same way you are?" Maguigan

b) *Depends on the case*

1. "Depending on his position in society. I would not sit down and review with the Boston Strangler what I was going to argue in his behalf. When I'm defending a lawyer, I would never fail to do that. Because you can never include everything, and if he's fixated on something he thinks is critical, whether I do or not, I'll fit it in there if I can without disrupting the whole structure." Bailey

c) *No*

1. "No. I always feel he's . . . the last person who knows what I should put in summation, because of his emotion and lack of objectivity." Kidd

C. Do you memorize any portion of your closing speech? (N=30)

a)	*Yes — at least some part*	5	.17
b)	*No*	25	.83

a) *Yes — at least some part*

1. "That part of the summation [the end], which may well be the most memorable, probably is the one part that ought to be committed to memory. You don't want to ever run the risk that you stumble there, or that you'll lose your place . . . That part which may run for five minutes, I know pretty well by heart. I worked at it very hard for emphasis." Fahringer

2. "I always memorize an opening, and I always memorize a closing. And much of the rest of it I will have been over so many times that it's really almost the same as memorization . . . The thoughts are there. It's not like a script that requires that you get every word in the same marching order. The *thoughts* are clearly committed to memory. There's not a conscious effort to memorize. There is in the beginning of the closing . . . I always know where I'm starting out, and where I'm getting out." Goldberg

3. "I memorize the material that I want to lean on most heavily." Bailey

b) *No*

1. "No — because it's an impromptu, extemporaneous kind of thing. You go with the feel." King

2. "Never. I like things to be fresh when I sell the jury something." DeSimone

3. "I've tried, but I always end up changing . . . I have a really good idea of what I'm gonna say without memorizing it. And usually it comes out the same as I had planned it, or close to what I had planned." Purnell

D. If there are several defense attorneys representing several clients, when do you prefer to give your summation: first, middle, last, doesn't matter? (N=27)

a)	*First*	8	.30
b)	*Last*	13	.48
c)	*Other responses*	6	.22

a) *First*

1. "I like to go first . . . That 'reasonable doubt' statement is very, very significant, and I think the first time they get it is the only time they're really going to pay attention to it. So that I think it has to be done right. And since I am in the habit of making a prepared closing, that I've worked on as the case has gone along, I invariably find myself in a situation where I think I will make it better than everybody else. And so I wanna go first to make it."

"I think I can set the tone better than most lawyers that I'm accustomed to seeing in courtrooms. If I was with somebody who I thought was as good as I am, and could do all those things just as well, I'd still wanna go first, because I'd wanna be the one who'd said it to the jury."

"I think that the best lawyer in the courtroom oughta be up there first — because he'll set the tone better than anyone else. And I think your second best oughta close." Goldberg

2. "It's better to go first. With multiple defendants, by the time you go last, they've heard everything, and they're really not paying attention." Kidd

3. "If I open first, and the others are only going to stick in something for their clients, then I'll carry the ball for the whole case. If I close — among the defense lawyers . . . I have the disadvantage of a tired jury (it tires you out to sit and listen to that nonsense), but the ability to clean up afterwards . . . Normally it's better to go first, because one doesn't like to walk all over the ground that they have used up." Bailey

b) *Last*

1. "Last. In my case, that's pure egotism. Sure, I know a lot of lawyers probably would say 'we want first' because of the primacy — or the lack of redundancy . . . but I happen to believe that the essence of persuasion is redundancy. Now what happens to the three hams that are squeezed between the two pieces of bread in the sandwich; to wit, the multiple defendants, referring to the three lawyers as hams? Deciding who goes first or

last is usually the ego trip between the three. Most of 'em wanna go last because they're so good — and I admit it; that they're gonna pick up the ball where everybody else dropped it. And that's exactly why I wanna go last . . . because nine times out of ten, I'll do a better job of summing up than they. Now, if I were with a lawyer though that I had high regard for, and thought he could do a better job at summing up than I, I'd leave it to him. But I've never had a co-defendant represented by a really good lawyer, except once, and that was Edward Bennett Williams . . ."

"I'll make that jury alert and fresh. I've never had a juror close an eye on me. I don't have that problem. They know they'd better not look down, or close their eyes when I'm talkin' to 'em. I'll intimidate them to that extent — by sheer force . . . I move around a great deal. I make the courtroom come alive . . . The jury and I, we move together, even with our eyes." Criminal Defense

2. "I like to go last. Can't control what other lawyers say — but I can correct if last." Peruto

3. "You give me the final word, and you're in big trouble!" Haynes

c) *Other responses*

1. "Doesn't make a bit of difference." Fitzpatrick

2. "First or last. More often than not, first. It depends upon the case. It's concerned with setting the tone wrong — or ending wrong." La Rossa

3. "Depends on who the other attorneys are — and how effective I think they are." Rudovsky

4. "Doesn't make any difference — there is a pecking order." He didn't really have a preference but didn't want a dynamic speaker going last: "He'll blow you right out of the water." DeSimone

E. Do you address your summation to one particular juror, all of them, or a few? (N=34)

a) *All of them*	19	.56
b) *All, then supporters*	10	.29
c) *Other responses*	5	.15

a) *All of them*

1. "All of them, one at a time. And then when I get them all together, I can move them all as one . . . The jury — which is a group of one . . . you must treat them as one. You must mold them into one. You must make their hearts beat together. You must make their souls blend together. You'd better tie the tubes to their veins, each vein and

each artery, just so it all flows with one. Otherwise they can't reach a verdict. They'll split. They'll polarize. I take out one at a time. I gotta connect the tube from their blood to [mine]." Preiser

2. "I view them as a unit; not as a group of individuals — but this may be that as a prosecutor I have to convince all of the unit." Lytton

3. "I would never take a chance on one feeling slighted." J.R. Carroll

4. "I speak to all collectively — and each individually. I think it's a mistake to focus on any one juror. That juror will become nervous — and the others annoyed." Rutter

5. "I spend some time with each juror in the course of an argument. I prefer to be in front of the jury box, about a foot away — two feet — sometimes with my hands on the rail, able to move about and address different arguments to different jurors, always before I'm through with the thoughts, sweeping, so that nobody thinks that he's been singled out. If I look hard at you and make a positive statement, you're gonna respond whether you want to or not." Bailey

b) *All, then supporters*

1. "I start out by trying to speak to all of them . . . By the time the trial is over, I think I have a sense of where my strength is, and I wanna reinforce that strength . . . I know who the leaders of the jury are — at least I believe I do — and I'll tend to concentrate on them. But I do make a conscious effort to have everybody on that jury feel at one time or another that I have looked at them, and have addressed a comment to them. But I will spend 80% of my summation with those three or four people that I believe are going to lead the jury, and that are, hopefully, in my camp."

"And if I detect any resistance on the jury, I won't fight that at all. I will ignore that person from thereonin, because it'll affect my confidence if I continue to struggle with them. The last case I tried, there was a woman on the jury that at one point, I turned to her and began addressing some remarks. And it was almost like she just shook her head and said, 'not by me, you're not', and then I just left her. Abandoned her completely. Because psychologically it's very bad to keep working with a person like that. You're never going to turn her around."

"There are some cases that are very bad, and what you're hoping for is the hold-out juror. And of course you will concentrate on that person, and try to give them all the arguments they're going to need in that jury room to sustain their position." Fahringer

2. "I bounce around the jury. You can tell when you're on the same wave-length. You can almost spot friendly faces. Not always, but sometimes. And you can spot the eyes that just look away from you ... I prefer to spend some time where I'm making impact ... and if they're looking away from me, then they're not going to notice I'm not looking at then anyway." Goldberg

3. "I speak to the whole jury. I make eye contact with everyone. If I'm making an emotional point, I might look at some of the women on the jury and get the eye contact with them . . . One of the things I am doing is literally just recognizing them — just giving them the human acknowledgment of who they are."

"I try to pick out a leader and focus in on that person . . . The leader will take six or seven with him, if not twelve . . . I will put in my summation a point, or an analogy, or an anecdote — or something having to do with recognizing that person. And I will look directly at that person when I make the point, and my message will be clear based on the anecdote, or the message that: 'You know that I'm speaking to you, and you know that I'm giving you the message that when you go back there, you're going to be able to explain this.' I am acknowledging them and recognizing them, which is a very important factor in getting someone on your side." Magarity

4. "There are pivot people. You may gear certain parts of your speech" to them. But "I think it's important, at some point in the argument, to look at each one of them. I'm just scared to death of them, because you cannot know what's in anyone's mind . . . because they're so unpredictable." Criminal Defense

5. "I look at all twelve", but "when you speak to a jury you don't speak to all twelve; you speak to maybe four or five . . . You anoint people, and you make them your disciples. And then, if they're strong enough, they can lead the rest of the pack."
DeSimone

6. "Try to hit everybody. Look for somebody who reacts, then key in with him, so you'll know when you're not getting your point across." Fitzpatrick

c) *Other responses*

1. "It depends on the case. If it's a case where you felt a particular rapport, and you know the odds are against you, and you have to hope for those one or two who will hold out, then you go for the individual jurors. In the case where, as best you can gauge, you have a good chance of swaying the entire jury, then you don't do that." Brown

2. "I look at the jury one time during the trial. The big chance you take is you might mis-read what they are thinking. You might get over-confident. And to avoid that, I don't look at them. I can feel them. I can tell when a jury doesn't like my opponent. They're rustling. They groan, or they grunt. It's a sixth sense. I don't have to look at them." King

3. "If I see a particularly hard customer, I go right into them, and try to force it down their throats: 'Okay, I'll give it to you. Since you made me so important by concentrating all on me, I'll give it to you'. He might not recognize that's what he's doing, but he loves the attention . . . I'm afraid of jurors who look like they're all for me. I've had the damnedest luck with that." Meyer

4. "I speak to all of them, and I speak to each of them . . . I've questioned my own judgment so many times about why I spend energy trying to move somebody whom I perceived to be any posture contrary to the one I'm advocating. So that may be a lost cause. I should perhaps concentrate on those who are receptive to the suggestions advanced in the hypotheses of closing argument, and ignore those who've already got their minds made up, and chalk it up to the fact they're less than adequate jurors. They have prostituted themselves and their oath, because they're not really supposed to reach ultimate decisions until they've heard it all." Haynes

F. Do you like to use a lectern? (N=29)

a) *Yes*	6	.21
b) *No*	23	.79

a) *Yes*

1. Yes, "as an anchor I come back to, to hang on, lean on. I like having a lectern. It's a good place to put things. It's like a woman carrying a handbag. It performs a useful function. It's a pain sometimes, but I leave it. I'm not gripping it and hiding behind it." Lytton

2. "I like some freedom of movement, but I don't mind using that as home base." Rudovsky

3. "I like the lectern only as a base from which to start — as a sort of home port to return to." Rutter

b) *No*

1. "I use the whole courtroom." A lectern limits you. I like to walk around. "They're analogizing you, that they like, with this bum that you represent. But the two of you together; a lot of your richness is going to rub off on him, when you're standing together and you've got your hand on his shoulder." Toro

2. "I don't think there should be anything between you and the jury, such as a podium or a lectern." If you must use one, "don't stand behind it. I move out to the side, come back, because I do have to follow my notes . . . I think there should be nothing between you and the jury."

"I'm not a 'leg in the jury box' man. I tend to stay about three to five feet back, because I think they like to watch a show. And I have sensed that if you get up here where you're within two feet of the jury, I've always detected uneasiness, and discomfort. And I think that that makes them nervous." Fahringer

3. I don't use the lectern because I am "mobile, agile and hostile!" Brown

4. "No. I hate it. I don't like anything that inhibits me. I find that I'm purely Italian in that regard. I use a lot of body English in my summation." Peruto

5. "I usually give a closing in motion." Christie

6. "It's a barrier between me and the jury. They already got one barrier between us — the rail separates us. And now if I've got another piece of wood separating me from the jury, that's another barrier between the lawyer and communicating with the twelve most important people in the world at that time." Haynes

G. Do you use notes during the summation? (N=27)

a)	*Yes*	2	.07
b)	*Yes — on hand*	13	.48
c)	*No*	12	.45

a) *Yes*

1. An outline: "I put that outline together on a single sheet of paper; no matter how long it is, it's on a single sheet of paper. I don't wanna be in a position of turning pages." Goldberg

b) *Yes — on hand*

1. "I use an outline type of thing so that I don't miss — in the fervor of an argument — I don't miss an area that deserves discussion. And I don't trust even my brain — which is almost a miracle of modern times! I don't trust it not to fail me in a time of stress, like a closing argument." Haynes

2. I work from an outline. "I need a guide in front of me. I've often thought perhaps if someone took it away from me — it's like Dumbo and the feather — I think probably I'd still be able to do it, but it sure does make me feel more secure to have it there in front." Fahringer

3. I make a detailed outline — "with certain trigger words; then a less detailed outline — typed. No thought spans two pages. I turn pages while not looking at them." Lytton

4. "I try to never use notes during the summation. I walk up there with my 'security blanket', and I put them down." Kidd

c) *No*

1. "I don't use notes. I use quotes — not notes. I got almost perfect recall of the facts. The first thing I wanna do is get relaxed; get into the subject matter; get into the nuances." King

2. "I want it to appear that I'm too sincere to use notes . . . If the other lawyer looks at his notes, he loses the sense of intuitiveness; he loses the sense of spontaneity, he loses the sense of sincerity." Meyer

3. "If you don't look at your notes than the jury thinks: Boy! — You really know what you're talking about." Purnell

4. "The reason I don't like to write things out is that I find the lawyers who do that are wedded to the paper. They become unthinking. They are focused more on seeing that what's covered is on that paper." Sprague

5. No notes; no outline. "I'm a great critic of anyone who uses crutches that isn't lame. I don't permit my lawyers to take notes to the podium when they're cross-examining someone . . . You don't learn to walk until they take their crutches away. And people that don't use notes keep their eyes where they belong — on the witness or the jury — because that's how you tell if you're winning . . . The unarticulated responses are legion. It's eyes; it's gestures . . ." Bailey

H. Do you like to use blackboards, large charts, overhead projector, props during the closing argument?
(N=33)

a)	*Yes*	18	.55
b)	*Sometimes*	4	.12
c)	*No*	11	.33

a) *Yes*

1. "Yes. The blend of showing and telling is what is essential . . . If you use psychology, which is what it's all about, you must, if you're gonna gain the edge, have a blend of showing and telling on everything you do in the trial. That's why we use transparencies; that's why we use blackboards; that's why we use charts; that's why we use photographs." Preiser

2. "I will get very emotional about it. 'Look at this exhibit back there . . . '; I hand it to them, so I have that personal touch, almost with them." Kidd

3. "What I want to do is project myself into the jury deliberation room, and I think that the exhibits are things they carry back with them to the jury deliberation room." Elizabeth K. Ainslie

4. "Many times, I do . . . I don't have the slightest bit of objection using whatever it takes to better communicate with the jury." Haynes

5. "Visual aids are always terrific in any teaching or persuading." Bailey

b) *Sometimes*

1. "Once in a while . . . Mostly however it would be with photographs or instruments — such as weapons used in the trial. Ordinarily, I don't like to . . . use blackboards or anything, unless it is something that I want to linger in the minds of the juror — and therefore present it as the one picture worth a thousand words that stays with them."
Peruto

c) *No*

1. "Not particularly . . . I don't like to get into awfully mechanical gadgets, because they always will get screwed up during a summation." Goldberg

2. Using props at this point in the trial is distracting. "You don't want the jury focusing on you and not on your case . . . When you have a rotten case, then you want them to focus on you. And then you just get up there and do this wonderful number . . ."
Temin

I. How long do you like to talk?
(N=34)

a)	*No limit*	1	.03
b)	*2 Hours minimum*	1	.03
c)	*1 1/2 — 2 1/2 hours*	1	.03
d)	*1 1/4 — 1 1/2 hours*	17	.50
e)	*30 minutes — 1 hour*	9	.26
f)	*About 30 minutes*	5	.15

b) *2 Hours minimum*

1. Q: Did the jurors get itchy? A: "Sure . . . but they signed up for it. They knew it was gonna be tough when they went in . . . I've argued as long as 8 hours." Q: Did you Win? A: "Sure." Criminal Defense

d) *1 1/4 — 1 1/2 hours*

1. "I'm very much aware of when the jury gets tired of listening to me. If they start fidgeting, or their eyes glaze, or their eyes close — I'll stop when I perceive that I'm no longer effective . . . I'm watching them to see their interest and how they're reacting."
Lytton

2. "They can't endure more than their butts can endure on the chair. Never, never — or almost never — more than one hour — regardless of the length of the trial." Peruto

3. "Depends upon the complexity of the trial; how many defendants involved, the issues involved . . . You cannot bore the jury, but you have to at least give them enough time to understand." McGill

4. "I have an awful lot to say and I think it has to be said . . . You should only talk for a long time if you have a lot to talk about." Purnell

5. "It depends on the complexity of the case. I've never gone over two hours . . . But normally, if you can't win a case in an hour, hour and a half, you're not gonna win it . . ." Bailey

e) *Thirty minutes — 1 hour*

1. "I think jury closings should be on the short side. In a rare case — in a rare case — should it exceed an hour . . . I think jurors are used to watching television and their attention span tends to be about an hour . . . Some of the best closing arguments I've ever seen take commercials. They do it in maybe four segments of fifteen minutes each, or twelve minutes each. In the segments, they'll try to make four points. In between segments, they'll take a breather for a minute or two and be a little light or humorous, and just try basically to get the jury to like them rather than argue." Dershowitz

2. "The days of those long four hour, winded, emotional pleas to juries are [over]. Juries are smarter. People are smarter. I think they resent it actually." Bergstrom

3. "You are given a certain allotted period of time. Not by the court, but by the attention span of the jurors. And it varies with the length of the case." Fitzpatrick

f) *About 30 minutes*

1. "The time that you spend in front of the jury is not the point. It's the affect you have." Meyer

J. What is your reaction to lawyers 'objecting' during summation?

1. "I try to take advantage of it. I want the jury to get annoyed at the other guy . . . Hopefully the jury is figuring: 'Shut up. We wanna hear what he has to say. Sit down, you nerd!'" Litvin

2. "I rarely object, no matter what the other lawyer said. I hate to do it. Unless it is the most God-awful thing, and I see a tactical advantage; it's gotta be more than the objection. And even if he's saying things that are improper or incorrect, I'll wait for my speech and come back hard as hell — and not interrupt him. It makes me look more effective when I speak — that I have not interrupted. It gives a certain calm, cool, collected approach on my part to the jury. Unless I see some real immediate advantage, I really do not believe in doing that. As a matter of fact, I go further. I relish being inter-

rupted by the other side in my speech, and staying absolutely calm, cool to the jurors as this lawyer rants and raves, because invariably the judge puts the lawyer down."

Sprague

3.7 General Statistics:

A. How many closing speeches do you make in the course of one year?

Number of closing speeches	*Number of respondents*
10 – 20	2
14 – 15	1
10 – 12	4
6 – 9 (median group)	3
5	2
3 – 5	4
1 – 3	1
1 – 2	1
1	1

1. "I've slowed down a lot. It takes me longer these days to try cases then it did back when I was younger . . . [Because] I know more about it now. I'm more careful. I know more about shutting the doors that pathological liars run out. To prevent the escape; to expose the lie — that takes a little longer."

Mr. Haynes (who reported 10 — 20 trials per year)

B. Number of lawyer-informants in study:

Women:	8
Men:	26
Total	34

C. Lawyer-informants by usual type of law practiced:

Criminal Defense:	22
Civil	4
Prosecutor	8
Total	34

For a summary of the data presented in this chapter, see 'Summary' at the conclusion of Chapter 5.

4. Learning and Teaching the Ways of Speaking Like a Lawyer

How one learns the ways of speaking like a lawyer is critical in terms of passing on the verbal tradition of summation to the next generation of lawyers. This chapter addresses the issues of how the accomplished lawyer/ speaker learned this way of speaking, and how he or she would teach the novice student to talk like a lawyer.

Because of the many law schools located in or around Philadelphia (there are five known to me), and because of a fairly recent concept of introducing practicing lawyers into the legal education process, more than one third of the informants in this study reported that they teach at university law schools on a full or part-time basis. Also, many lecture regularly at seminars on the "summer peas and cold roast beef" (Haynes) speaking trail.

The data in this chapter will be treated in the same manner as was the data in Chapter 3. As before, a summary indicating what was significant to the users (teachers) of summation can be found at the conclusion of Chapter 5. The evaluation of what the researcher believes is the essence of this information will be discussed in the final chapter.

INDEX FOR CHAPTER 4

4.1 How you learned to speak like a lawyer summing up:

	Responses Given	*Informants*	
A.	Observing other lawyers	24	(71%)
B.	Doing it	14	(41%)
C.	Reading transcripts of closing speeches	11	(32%)
D.	From books, tapes and records	7	(21%)
E.	Public speaking course or debate in high school	5	(15%)
F.	Trial practice course	5	(15%)
G.	Thinking about the content	2	(6%)
H.	Reading in general	1	(1%)

A. Observing other lawyers

1. "I learned by doing it and by watching others do it . . . I tell most people that I lecture to on summations that most of what I do that may seem good or clever, I have probably stolen from somebody else. And I encourage people to go and watch — the good defense attorneys and the good prosecutors — and if something looks good that you think fits in with your personality and style — steal it!" Lytton

2. "I can't say that I ever 'learned' really . . . You get to learn a lot from the people that you try against, and the more you try cases, the more you are exposed to opponents

— the most stupid of which can give you one little clue or inkling into something that perhaps he didn't even manufacture himself, but learned from someone else. And I think that I could best call myself a composite of the people that I tried against with the embellishments — or whatever you want to call it — of my own." Peruto

3. "Watching other good lawyers who are doing it. Adapting what they do to what is natural to you as a person, in terms of your own persona — your own style — and then doing it." Rutter

4. When I had the chance, I did "watch other lawyers — how they handled themselves in a courtroom — to see what it was, usually, that I did not like — the things that they were doing that I thought were not effective, or wrong. And sometimes picking up things that I thought were good. A great deal of my experience has really come from my opponent in the cases that I have tried; watching what he has done and deciding what is good or bad about that, and to the extent that there is something good, taking it for use subsequently." Sprague

B. Doing it

1. "I don't think you learn to do it anywhere. I think you learn to do it in a courtroom. You do it by doing it . . . I think you can learn a certain amount by watching, and you can learn a certain amount by reading, but I don't think there's any comparison to what you can learn by doing, however well or not well you do. If you do it right — fine. If you do it wrong — do it right the next time." Christie

2. "I don't know that you learn to do it anywhere. Much of it is by osmosis, and much of it is by the same manner that we learn to do other things as lawyers — that is, we practice law, and the verb practice is accurate to describe what we do." Rutter

E. Public speaking course or debate in high school

1. "I've always been a communicator; high school debate, president of class . . . made lots of speeches even before I started practicing law, so I had some — advantage, I think, in terms of overcoming the built-in inertia all human beings have about getting up and making an ass of themselves before strangers." Haynes

2. "I was always involved in public speaking, oratory, debate, dramatics. My undergraduate major was radio-television. It was something that really came naturally to me." Bergstrom

F. Trial practice course

1. "Really learned by going to seminars like the American Trial Lawyers puts on . . . If there's ever a seminar near enough for me to be there, I'm gonna be there. Because I'm gonna listen to the other lawyers; Cause every lawyer I know, knows something that I don't. And as long as I can hear him say it, I'll be that much better for my client." Preiser

H. Reading in general

1. "I believe in a liberal arts education. By a study of literature and history and poetry and music and art, we develop a much more broad vocabulary. I'm not talking so much about the correct use of words as I am about the selection of words, and the way we put them together. And using examples, and using battle metaphors, and using even art metaphors . . . I've always been very much preoccupied with the beauty of language . . . I read as much as I can, and see how other people use words effectively; [I] try to match their style." Fahringer

4.2 Educating the novice lawyer to this way of speaking

Below are listed the responses the informants gave to the following question:

> If you were teaching a young lawyer how to deliver a closing speech, what would you tell him or her to do, or never do?

A. Positive factors: What a lawyer SHOULD do in the summation

Some statements are followed by the number of lawyers who specifically named this factor. However, many of the same factors were mentioned often within other contexts throughout the interviews. Therefore, each number represents a minimum of responses.

1. Be prepared; plan out carefully ahead of time 8

"More summations are imperiled by a lack of preparation than by a lawyer's skills or presence." Fahringer

"Doesn't do you any good to get up there and harangue if in fact you have no message. You better have a message of some sort. You'd better plan and think out what it is that you wanna say. You'd better have some idea of what *needs* to be said. You better have some idea about what the accused deserves to have said about him or her." Haynes

"Put your case together properly. If you haven't put your case together properly, you're not going to be able to give an effective closing argument. Because all the points you want to be able to raise in your closing argument may not have come out during the case." Purnell

2. Be yourself 7

"Do not be, ever, anybody but yourself. You can't be me. You can't be some lawyer you admire. You can take some part of the technique, the approach, the dynamics of the communication from another lawyer. But you have to do it as yourself.

You can't be somebody else, because if you're not yourself, you don't have the candor that jurors require to consider you effective." Haynes

"You have to use your own style; you have to be yourself. The most important part of a speech is the jury believing you — and trusting you. If you're not yourself, if you're affected in any way, the jury is not going to believe you." DeSimone

3. Use very good language 5

"I think if you're going to be a lawyer, you'd better learn to talk like an — educated person. Not in the sense of being snotty, snooty, stuck-up and all of that. And that's not to say you shouldn't use some vernacular . . . I don't think you should use words like 'foresworn' — cause they don't know what that means . . . I think you've got to be *very* good to get away with that." Lytton

"Use the King's English. Not in a stilted way, but like you were sitting at a cocktail table with people that you knew had half a brain trying to persuade them of something you really believed in. Don't be stentorial [sic]. And don't throw out good lines just because they're good lines. You win a superficial near-term victory, and it dissipates." Bailey

4. Develop an effective theme or theory 5

"You must have an understandable, persuasive theory of the case." Rudovsky

"I don't believe in arguing inconsistent defenses, or giving them alternative defenses; 'Well, if you don't believe this, then go for that.' You have one theory; and stick to that." Purnell

5. Know your case 4

"The first thing that would come to my mind, which would overwhelm all of the other considerations, is to know your case. Don't try to wing it or bluff it." Toro

"Know your case so well that you are empty-handed in front of the jurors. Don't have an outline — except to have your colleague check and see if you covered the points." Bailey

6. Select your arguments very carefully 4

"You don't have to make every argument that you've got. Pick your best argument and go with it. Get out of there the things that clearly don't belong there." Fitzpatrick

"Give arguments that go to the heart of the case. That is, what the lawyer thinks the jury is going to be concerned with when they get back in the deliberation room . . . Make the meaningful arguments; the arguments that will grab the jury by the brain; that will be persuasive. Now how do you do that? By listening to yourself, and running it through your own computer, your own brain. Certain arguments turn you on, and other arguments sound like lawyer arguments, or technical arguments, or ridiculous arguments. A lawyer has to make that difficult judgment of selecting the arguments that really make sense and are persuasive." Litvin

7. Maintain eye contact 4

8. Speak as extemporaneously as possible 3

"I think it's important to have that closing appear as extemporaneous as possible — and yet it's very significant to have an outline, so that if I get off the track, I can get back on the track." Goldberg

9. Believe in what you are saying 3

10. Use phrases the court will use; tie in with the judge 3

"Cite the law in the same words as the judge will use, therefore reinforcing the idea that, 'I can really trust that lawyer. He told me — and the judge told me — the same thing.'" Rutter

11. Try and keep to an hour and fifteen minutes 3

"Normally, if you can't win a case in an hour, hour and a half, you're not gonna win it." Bailey

12. Use some stock phrases 2

"I give them [new lawyers] some stock phrases that are crutches to help them when they start bailing out of their closings, because they get really frightened at the beginning [of the closing speech]." Maguigan

13. Use metaphors, examples, analogies 2

14. Use rhetorical questions 2

"The rhetorical question is probably the prosecutor's best friend . . . 'Do you believe this? Can you believe it? Would you believe it?'" King

15. Persuade 2

16. Communicate 2

17. Get as physically close to the jurors as possible 2

"The closer I get to a jury, the better I feel about it, in terms of physically . . . I stand near them; near as possible to them as I can. And I also stand in one position, and the only time I move is for affect." DeSimone

"Do not stand away from them. Don't appear like you're afraid of them. Because if they feel that you are afraid of them — it's like someone who will not look you in the eyes — you have something to hide." McGill

18. Anticipate the other closing speech(es)

"You've gotta anticipate what the prosecutor's gonna say, and then be ready for it, and knock 'em down." Toro

19. Watch the line between too much legal argument and avoidance

20. Be very enthusiastic

"They wanna see you up there being enthusiastic about your case. Be very, very enthusiastic about your presentation — to let the jury know that this is something that you as a nice guy believe in. You're not just doing a job. You're not a hired gun that came up here and speaks well in front of the jury. But your client *should* win. And if the jury likes you, they're going to like what you said." Toro

21. Begin and end dramatically

22. Treat the judge and your opponent with courtesy

23. Use whatever has a chance to succeed

24. Watch and steal!

"I tell most people that I lecture to on summations that most of what I do that may seem good or clever, I have probably stolen from somebody else. And I encourage people to go and watch — the good defense attorneys and the good prosecutors — and if something looks good that you think fits in with your personality and style — steal it!" Lytton

25. Plan your choreography

"Where to stand, how to stand, how many steps to take." Lytton

26. Use silence

"Silence. You know — not speaking, and letting a phrase reverberate through the courtroom." Lytton

27. Be redundant — which is the essence of persuasion

28. Use a mixture of passion (emotion) and logic

29. Get them to like you

"I've never seen a jury do anything for anybody where they hated his lawyer."
Peruto

30. Entertain them

31. Make the jurors care about the victim

"Who the victim is makes a difference to the summation. If the victim is a female, an elderly person, a child — from an emotional standpoint, people are outraged more at the death of a child . . . And you get into the manner of death . . . Make those people care about your victim." King

32. Give the jurors ammunition for the jury room

"The style and histrionics are important, of course, but they should be secondary to a rational marshaling of the facts, that are going to stick with the jury, and to give those jurors that are particularly on your side ammunition in dealing with their fellow jurors during the deliberations. You've gotta give them something of substance."
T. C. Carroll

33. Be honest — even about damaging evidence

"It should not avoid — it should attack — the weakest parts of your own case, and deal with them. Because if you don't, the jury will." Temin

34. Control your facial expressions

"One of the toughest things for a young lawyer to learn is how to control facial expressions. You can't show a disappointment . . . If I'm winning a case, I am keeping the same demeanor I am if I'm losing. Because jurors have a tendency to pick up on your uncertainties. If you are uncertain about your case, how can you conceivable convince them that they should be sure?" King

35. Point out weaknesses of other side's case

"Pick out where you feel the weaknesses in the government's case are, and really hammer that home." Bergstrom

36. Go through the facts (evidence) of the case

37. Know your jurors as well as possible

38. Convince them that they are the people who matter

39. Explain that you can't select your witnesses

"Explain to the people that your witnesses are average people, and they're real people, and this is the way these people are; that we didn't do around picking our witnesses. And if our witnesses are kinda trashy, that's because that's the people who were there. You know, you don't go out and select them." Rubino

40. Understand and use the law as the framework of your argument

B. Negative factors: What a lawyer should NOT do in the summation

1. Do not read your closing speech All

"I constantly teach people — don't ever write a speech and then read it. Because that's not a good oral delivery. It leaves no flexibility to react to a juror's response." Bailey

2. Don't use legal jargon; don't speak over jurors' heads, or beneath them 7

"Not to get too high flung in you language to the jury. And then again, not to talk down to them . . . I don't think you can talk to a jury the way some of the fellows around here [in the District Attorney's office] talk to each other. I think jurors resent it. Especially if you have older women on the jury who aren't used to hearing that." Rubino

"Don't treat the jurors as less than equal . . . Lots of people, upon getting a law degree, think that they've been specially annointed. You have to break them of that . . . You are best persuasive when you're talking person to person — people to people." Rutter

"Avoid being patronizing to the jury. You're not Mr. Big Deal or Mrs. Big Deal lawyer. Avoid being too humble. They know that you are a professional who's proud to be there." Temin

3. Don't use (or look at your) notes 5

"Don't take your eyes off the jurors at any time, except for the brief moment that you may refer to an exhibit and draw their attention to it . . . Keep at them all the time. They will tell you things. You may rescue one." Bailey

"Don't use notes. The first thing a trial lawyer must do is understand that notes are disastrous. You must have contact with your eyes. And if you forgot something, so what? It's a tempo; it's a persuasive procedure. The art of applied psychology." Preiser

"Don't use notes — because then there's no communication with the jury . . . They ought to be looking at the jury to see what a jury is responding to. Sometimes I'll be on a certain point which I don't think is too important and somebody is real interested in it and so I may continue on it — or I may speak directly to that person . . . You don't get that unless you're really looking at them and having some communication." Rudovsky

4. Don't get nose-to-nose with the jurors 4

"I don't, for my personal style, like to lean on the jury box. Even in questioning of a witness . . . I would feel like it's an intrusion of my space. You've got precious enough little room in the jury box to begin with without somebody leaning over the jury box . . . somebody staring you right in the eyeball if you're sitting in the front row . . . that's a little bit too much contact with the jury." Christie

"Never try to offend their space. If you stick your finger right up under their nose, you're asking for trouble . . . that's a form of intimidation." Fitzpatrick

"People have their own little shells, and they don't want you to come too close to them, cause it makes them nervous." Purnell

5. Give no hint of insincerity 3

"Any time you do anything that remotely doesn't resemble sincerity, you lose it. You can't be dishonest." La Rossa

6. No ranting or raving; don't be too theatrical 3

"If you get over-theatrical, it's insulting." DeSimone

7. Never lie 3

8. Do not recite a relentless chronology of the case 2

9. Do not memorize 2

10. Don't depend on oratory 2

11. Don't name-call 2

"Never indulge in discourtesies unless they're thoroughly warranted by the evidence. If you're picking on a witness as a liar, make sure there's a good justification for that that occurred in the courtroom." Bailey

12. Never refer to the opponent as the United States Government (for defense attorneys)

"Never refer to the 'government of the United States' as the 'government'. That's too overpowering. Never refer to your client as the 'client' or the 'defendant', but by name. You have to humanize people." Fahringer

13. Beware of lack of preparation

"Nothing should happen by chance in the summation. There is an enormous amount of work that has to go into the planning and structuring of the summation."
Fahringer

14. Never deceive

15. Don't pace or move around too much

"I don't like to wander around. I just think it's awfully distracting. I like to find a spot and stay in the spot . . . I don't see any point to moving around." Goldberg

"I don't like people movin' around a lot. It's very distracting. Your voice trails off, and you look nervous and fidgety." Purnell

16. Never bore the jurors

"It's inexcusable to ever bore a jury." Litvin

17. Don't overstate your case

18. Beware of a lack of objectivity

There must be objectivity. "When the lawyer identifies too much with the client, he might as well let the client make the speech. The lawyer has to step back, and view from the jurors' distance what the witnesses have looked like from the stand . . . If they're too partisan, it looks like they're making the speech for the fee instead of the jury . . . Get that distance between you and client — manifest objectivity . . . and that you get by being manifestly honest." J. R. Carroll

19. Don't answer every argument of the other side

"Don't answer tit for tat defense's closing. I don't feel that that's a productive thing to do, because I think it detracts from the points that you are trying to make — and it also appears it's a defensive move . . . Why do that when you have your own points to make?" Christie

20. Don't review witness testimony which is against you

"I tell defense lawyers, those who are going to defend people in criminal cases, certainly do not simply go back over — in what is supposed to be a closing statement and paraphrase what all the witnesses against you have said . . . all they do is reemphasize the prosecutorial theory. It may be a summation of some sort, but it's not the kind you're obliged to make. It's a summation for the other side." Haynes

C. General comments about learning and teaching to sum up

1. "Experience will *not* a trial lawyer make . . . you need a good mentor."

"I happen to think that trial law is the aristocracy of the bar; the majesty of everything that comes along in the courtroom . . . You can't read the law from the cold printed word in the case book, or in the law review articles. The law lives and breathes; it has a soul; it has a brain; it has a heart. Unless you've seen that soul, seen that brain, felt the heat of the whole body of law, you can't interpret what you see in a book."

"Law schools are totally failing in their jobs because all they're doing is teaching law, and not teaching lawyering . . . We need more lawyers teaching in the law schools, and less academicians . . . Teaching too much law and not enough lawyering." Preiser

2. "There is no such thing as *a* closing speech . . . It's stunning to see how different personalities can be enormously effective when you'd never think they could be. I really insist that my students go to court and watch, so they can see the incredible range . . . To see who can have the jury's attention totally riveted for an hour and a half." And then "a much more flamboyant, apparently more powerful personality loses them after twenty minutes — and doesn't notice. You see these people gesturing wildly and being very emotional, and the jurors are looking around." Maguigan

3. When asked to talk about how to teach law students: "That's too late. The book *To Be A Trial Lawyer* [his book] is targeted for college students, who can still rescue themselves from the disabilities with which they will otherwise wind up with in law school; with their flaccid memory and a very poor command of the written and spoken word. A lawyer's command of language is a huge part of his arsenal. If he's got a brain to drive the mouth or the pen, he's probably going to be a very successful lawyer." Bailey

4. "We discuss, without my trying to impose my views on the students, things like: Do you use the lectern? Do you stand in a stationary position? Do you walk? Should a woman be better dressed than the female jurors? Should the lawyer hang over the rail of the court with women in short skirts? — because women are sensitive about that kinda stuff. Should the lawyer conduct his speech in such a way that the jurors are paying more attention to him or to her then to what he is saying?"

For some of the students, "you just have to get them to stand up, to remember to keep their hands out of their pockets, or to stop slouching, and to talk! And to not read."

T. C. Carroll

5. "I think too few lawyers have a theory of summation and really think through the strategy of what it's intending to serve. Lawyers often just do what they've been taught to do, and what they've seen other people do, and there's become a kind of form for the summation, and I think you really have to think it through anew for every case. I don't think there are formulas that work. I think every case needs its own approach to summation."

"There is a trial practice course at Harvard. They just bring in the Old Greats —

and they say, 'Show us'. You ain't the Old Master. I'm much more of an advocate of *a priori* learning, of starting from the beginning and thinking the whole strategy through for yourself — every time . . . I've seen too many imitative closing arguments."

Dershowitz

For a summary of the data presented in this chapter, see 'Summary' at the conclusion of Chapter 5.

5. In the Words of the Senders: Significant Other Issues

> An informant should be used as a window into a culture . . . His contribution to the research is indispensable. The investigator must constantly remind himself, however, that his informant is an adherent, not an objective interpreter, of his communicational system. The report of an informant about his behavior is itself behavior; such reports are data and not evidence. And the fact that all informants agree does not make their statements true, except insofar as agreement indicates conventional understanding (Birdwhistell 1970: 191).

As in the two previous chapters, here are the words of the lawyer, "an adherent, not an objective interpreter, of his communicational system", describing other dimensions of summation which he or she believes important in understanding this speech event. Only the topics of metaphors, rhetorical questions, and summation as a two-way communication were introduced by me. All of the other topics were interviewee generated.

The reader is advised once again that a summary of the data collected according to the topics discussed in Chapters 3, 4, and 5 will appear at the conclusion of this chapter, and an interpretation of the data can be found in the final chapter.

The index for this chapter appears on the next page.

INDEX FOR CHAPTER 5

a) For several of the topics listed in the index, the reader can find discussion on the listed page. For example, on page 98 a discussion of the metaphors of summation begins, and on page 110 one can find a discussion of the summation as a two-way communication.

5.1 The metaphors of summation:

"The essence of a metaphor is understanding and experiencing one kind of thing in terms of another", state George Lakoff and Mark Johnson in *Metaphors We Live By* (1980:5). Furthermore, they wrote, "its primary function is understanding." Metaphors allow us not only to elaborate a concept, but also to highlight or conceal some aspects of an experience. There is a directionality in metaphor, such that we structure the less concrete, more vague concept in terms of experiences which are more clearly delineated in our lives.

Their criteria for metaphor are (a) a difference in activity and (b) partial structuring by use of only selected parts. For example, summation is a picture puzzle, but a lawyer can only use the pieces which he has — and those are the ones which were submitted into the game as evidence.

One of the metaphors which Lakoff and Johnson posit in their book is ARGUMENT IS WAR, for which they give examples with expressions such as 'I *demolished* his argument', 'I've never *won* an argument with him', or 'He *shot down* all my arguments.' They go on to say that we don't just talk about arguments in terms of war, but, as in war, we actually do win or lose arguments. We see the person we are arguing with as an opponent. (The lawyers in this study repeatedly referred to the other lawyer in a case as an opponent.) We attack opposing positions and defend our own. Lakoff and Johnson believe that not only are metaphors grounded in the physical and cultural experiences of our past, but that they also influence our future actions.

During the interviews with the informants in this study, it often became clear that their understanding of the speech genre summation was made coherent for them by experiencing the summation in terms of another event. Sometimes the metaphors of the legal informants would be revealed only briefly by the use of certain vocabulary items at different times throughout the interview. Sometimes entire descriptive passages would be used to elucidate their metaphor of summation.

Some lawyers had more than one metaphor for the speech event summation (Bailey in 1, 2 or 5, below), perhaps because one metaphor would not do the job, i.e., there might not be a single metaphor which coordinates with both the direction and the content of his or her argument. Also, dif-Also, different kinds of cases, e.g., murder or mail fraud, might dictate different kinds of metaphors. During the summation, the lawyer may switch metaphors just because it is satisfying to the speaker to do so, or because he notices a lack of attention from the audience, or because he wants to make a point in a different manner. Often the metaphor for the trial and the metaphor for the summation coincided, lending coherence to one another (such as 1, 4 and 6 below).

Lakoff and Johnson stress that "issues of truth are among the least relevant and interesting issues that arise in the study of metaphor" (p. 175). What is significant is that these structures can give meaning to ones past and present activities, and to what one knows and believes.

In the words of the informants which follow are the metaphors of summation as indirectly conveyed to me. The classifications of the metaphors, such as, 'summation is an act of intimidation,' are those which I interpreted from what was conveyed to me by the informants, although never explicitly stated as such, i.e., "This is my metaphor for summation."

1. *Summation is an act of intimidation*

"I get tough with them. And they get intimidated. But I get the judge to back me up."

"It's an intimidator's moment of threat."

"If I look hard at you [as a juror] and make a positive statement, you're gonna respond whether you want to or not."

[Although the following was related in reference to cross-examination, it has been included here because it so well conveys this lawyer's metaphorical view of the sense of intimidation which seemed to so often permeates his vision of what transpires in a courtroom.]

"If the purpose of the cross-examination is to impeach the witness, I want something more threatening . . . The witness is facing an adversary, and everything that will intimidate him and make him afraid to deviate from the truth is useful. The manner, the approach, to convince him that I know so much about him, he'd better walk the God-damn line, or I'll cut his legs off! . . . And the way you do that is to take his prior statements, memorized, and say, 'Didn't you say — boom, boom, boom, boom, boom?', verbatim. And immediately, if the witness perceives this is like Boswell said of Johnson, 'This is a dangerous person to disagree with', you have him disciplined, and afraid to innovate . . . You want to frighten him out of trying to do that." Bailey

2. *Summing up is an act of hostility*

"Attitudinal and physical pumping up that occurs prior to the final argument . . . it's like somebody getting ready for a fight. The best thing to do if you're going fight somebody is stretch."

"If you have to land on the other lawyer, do it reluctantly, but courageously . . . "

[About cross-examination]
"The best cross-examiners are those who fight the burden of proof; who attack, rip apart, who cast doubt. That's their function. That's why prosecutors who build houses instead of tearing them down aren't that good at it." Bailey

3. *Summation is a dramatic production*

"I feel that I am the producer of a drama. I'm producing a play, and I have an advantage as the producer of this play. My cast of characters; is it better to start with a little wife first — or a dynamic person? Is it better to end the play on a high note — a low note? The drama being produced is because I want to convey my message."

"I have one big advantage over a playwright or a producer. They are subject to whoever buys tickets and comes in. To some extent, I get to pick my critics, or my audience, which the normal producer doesn't get to do. And that is also lining up for the final summation the kind of juror who's going to be receptive to *my* play. Of course my opponent's producing his play. And it's these two plays. And as the jury ends up — you know, The Lady and The Tiger — which side was able to be more persuasive as to their side." Sprague

4. *Summation is a picture puzzle*

"The trial is like a jigsaw puzzle. It has a bunch of tiny pieces of evidence all coming in at different times, and really meaning less to a jury. And when you put it together in the summation, it becomes a great big painting. A beautiful painting is what you want them to see. But how do you know what pieces to put in that jigsaw puzzle unless you know what you're going to tell them at the end?" Preiser

5. *Summation is an act of selling*

"It's a salesman's moment of persuasion." Bailey

"How well are you able to sell what you are saying?" Sprague

[Selling vegetables, or bread?] When lawyers repeat stories in their summations, "It comes over stale. I like things to be fresh. When I sell the jury something — I want it to be fresh. I want them to have freshness about — crispness in my words." DeSimone

"It depends on what you're selling." Fitzpatrick

6. *Summation is war*

"Billy had the ability to command a jury. 'You will go out there — and you will return with such-and-such a verdict.'" King

"The last word is always the best word . . . I don't want a dynamic speaker going last. He'll blow you right out of the water." DeSimone

"Because the greatest weapon in the world is to have a head full of facts . . ." Bailey

"You're in an uphill battle from the day you start." Goldberg

7. *Summation is an athletic competition*

"I had kinda an advantage coming from an athletic background; and from that particular background, there's a competitive nature there — there's a kinda toughness . . . I think it's [trial work] the closest thing I have done since athletics to keep the competitive fires burning." King

8. *Summation is a conversation*

"Nobody likes to be talked to like it's a speech: 'How nice. He's giving it to us like you talk with someone in a living room.'" Toro

9. *Summation is a Bach fugue*

"Usually the whole case is geared into my jury speech . . . It's like a Bach fugue. There is a theory about Bach fugues. That Bach wrote all the stretti first, and worked backwards. In a Bach fugue, a stretto is when all the voices come together. And the Bach stretti just work; they just always work; and people marvel at them . . . and in a way, I compose my case backwards." Temin

10. *Summation is an exercise in pride of personal accomplishment*

"I can't wait to get up in front of the jury, because I know in my mind at that point in time that I'm going to outspeak the other guy — or the other lady . . . You always get that twinge in your stomach, and if you don't have that twinge in your stomach, you're not going to give a good speech. Because it's gonna come over flat . . . At the end of the speech, I'm totally spent. I'm a babbling fool for about a day after that. I can't even put two sentences together. I just *know* that it's coming. It's from the sense of sincerity I have about my case, especially when I was a prosecutor . . . A belief that I'm right, and a belief that the jury is going to understand this before I sit down. That our side is absolutely correct, and that what they've just been hearing is hogwash for forty minutes. And the next forty minutes, they're going to hear a torrent of truth coming out."
DeSimone

11. *Summation is an exercise in psychological persuasion*

"Of course you have to have the evidence to use in your summation, but having the evidence in the hand of a skillful lawyer can mean very different results. And the use of the psychological principles of persuasion, knowing for example *when* to argue what points, can be critical to what the jury might do. All lawyers are eloquent; they can speak well — all the trial lawyers — but the difference between the greats and the average is the thought process of using the various types of psychological principles of persuasion, such as primacy; lastness."

"The blend of showing and telling is what is essential . . . If you use, again psychology — which is what it's all about — you must, if you're gonna gain the edge, have a blend of showing and telling on everything you do in the trial." Preiser

12. *Summation related to food*

"Gastronomic jurisprudence: what's your gut feeling about it?" Fitzpatrick

13. *Different metaphors for different cases*

"There are some cases where you have to *sell* the nice guy, other cases where you have to *be aggressive and attack*." Kidd

5.2 Legal missteps in closing arguments:

Speakers are not free to say anything they wish in summing up to a jury. Their choice of topics and manner of speech are constrained by legal strictures. One of the informants interviewed for this study, Harvard Law School Professor Alan M. Dershowitz, restricts his courtroom activities almost exclusively to the appellate courts. These are the so called higher courts to which an appeal is made when the validity of the results of a trial in the so called lower courts, for example the United States District Court, are questioned. Lawyer error in the closing speech can be one cause of invalidation of a verdict. Below are some of Professor Dershowitz's comments on closing speeches.

"I'm like the pathologist who performs autopsies . . . I read only the cases that are lost below. Only when they lose, and somebody comes to me and asks me to evaluate the record for appeal. So I know everything you wanna know about losing arguments."

About the kinds of reversible error which can occur in a closing speech:

1. "When the prosecutor testifies. When he basically puts facts into evidence that weren't previously in evidence . . . such as when he says to the jury, 'Let me tell you, ladies and gentlemen of the jury, from my experience - - - .' He's not under oath and he's supposed to just be arguing from the facts . . . More importantly, when he puts his credibility on it, when he says, 'Believe me, I wouldn't be telling - - -.'"

"It's [summation] to describe the facts, and then call it an inference from the facts . . . Inferences sound inexorable. Of course they're not. They're often opinion based on experience. Normally many inferences can flow from a given fact. But a good and effective advocate will make an opinion sound like inescapable conclusion. But a very bad advocate will say, 'It is my opinion, ladies and gentlemen of the jury, that - - - .' We don't want to hear his opinion."

2. "When a prosecutor says things like, 'Ladies and gentlemen of the jury, unless you convict this man, he will be out on the street - - - .' Sentencing is not the function of the jury. In the Big Dan rape case: 'Your verdict in this case will send a message to the community'. I think that's wrong argument. Jury verdicts are not supposed to send messages to the community. They are supposed to resolve issues of guilt or innocence . . . 'Messages to the community' should be regarded as an impermissible method of argument."

3. "A personal attack on the opponent — unduly disparaging your opponent."

Dershowitz

A woman attorney discussed argumentation before an appellate court:

"I think I am best at appeals, and I can argue to a court of appeals, I think, *far* better than to a jury of twelve people. I don't feel that I'm very good at persuading people that I'm right and they should do what I want . . . I feel more comfortable because I only have to come up with an intellectual argument. They're not going to be impressed with what I'm wearing, or how I talk, or the fact that I'm a woman as opposed to a man."

Higgins

Another lawyer discussed the same issue:

"It's a different kind of an argument. You're arguing to a sophisticated audience. I don't leave emotion out just because they're judges and not jurors. It's an entirely different approach. You've really gotta be very straightforward with the court, or else you lose the court."

"You're much less likely to fool a group of judges than you are to fool a group of jurors, because the judges have heard it over and over and over again, and they're going to be quick to detect a false note."

Goldberg

5.3 Rhetorical questions:

The use of rhetorical questions in summation was frequently mentioned by the informants. I also observed that rhetorical questions occurred in over 40% of the 66 closing speeches which were included in this study. The reasons for such frequent use of this speech form are explored further in Section 2.

1. "The rhetorical question is probably the prosecutor's best friend. Rhetorical questions — that's the savior."

King

2. "Not only tell them, but let *them* come up with the answers. Ask the rhetorical questions."

"I was speaking one day, and I was asking rhetorical questions. And I would say[7] to them: 'You know what you didn't learn in this case? - - - You know what you didn't hear. You know I don't have to tell you. You didn't hear that, did you?' And a juror responds, 'Yes!'[8] You make them part of your speech." DeSimone

5.4 Civil/Criminal, Plaintiff/Defense, Prosecutor/Defense differences:

The needs of the prosecutor and defense attorney differ in regard to persuading jurors. The prosecutor must convince every juror that his or her argument is correct in order to win the verdict. The defense attorney would also like to convince every juror of the rightness of his or her position, but if s/he is successful at convincing only one juror, then a hung jury can be achieved, thereby earning a second chance for a not-guilty verdict in a new trial. Therefore, this can also be considered a result well worth working towards when all else fails.

The summation differs according to the direction in which the speaker wishes to lead his or her audience. There are three dimensions which affect the form and content of the closing speech:

A. Civil/Criminal differences

1. "In a civil case, you're portraying the client's injury. It's always the client; the client; and you paint it in a very dramatic fashion. In a criminal case, you want the jury to like you personally, and you keep away from the client. Because unfortunately, usually in a criminal case, your client is guilty." Toro

2. "In civil litigation, winning the case means not only getting a verdict . . . but getting an adequate award." Litvin

3. "From the plaintiff's standpoint, and from the criminal defendant's standpoint, you need an adequate time to discuss the evidence and to persuade, in order to obtain an adequate verdict on the plaintiff's side, and to talk a jury into doing that which they came there *not* to do — to acquit — on the criminal side. And you need time to do it." Preiser

4. "In the criminal process, summation is, I believe, much much more important for the defense than for the prosecution. Because the prosecution has the benefit of first impression and majority of the evidence. On the criminal side, you are truly defending." Magarity

B. Plaintiff/Defense (within civil litigation)

1. "The purpose of the summation is, on the plaintiff's side, to sum up what makes his claim a valid claim. To tie all the points on which he thinks, during the trial, he scored

— in terms of presenting either the legal bricks that supply the foundation for his claim, or on top of the legal bricks, the episodes or incidents which may have been described or occurred, which in his judgment appeal to a jury as people. Including an emotional appeal."

"From a defendant's standpoint, the purpose of the summation is to summarize the defendant's defense. Which means to shoot holes in the plaintiff's case. And also, to try to create a rapprochement with the jurors. The plaintiff has an enormous advantage from that standpoint." Levy

C. Prosecutor/Defender (within criminal trials)

1. "It is the first opportunity since the opening statement — which is merely a hopeful indication of what the future may hold — to demonstrate . . . that you have delivered on your promises — which is very important. Whatever you promised in opening, you have buttressed with some evidence which the jury's heard . . . So you can construct a paradigm and fit everything into it, which should give rise to a reasonable doubt in a criminal case."

"Or if you're carrying the burden of proof as a plaintiff or a prosecutor, you try and show why the house you have built is strong enough to support your premise." Bailey

2. "The longer a speech, from a prosecutor's standpoint, the more chances for prosecutorial misconduct. The more chances for an opinion to slip in." King

3. "As a prosecutor in a first degree murder case, you're going to ask them to put the man to death. Or you're going to ask them to come back with the verdict of murder in the first degree. You have to give them courage. On the defense side, you want to personalize the defendant." DeSimone

4. "We have to be so careful as prosecutors in our closing arguments not to appeal too much to the passions, because we can get into legal trouble with the Court of Appeals if we do . . . During the rebuttal, more is forgiven us — and for that matter, we are more likely to have the jury with us if we engage in passion. So that if the defense lawyer has, God forgive him, engaged in some sort of unfair tactic in the closing argument itself, then they expect and relish a certain amount of righteous indignation." Ainslie

5. "I tell defense lawyers, those who are going to defend people in criminal cases, certainly do not simply go back over, in what is supposed to be a closing statement, and paraphrase what all the witnesses against you have said . . . all they do is re-emphasize the prosecutorial theory . . . It may be a summation of some sort, but it's not the kind you're obligated to make. It's a summation for the other side." Haynes

6. "As a prosecutor, I wanted intelligent juries, because I had the feeling — the suspicion, if you will — that defense generally wanted — if they could confuse the jury, they'd win. And I wanted somebody that would not be confused, but that had a great deal of common sense." Lytton

7. "To be a good prosecutor doesn't necessarily mean very much. Because I think it's a much easier role to play. And the fact that you're a good prosecutor doesn't mean that you'd be a good defense lawyer. I think any good defense lawyer could become a good prosecutor - because you have the facts . . . you've chosen to bring the case. So that you're not walking into a courtroom because somebody paid you to come in there. You're walking into that courtroom because you've decided this is a case worth bringing there. A defense lawyer is brought there because he's been hired to go." Goldberg

8. "It gives the opportunity for the attorney for the commonwealth to place the pieces of evidence into a fabric of the whole of the case . . . The case is not about personalities. The case is about evidence, and witnesses, and their demeanor . . . and you're just a mechanism for presenting evidence in the courtroom." Christie

5.5 Sincerity/Credibility:

The issue of being, or appearing to be, sincere when speaking with the jury, and thereby earning credibility, appeared again and again in the lawyer interviews.

Sincerity

1. "My son told me, 'The most important thing about being an actor is sincerity. If you can fake that, you can fake anything.' I think there's a great danger — if you try to act too much — a jury may think you're faking, and I think *the* number one cardinal sin for a trial lawyer is to seem insincere . . . is to think you're trying to put something over on the jury — that you're conning them." Dershowitz

2. " . . . assets that I think I have. Which I think are primarily based on my common sense and my sincerity. Because I do not say anything that I do not mean . . . I think it's [sincerity] everything." Ainslie

3. "I wanna be sincere. I want them to understand that I absolutely, fully am convinced of the rightness of whatever it is I am arguing ... It's a matter of sincerity. I wanna convey sincerity." Lytton

4. "I think [in a civil trial] an emotional approach can be a very dangerous thing to do, because if a jury sees through you — To me an emotional approach is something that's not quite sincere, not based on reason . . . I don't ever wanna say something to a jury that doesn't persuade me and I don't believe." Litvin

5. "A juror once said to me, 'We thought you cared.'" He considered it the best compliment he ever had." King

Credibility

1. "If you try to change character in the middle of the trial, or between the trial and

the closing, I think you're in trouble. I think you lose credibility. Jurors don't like the feeling they're being conned." Dershowitz

2. "I think it's important that you build up your credibility during the trial, so that by the time you stand up there at the time of closing argument, they are ready to believe what you tell them . . . If you have given them the impression that you are competent, reasonable, and can be depended on, they're much more likely to accept your closing argument." Ainslie

3. "A heavy handed sell from one in the posture of an advocate is not very effective, because lawyer's arguments are greeted with scepticism. Everybody knows that they are doing a job whether they believe in it or not as a surrogate for a silent client with a lot at stake. So, credibility usually starts very low, and you have to build it constantly. And the way you do it is to remind them, 'At the beginning of this case I made a promise to you. I said these things would happen. Now look . . .'" If they didn't happen, "then I have to explain them, and if necessary, apologize."

"And I usually differentiate between what I know I can prove, and what I hope I can show. Because you see, I'm not carrying any burden [like the burden of proof the prosecutor has]. I'm entitled to assume the burden of proving innocence, if I can handle it. If I've got the Pope as an avid eyewitness, I'm not going to leave him out." Bailey

5.6 Persuasion:

1. "At the bottom line, it is nothing but persuasion. Its whole purpose, its whole function is to persuade a group of people to go in a certain direction. And there are two ways to do that. One is to order them, and the other is to show them the wisdom of behaving in a certain way . . . A suggestion is the foundation of hypnosis. If somebody accepts your suggestion, you are controlling their contact."

"Many call this a final argument. But an argument presumes that two people are arguing with each other. 'You aren't going to argue with me. And you're never gonna tell me what your argument is, except as I may pick it up from little indications in your eyes. This is a summary of where we are from my view, and if you find it to be more persuasive than the one you're gonna hear from my — uh — learned friend, you'll acquit the defendant. And if you're not, you're gonna convict him. And that's where we are. I only have a little time ...'"

"Lawyers will get up and fawn all over the jury, and *ask* for their attention. I don't do that. I require it. 'I want your attention every single minute.' Because if I'm successful, by the time 'my boy' [opponent lawyer] gets up, I'll have tired that jury out to the point where it's really hard to sit and give him the same amount of attention." Bailey

2. "I honestly believe that in the process of persuading the jury — which is virtually your total goal in trying a case — your total goal is to win — is to get the twelve people to decide the way in which you want them to decide. So the whole process is persuasion. The elements of that are facts, and logical argument from those facts. So what you're

doing in the summation is, you're saying, 'Okay, now all that stuff that's gone up until now, let me put it into perspective for you, and show you why you should decide my way'. So it is probably *the* most important element in the process of persuasion, and persuasion is what you're trying to do the whole time. You're trying to convince them that you should get what you're asking for." Magarity

3. "I am totally convinced that you cannot persuade or convince anyone emotionally or intellectually until you can move them first physically . . . If I can make you move physically in a summation, respond to me, . . . then I can talk to you intellectually and emotionally; then I mold it together." Preiser

4. " . . . being persuasive. What that comes down to is having a point of view. We call it 'theories', a theory of the case — or theories of the case . . . and not making every possible argument that can be made . . . I think it's important for the lawyer to make the meaningful arguments. The arguments that will grab the jury by the brain, that will be persuasive." Litvin

5. "Most people don't have an ability to speak. Very few lawyers are good at it . . . I think a lot of summations are God-awful. Most lawyers don't have an ability to become effective salesmen, persuaders to a jury. Those that do (depending again on what kind of a jury they got for that case), can make a very persuasive speech, which can be extremely compelling to the jurors in that particular case."

"It's not just the words that are part of the persuasiveness in that speech . . . If a jury listens to a speech that I give them, and it's persuasive, the words are part of it. But I think the rapport is part of it; the way they have perceived me during the trial is part of it. The degree to which I become a symbol, or I made my part of the case become some sort of a symbol . . . Who seems to be the guy that is in control over what happens in the courtroom? Those things — body language — are part of a speech as well. Not occurring maybe at the moment of the speech, but they affect the listener in his receptivity." Criminal Defense

6. "I think that they [jurors] start out like most people — on the side of the prosecutor; that they believe like most people that the defendant must be guilty or else he wouldn't be brought here for trial. So I think you're in an uphill battle from the day you start, and that what you're trying to do is really to convert minds to your cause, bearing in mind that they've already sworn that they're evenhanded and are not starting out against you. I think that they are, and I think they have to be moved." Criminal Defense

7. "You are certainly more likely . . . to persuade a jury with an argument that doesn't make sense, then you are to persuade a group of judges . . . You can fool anyone at any point in time by making an argument that really . . . if time is taken to it by a good mind will see the holes in it. And you make the argument, and you hope no one sees the holes in it. And you kinda hold your breath when the prosecutor stands up."

Criminal Defense

5.7 Truth versus justice in the courtroom:

1. "These are all arts of persuasion not to do a wrong, but to do a right. To make the jury do what they came there *not* to do; to render justice. It's not a search for the truth — it's not at all. It's a search for justice. And justice is a lot more than truth. Justice includes within it mercy. Justice includes the application of the mores of our society in a given place and time. It includes the reflection of the socioeconomic conditions of the given time."
Preiser

2. "If you take the goal of the trial process as being the finding of truth, or as close a proximity to it as you can, then the elucidation and clarification part of closing is the most important . . . you have a chance to crossruff, so to speak, from your argument to the evidence, and back to your argument . . . this should be a very illuminating experience to the jury."
Prosecutor

3. "Truth is an important part of justice, but I think we put justice before truth . . . It's a system based on means. It's a process, not just a result — and it's not just a scientific testing, weighing."
Dershowitz

5.8 Summation as a two-way communication:

Although the summation has traditionally been conceived of as a one-way communication, many of the lawyers interviewed expressed the belief that a relationship of sender and receiver holds between lawyer/speaker and juror/hearer. Only the lawyer is speaking, but messages are clearly being sent and messages are certainly being received — in both directions. Therefore, it seems appropriate to identify the summation as a two-way communication.

Joel Sherzer (1983) wrote of the two participants in Kuna curing and magical rituals, the addresser and the adressees. Just as he describes the addressees, one could describe the jurors during summation: "The addressees do not speak during the performance — they are listening and understanding members of the dialogue" (p. 196).

1. "It's a very intimate relationship. I was absolutely unaware of anybody else in that courtroom, except me, the jury, and the defendants - and the judge, of course. But beyond counsel table, I noticed there were people standing. I knew the reporters were them. I knew my wife was there — the first time she ever came to court. But they disappeared . . . It was as if I was in their minds — I was hearing what I was saying as if I were a juror . . ."
Lytton - Prosecutor

2. "A lot of times lawyers don't pay attention to the effect they have on the people

they're arguing to . . . I had to be very disciplined to watch the jurors all the time, and if I saw their attention wandering, figure out what I could do to pull this one back at the risk of losing that one — and pull that one back . . . You know who's looking at you and who's not, and you can tell if they're looking kind of politely, or if they're really interested." Maguigan — Defender

3. "I try to pick out a leader and focus in on that person. The leader will take six or seven with them [during deliberation], if not twelve. The non-verbal communication should be saying to the leader: 'You understand what I'm saying, and when you go back there [in the jury room], you're going to be able to explain it to them [other jurors]'. I will put in my summation a point or an analogy or an anecdote, or something having to do with recognizing that person. And I will look directly at that person when I make the point, and my message will be clear based on the anecdote or the message that, 'You know that I'm speaking to you, and you know that I am giving you the message that when you go back there, you're going to be able to explain this'. I am acknowledging them and recognizing them, which is a very important factor in getting someone on your side . . . something like having a one-to-one conversation." Magarity — Defender

4. "The eye contact of a juror is a signal to me that they are paying attention to my argument . . . Some jurors are more expressive than others. I will often end up talking to that juror or jurors more than the others. If they have been maintaining close eye contact with me but then look away, then I think, 'I'm boring them and they're already convinced at this point. I should move on to something more'. Or they look confused, and I will go back and try to say the same thing more simply . . . I pitch my closing to those jurors who are willing to give me feedback about how the closing argument is going."

"I think I should definitely focus on those who are not with me yet . . . but I have no way of knowing before hand which those are ... I have no sense probably of how the great unwashed — you know, the remaining nine or ten — are feeling, and I'm simply going by the most expressive face in the group and trying to gauge my closing speech according to him or her." Ainslie — Prosecutor

5. "I cannot picture a good trial lawyer who during a trial isn't observing his jury and looking to see what is the effect — of everything that transpires in the courtroom . . . To a certain extent, while there is no ability to 'talk to' the jurors, during a trial that is at least any length of time, there starts to become almost an unspoken communication at times between the lawyers and the jury." Sprague - Defender

6. "You can tell when you're on the same wave-length. You can almost spot friendly faces. Not always, but sometimes. And you can spot the eyes that just look away from you." Goldberg — Defender

7. Q: How do you know if they're not paying attention? "The usual way; if they're not looking, or they're looking at their feet. Usually if they're looking at their feet, something's wrong. They're not bored. It may be that they've already decided that your client

is guilty, or that you're going to loose the case, or whatever it is, and they just can't bear to look at you." Temin — Defender

8. ". . . people that don't use notes keep their eyes where they belong on the witness — or the jury . . . because that's how you tell if you're winning . . . The unarticulated responses are legion. It's eyes, it's gestures . . ." Bailey — Defender

9. "They ought to be looking at the jury to see what a jury is responding to. Sometimes I'll be on a point that I don't think is too important and somebody is real interested in it, and so I may continue on it — or I may speak directly to that person. You don't get that unless you're really looking at them and having some communication."
Rudovsky — Defender

10. "The constant contact with the jury is necessary. The tone of voice. There are many ways in which you do it. As you walk down in front of the jury box — I would attempt to look at each of them. But walk back. They'll be a change of voice. Or there'll be a pause for emphasis at times. There will perhaps be a louder point — or a softer point — in order to make sure that they are contacted. To reach around and get a picture, or something physical, or something they can see or feel. Jurors seeing, feeling — and almost touching — to make them feel a part." McGill — Prosecutor

5.9 Style:

1. "I prefer to think of them as arguments — the final argument. I probably personally like 'argument' better than I do 'summation' because I probably argue more rather than I sum up. That's my style as opposed to other people's styles." Haynes

2. "This [mine] is not everybody's style. This is just what I like to do. I know there are other styles. But I know that I could not be anywhere as effective using anybody else's style." Meyer

3. "I still think the summation is extremely important . . . There might be a different verdict in *some* cases, . . maybe less then five percent. Because I think there are some criminal defense lawyers who are extremely able orators and that they may just be able to pull away one or two cases out of every one hundred based on their skills in closing. Sometimes it'll be based on emotion, and his style . . . in the summation." Kidd

4. "I think that lawyers who have firm rules are not people for all seasons. I think you have to make the rules as you go along, pending on whether a factorial approach would help, or whether an emotional one would help." Dershowitz

5. "A great part of my experience has really come from my opponent in the cases that I've tried. Watching what he has done and deciding what is good or bad about that, and to the extent that there is something good, taking it for my use subsequently." Sprague

6. "I'm comfortable that way [with hands in pockets], and I kinda think that it looks 'comfortable' to the jury. It looks like I'm comfortable in front of them. But I'm comfortable with at least one hand in a pocket, in a very masculine kinda strut or pose. It's individual style. Individual style!" Carolyn E. Temin

5.10 Performance:

1. "I'll spend the whole night working, really just getting it in good tune. And next morning, the trick is to try to stay up for it. I will not go to the office that day. I don't want any phone calls. It's a performance. Just like you don't speak to actors backstage, or singers." Fahringer

2. "If I am an actor, it is in the John Wayne genre: I just play F. Lee Bailey." Bailey

3. About feeling a sense of power: "Oh yes. Absolute — because you're on the stage. This is my time. If somebody interrupts me, they do it at their peril . . . All eyes are on you . . . I mean it's that being an actor again; being an egotist and enjoying the attention. Anybody who denies that they don't like all that attention when you get up to give an argument is not being truthful. I love it. I *love* it. And the more people in the room, the better. It's a cheap high!" Lytton

4. "What happens to me by the time the summation comes up, I'm so accustomed to the stage — where I've been — I've tried so many cases — that I can't wait to get up in front of the jury, because I know in my mind at that point in time that I'm going to outspeak the other guy — or the other lady." DeSimone

5. "Unless the adrenaline is flowing, the whole thing doesn't work... It's what a courtroom sets off in you that makes you different in a courtroom than you are in the office, at home, or anywhere else — and it *is* glandular . . . You react differently when you have a crowded courtroom. You react to the crowd."

Q: Do you like to have an audience? "I love it . . . I've tried cases in empty courtrooms. They try differently. It's really hard to get up a real head of steam in an empty courtroom. Very upsetting."

Q: If you're speaking just to the jury, why should that matter? "Well, I guess you could say the same thing to an actor: Does it matter whether you have one person out in the audience or a packed house? I would think most of them will tell you that a packed house matters. And it matters as a lawyer too."

"I think that there's enough ham in all of us that we respond differently when we have a full audience, just as I am sure that lawyers would respond differently if they're televised — as I'm sure that witnesses would respond differently if they're televised . . . I'm clearly focusing on those twelve people. There's no question about that. But the performance that comes out, and getting up for that performance, and it is a performance!, is, I think, gonna come out differently depending upon whether or not you've got a full courtroom — or an empty one." Goldberg

6. [During closing argument] "you should be the center of attention, and nothing else. It's like you're on stage at that time." Purnell

7. "When I'm standing up there, I suppose it's something like being in a play, or being an actress — or something like that — that you just get a feel of some time parameter that has nothing to do with the clock . . ." Temin

8. "You bet it's stressful. You are what stands between the defendant and the state. You are the guy who is there charged with the responsibility of this guy's liberty . . . It's the time when you're really called on to perform — in a sense that is more an acting kind of performance than you've been involved with throughout the trial . . . Here you really need the theatrical skills." J. R. Carroll

9. "It is on the stage . . . I hate to think of it that way, but I'm compelled to confess — yes, it's a great deal like the stage. You've got a script, and you want a review — that is *kind*!" Haynes

10. What they say about the closing speech when you lose the case: "He was a great actor, but the show stank." Fitzpatrick

SUMMARY OF DATA PRESENTED IN CHAPTERS 3, 4, AND 5

In Chapters 3, 4, and 5, the opinions of the interviewed lawyers were presented in their own words. Below is a summary of what they reported that they believe about summation. To put this summary into proper perspective, I repeat Birdwhistell (1970: 191):

> The report of an informant about his behavior is itself behavior; such reports are data and not evidence. And the fact that all informants agree does not make their statements true, except insofar as agreement indicates conventional understanding.

After each of the summarized findings below, a page number is given. On that page, the reader can find the complete findings and related comments.

The value of the summation to the trial process

* Three-quarters of the lawyers interviewed believed that the summation is extremely important to the trial process. No one stated that it is unimportant. (p. 38)

* Two-thirds of the lawyers reported that the outcome of the trial would be different without the summation. The others said maybe. (p. 39)

* To persuade, to clarify or explain your theory of the case — these were the most frequently expressed reasons for what the lawyers are trying to do in the closing speech. (p. 41)

Style of presentation of the speech event

* Eighty-one percent of the informants were able to describe their own style. (p.43)

* In answer to the question, "Are you good at it?", half of the lawyers interviewed said, "yes", or "I've heard it said about me." Only twelve percent wouldn't comment, or answered, "no, not yet", or "I'm getting better at it." These last comments came primarily from women lawyers. (p. 44, and see discussion of Women Trial Lawyers in Chapter 10.)

* Half of the informants preferred to give an intellectual closing speech. Another thirty-six percent stated a preference for a combination of intellectual and emotional. Few were interested in a purely emotional summation. (p. 47)

* Half of the lawyers use humor sometimes, with forty-four percent saying they never use humor in the closing speech. (p. 49)

* Two-thirds of the lawyers never disparage the opposing counsel. (p. 50)

* When asked if they experience stage fright just before the summation, the answers split fairly evenly between 'yes', 'some anticipation', and 'no', with a slight edge going to 'yes'. (p. 51)

* Seventy percent of the lawyers stated that they are attentive to the way they dress for summation. (p. 52)

Women in the act of summing-up

* Two-thirds of the respondents believed that women are different from men in effect in the courtroom, but in a positive way. (p. 53)

* Seven of the eight women interviewed said that being female in a traditionally male arena made a difference to them. (p. 54)

* Seven of the eight women interviewed said that they are attentive to the way they dress in the courtroom — with an awareness of being a woman. (p. 55)

Lawyers' views of the receivers (jurors) of the closing speech

* Two-thirds of the informants expressed very high regard for the jurors and the jury system. (p. 56)

* Almost two-thirds of the speakers said that they thought there was a relationship between liking someone and believing them, and expressed the view that if you can get the jurors to like you, they will do what you want them to do, i.e., decide in favor of your argument (client). (p. 60)

* When asked if they believed in using social scientists for selecting jurors, exactly half said yes and the other half said no. (p. 62)

* Almost two-thirds of the informants believe that jurors should be allowed to take notes. (p. 63)

Content of the closing speech

* Eighty-one percent of the respondents said that they do have a usual way of opening or closing their final arguments. (p. 65)

* A few more than half of the lawyers do not thank the jurors for their jury service. (p. 66)

* Exactly half of the speakers like to use metaphors, stories, poetry, biblical or literary quotations. (p. 67)

Methods employed for the speech event summation

* Better than two-thirds of the lawyers begin working on the summation when they accept the case. Twenty-three percent said just before they begin to speak. (p. 68)

* Three-quarters of the lawyers said they never include the client (or anybody else) in the preparation of the summation. (p. 70)

* Eighty-three percent said they do not memorize any portion of the closing speech. (p. 71)

* If there are several defense attorneys representing several clients, almost half of the lawyers said they prefer to sum up last. Thirty percent said first. The others had no preference, except no one wanted the middle slot. (p. 72)

* More than half of the respondents said they address their summation to all of the jurors. Almost another third said they start out by addressing all the jurors, and then focus on their seeming supporters. (p. 73)

* Seventy-nine percent of the informants reported that they did not like to use the lectern. (p. 76)

* In answer to the question, 'Do you like to use notes?', the answers split just about evenly between 'no', and (with a slight edge) 'yes — on hand'. (p. 77)

* More than half of the lawyers said they like to use blackboards, large charts, overhead projector and other props during summation. (p. 78)

* Half of the respondents stated that they like to talk 1 1/4 — 1 1/2 hours. Another quarter reported 30 minutes to one hour. The complete range was from 'seventeen minutes' to 'all day'. (p. 79)

The factors that were agreed upon by at least two thirds of the informants are listed below:

Women are attentive to the way they dress in the courtroom — with an awareness of being a woman, 88% (p. 55)

Do not memorize any portion of the closing speech, 83% (p. 71)

Can describe their own style, 81% (p. 43)

Do have a usual way of opening or closing the final argument, 81%, (p. 65)

Do not like to use the lectern, 79% (p. 76)

Believe the summation is extremely important to the trial process, 76% (p. 38)

Do not include the client in the preparation of the summation, 73% (p. 70)

Are attentive to the way they dress for summing up, 70% (p. 52)

Believe the outcome of the trial would be different without the summation, 68% (p. 39)

Begin working on the summation from the moment they accept the case, 68% (p. 68)

Do not disparage the opposing lawyer, 67% (p. 50)

Believe that if women are different from men in effect in the courtroom, it is in a positive way, 67% (p. 53)

On some issues, the informants differed on a 50/50 basis:

* The issue of using social scientists for selecting jurors (p. 62)
* Using metaphors, stories, poetry, biblical or literary quotations (p. 67)

On some issues, the split was almost 50/50:

* Using humor in the summation (p. 49)
* Thanking the jurors for their jury service (p. 66)
* Using notes during the summation (p. 77)

* Most of the informants (71%) reported that they learned how to sum-up by observing experienced, well-known courtroom lawyers when they were beginning to practice law. (See section 4.1, pp. 84-86.)
* No one believed that the summation was not at all important. (p. 38)

Seventy-five percent of the lawyers who know this way of speaking and were interviewed for this study concurred that the summation is an extremely important part of the trial, especially in what was termed a close case.

The data in Chapters 3, 4, and 5, which represent the views of summation according to the users, will be evaluated in juxtaposition with the views of the observer (Section 2) and the jurors (Section 3) in the final chapter.

SECTION 2: The Observer

6. Observing Summation

One of the two related issues investigated in this study is the description of summations as I observed them within the context of actual courtroom trials. Hymes (1972: 59) wrote that "...*how* something is said is part of *what* is said". Although how some things were said during summation can be reported, what was said exactly cannot be. There is a proscription against using electronic recording devices in the Pennsylvania courts (Pennsylvania Code of Judicial Conduct, Canon 3A-7). Several judges were extremely helpful in assisting with the data collection for this research and I did not wish to impose my presence further into the judicial process than necessary, and thereby perhaps lose the privilege of interviewing jurors for Section 3 of this study. However, very accurate notes of speech were taken.[9]

Subjects

The population for this part of the study was selected in one of two ways. First of all, almost half of the interviewed lawyers were observed in the courtroom. Many criminal trial lawyers try very few jury cases, some only one or two a year. They report that they consider themselves having served their clients better if legal matters can be resolved outside of the courtroom. 'Going to court' is to be avoided if possible. Therefore, many of the interviewees were rarely on trial during the period of the data collection and could not be observed in summation. However, sixteen of the thirty-four lawyers were observed, and three were observed twice.

Nine of the interviewees were observed in the courtroom after the interview. However, on occasion I observed lawyers in the courtroom who I determined should be interviewed and included in the study because of some special quality of the summation. There are six of these lawyers. One lawyer was first observed, then interviewed, and then observed a second time.

The second group of lawyers observed was selected by chance. Three judges permitted the use of their courtrooms for this research and the lawyers observed were those who happened to be appearing in a courtroom the day I was present. In every criminal trial, there is always one prosecutor and at least one defense attorney who will sum up, depending on the number of defendants being charged in the case. Therefore, I had the opportunity to observe a variety of lawyers, some of whom were outstanding in the verbal art of summation, some only perfunctory, but most of average ability. This provided very good information for comparative evaluation of summation quality.

Only attorneys in criminal cases were observed. Criminal cases terminate with guilty, not guilty or hung jury decisions. Civil cases result in a monetary award which can be great or small in consequence, or no compensation at all. Therefore, criminal cases as opposed to civil cases assure an either/or result against which the quality of a summation may be considered, but as we shall see later, not necessarily as an indicator of a good or bad closing speech. Many factors influence the result of a case, e.g., the facts in the case, the judge, the witnesses, the jurors, other lawyers, and the closing speech is but of these.

However sometimes it might be informative to know if a speech was part of a winning or losing case. For example, it would be interesting to know that a closing speech considered to be spectacular by speaker and observers was embedded in a losing trial.

The summations in twenty-four trials of the thirty-one included in this study were spoken in City Hall courtrooms in Philadelphia, which are state courts. Within the structure of the criminal code of the State of Pennsylvania, defense attorneys sum up first, being afforded the advantage of primacy, followed by the prosecutor representing the Commonwealth, who has the advantage of recency (Costopoulos 1972, Erlanger 1970, Hayes 1972). There is no rebuttal summation in the state courts.

The summations of seven trials were observed in the federal courts of Philadelphia. Instead of crimes against the laws of the Commonwealth of Pennsylvania, such as murder, rape and robbery, these courts concern themselves with those who are accused of having committed crimes against the laws of the United States government, such as income tax evasion, mail fraud and theft from interstate commerce. These courts are structured so that the prosecutor sums up first, followed by the defense attorney(s) representing the accused, followed by a brief rebuttal from the prosecutor.

The judges in the federal courts are appointed for life as opposed to being elected for a ten year term as they are in the Pennsylvania state courts. The prosecuting attorneys in the federal courts work for the United States government, while the prosecutors in the state courts are employed by the District Attorney's office.

City Hall courthouse serves many functions for the local citizenry and its physical environment encompasses the hustle and bustle that one would expect within this historic edifice, well used and supposedly responsive to the needs and complaints of the local population. The federal courthouse is austere, modern and unyielding, as one might also expect of a legal institution which requires the accused to respond to charges made by the government of the United States of America.

It is noted that in only one of the trials observed in both court systems was the defendant female, and she was a co-defendant with a man in a murder case. Also, all trials observed in City Hall concerned black defendants except two, one of which dealt with a teenage gang related murder and the other a burglary and car theft, for which the defendant was found not-guilty.

In contrast, the seven cases observed in the Federal Courts all concerned white defendants, except for one, a drug-related crime. The only interpretation that the reseacher can attempt with this very limited but very real data is that women do not appear to be involved in crimes which result in arrest and trial to the same degree that men do, and that white and black males may involve themselves in different kinds of crime. This difference may be a consequence of racial or ethnic distribution, or of socio-economic characteristics of the inner city, or an interaction of the two. According to the Statistical Abstract of the United States, 1986, Philadelphia has a population in excess of one and two-third million residents, 37.8% of whom are black. This city, as most congested metropolises of the East Coast, contains large pockets of poverty, and it is poverty which often forments criminal activity. However, since poverty is known to both whites and blacks in Philadelphia, it is admitted that an explanation of this observation is beyond the scope of this project and better left to those who study the sociology of crime.

Procedure for Data Collection

Information about each trial was obtained in three ways: (1) I observed the closing speeches; (2) a questionnaire completed by the alternate jurors immediately after they had been excused following the closing speeches and the judge's charge; (3) an almost identical questionnaire was completed by the remaining jurors after their deliberations and the verdict rendered. This chapter and the next are concerned with (1), the observations of courtroom summations. The other two matters are discussed in Chapter 9.

Jurors, the persons to whom the attorneys direct their closing speeches, the receivers of the speech event summation, are required to be fellow members of the community who may or may not have knowledge of the law. This description fits me, the researcher, as well and qualifies me to be a participant-observer in the courtroom. It is also relevant that I had served as a juror in the same jurisdiction only two years earlier, and was far more than a naive observer of the jury (Goldberg 1981).

I sat in the front row of the courtroom during summations, very near the jury box, where I listened as a juror might listen to the closing speeches of the lawyers. As well as taking notes of what the lawyers were saying, I also attended to the facial and body gestural behavior of the speakers. The responses of the jurors were also noted. Although unable to tape-record the speeches, selected utterances were accurately transcribed, to be used as examples of observed features.

In most cases, the lawyers did not know me, or realize that their speeches were being observed for linguistic analysis. In these instances, I could observe anonymously and be assured that I had no effect on the speech event.

However, when the informant and I knew one another in other contexts, or when the interview took place before the observation, I felt that sometimes there was an observer effect. Some lawyers appeared to be performing for me, even seeking eye contact from time to time. One or two of the speakers included features in their summations which we had discussed in the interview, such as not opening with the traditional formula, or discussing the speech event summation and explaining it to the jurors. One lawyer even referred to the fact that a person studying summations was in the courtroom. Another discussed the fact that summation was a topic of study, and related this to his speech, i.e., ". . . and I am told even by those who study closing speeches . . ."

Even though there may have been some participant-observer effect, I felt it to be minimal, for soon after the lawyer began speaking, he was well into the direct communication with his or her juror audience. However, after the conclusion of the summation, several lawyer-informants did discuss their closing speeches with me, asking my opinion of the speech, and volunteering information about what they thought they could have done better, which was usually a matter of including certain arguments, or deleting others. As one defense attorney told me, "The fear is that you will leave out something that you should have mentioned that would convince one juror, who will then go the other way."

Difficulties of Data Analysis

The utterances and observations were collected, analyzed and sorted into those features which I observed to occur frequently and which I deemed to be relevant to the communicative behavior of the persons involved in the presentation of a summation.

The sorting of the features into meaningful arrangements was complicated by the multiple functions which even apparently simple utterances can serve. The function of reference and conditions of truth or falsity of utterances has been studied for much of this century by British and American linguistic philosophers. The late British philosopher John Austin called attention to the fact that many everyday utterances escape such a focus. Utterances such as 'I now pronounce you man and wife' cannot reasonably be said to be true or false, but can be said to be felicitous or infelicitous. The conditions which apply to them have to do with appropriateness and inappropriateness -- whether or not they are said by the appropriate person under proper or improper circumstances in an appropriate or inappropriate way. Austin called this kind of utterance 'performative.' His classification and approach (Austin 1962) has been widely discussed, and a number of alternative classifications and interpretetions of such phenomena developed. This general area is commonly called Speech Act Theory.

Austin noted a distinction between the illocutionary force and the perlocutionary effect of utterances. The illocutionary force of an utterance is the work it accomplishes in being uttered in a specific context. The perlocutionary effect is its effect on the hearer. For example:

(a) "I thank you for your attention."
(b) "I urge you to consider the evidence carefully."

This set of utterances which were spoken during summation focusses on illocutionary force, and appear to be explicit in that a verb that names and does the act of thanking or urging is present.

The next set of utterances, (c,d,e), seems to focus on the perlocutionary effects. They are implicit in that insult, compliment, apology enter into them as effects.

(c) "Mr. L stood up there holier than thou."
(d) "You are kings, queens, emperors and empresses — presidents of the United States."
(e) "I don't pick or choose my clients."

But the relation between the doing of a speech act and the effect the act has is complex. Notice that the act of thanking or urging (a,b) could have the effect of an insult, compliment or apology, given various sets of circumstances. For example, (a) said when it is obvious no one is paying attention could have the effect of an insult; spoken when paying attention was difficult, and the fact of being attentive was of special merit could have the effect of a compliment; or an apology when the speaker thinks or intends to convey, and succeeds in so doing, that he really didn't deserve the attention, and feels apologetic for having received it.

In the second set, each of these also could have a different perlocutionary force. Utterances (c and e) could be 'assertive' in their illocutionary force, statements which could be deemed true or false in relation to how they fit the world, i.e., the speaker in (e) really doesn't pick and choose his clients; he works for the Defender's office. His cases are assigned. A hearer usually can identify the appropriate perlocutionary force because something else is know to that hearer which enables him or her to do so.[10]

Observed Features

Below are listed the features which I noted as recurring and meaningful during my observations of summation. By placing what I saw and heard into these categories, I was able to observe sameness and differences between speakers.

The features are divided into four categories:

(1) Their choice of words
(2) Apart from words
(3) Hearer response
(4) Topics for argument

This chapter is a partner to the next chapter. Here are listed the features according to category, and in Chapter 7 the reader can find real world examples of most of these features that were spoken during actual summations. The link between the features listed in this chapter and the examples in the next is the page number placed after the feature. In this manner, the reader will know not only which features were significant in summation, but how they were expressed.

(1) *THEIR CHOICE OF WORDS*

A. Structural slots in the summation

Opening words: traditional (147)
nontraditional (146)
Signals close (152)
Closing words: assertion (139)
imperative (139)
request (140)
urging (141)

B. Small genres of speech

Apologies (138)
Compliments: jurors (142)
opposing lawyer (142)
Descriptions
Enumerations
Insults: other lawyer (143)
witnesses (144)
Jokes (144)
Politeness formulae: thanks jurors (154)
Requests (140)
Rhetorical questions (150)
Sarcastic comments (152)
Suggestions (153)
Urgings (141)

C. Modes of discourse management

1. Channel: Comprehension checks (142)
   Hedging (143)
   Repetition
   Self-correction (152)
   Slang (153)

2. Message form: Direct quotes (148)
   Latin used
   Memorized material repeated
   Reads from written material

D. Syntactic and lexical choices

Imperatives (139)
Metaphors (145)
Terms of address: deceased (149)
defendant (149)
other lawyer (149)

(2) *APART FROM WORDS*

This dimension includes features, apart from words, which were identified with speakers.

Body motion used for emphasis
Charts, photographs, exhibits and maps used
Checks own notes
Does not look at jurors' faces
Extensive use of hands
Hand props used (i.e., pencils, eyeglasses)
Silence: Loses train of thought, changes topic of discourse
Missing words: No discernible closing
Objections made by opposing attorney
Recess during summation
Sidebar conference during summation
Speaker bangs on lectern or rail with hand
Stance (in relation to jurors):
- Sits down at own table (desk) during
- Sits in witness box during
- Speaker at rail of jury box
- Speaker at lectern
- Speaker across the room
- Not too distant (6 to 10 feet) from jurors — moving
- Not too distant (6 to 10 feet) from jurors — stationary
- Speaker stationary

(3) *HEARER RESPONSE*

This category incorporates the responses from some of the hearers of summation, jurors and observer. One of the dimensions, termed Tone, coordinates with key in Hymes' mnemonic device SPEAKING discussed in Chapter 1: "The tone, manner, or spirit in which an act is done" (Hymes 1972: 62).

The (a) list of adjectives under the heading of Tone refers to this observer's response to the overall tone of the *speaker* throughout the summation, such that at the conclusion of the summation, one of the listed adjectives could descriptively complete the phrase, "I thought the speaker was (angry, brusque, defensive, etc.)"

The (b) list refers to my response to the overall tone of the *summation*, such that the adjective could complete the phrase, "I thought that closing speech was (contrived, perfunctory, etc.)"

A. Juror response:

Juror(s) answer aloud lawyer's opening greeting
Appearance of jury attentiveness
Very attentive
Moderately attentive
Paying less attention than at start

B. Observer response:

(a) Tone of speaker was
Angry
Brusque
Defensive
Direct
Dramatic (154)
Gentel/soft
Impassioned
Informal
Intense
Formal
Logical/intellectual
Passive
Sweetly feminine
Timid/unsure of self
Unemotional

(b) Tone of summation was:
- Contrived
- Patriotic
- Perfunctory
- Very believable

These are not the only tones to be observed in speaker and summation to be sure, but these are the ones to which I responded and so indentified in the sixty-six summations observed.

(4) *TOPICS FOR ARGUMENT*

Appeals to emotional issues
- Attitudes toward opposing counsel
- Courage: Have courage to do the right thing (142)
- Discusses using '(good) common sense' (141)
- Emotion (143)
- Morality
- Onus placed on jurors: You are responsible (146)
- Patriotism (147)
- Pity my poor client (147)
- Qualification of presentation during summation (148)
- Religion: God's name evoked (150)
- Solidarity: 'We' — you and I are a team (153)
- Television: This is not like Perry Mason (154)

Appeals to intellectual issues
- American legal system (138)
- Credibility (143)
- Discusses evidence or facts (149)
- Follow the law as the judge presents it
- 'Metasummation' discussion of summation (153)
- Reviews witnesses through testimony (155)
- Recollection: yours controls (148)
- Type of witnesses (155)

Legal definitions (or discusses)
- Accused does not have to testify
- Burden of proof (139)
- Presumption of innocence (147)
- Reasonable doubt (148)
- Robbery
- Scotch verdict

Refutational arguments

Refuting arguments which were made or might be made by opposing counsel (150)

Setting the Scene

The physical context in which summations are presented is significant. As almost any movie-goer or television-watcher knows, the judge in a courtroom sits at a raised and usually massive desk at the front of the court, with the flag of the United States of America prominently displayed nearby. The jury is seated in the jury box, a waist high enclosure, usually wooden, topped off by a railing, which is positioned to one side or the other of the 'arena', and is where all the activity takes place. The witness stand is placed next to the judge and facing the jurors. (See Chapter 10 for a description of differences in the Old Bailey Courts in London.)

The lawyers each have a table near the center of the arena facing the judge, at which they are seated when they are not immediately involved in the activity in the courtroom. They usually stand to speak (always in federal court). The accused sits near the defense attorney at his table across the room from the jurors. If the defendant is not in custody, however, he may sometimes sit elsewhere in the courtroom. The prosecutor normally sits alone just in front of the jurors. This is by tradition, and not by law. One defense attorney reported that he demanded the table nearer the jurors in one instance in the state of Texas, and was granted that position by the judge only after much argument, followed by finally sitting on the prosecutor's lap.

When the lawyers rise for the summation, they have a choice of where to stand to speak. They may stand at their tables, or at the lectern positioned near the center of the arena. They may approach the jury box and select a spot not too distant (six to ten feet) from the jurors, or they may walk right up to the box, and even use the rail for a desk for their notes. They may walk around the arena while they speak, or take a spot and remain there. Some prefer to pace; some do not. This is regulated only by the preference of the sitting judge and the style of the lawyer. Although the use of a lectern is officially required in federal court, the judge may not demand compliance. It is truly the judge's courtroom.

From the moment that the judge informs the jurors that the lawyers are to begin their closing speeches, the courtroom becomes silent. Judge, jurors, attorneys, the accused, and all those present often visibly settle back in their seats, preparing to listen. What happens next depends on what kind of a courtroom you are in. I saw courtroom clerks in the Pennsylvania state courts alter the seats of the jurors to be certain that they were fully facing the speakers. (In federal court in Philadelphia, the chairs are affixed to the floor.) In some courtrooms, the judge instructed the bailiff to lock the doors so that no one could enter or exit, and sometimes ordered that the telephones be removed from their hooks. One bailiff announced, "If anyone wants to go to the bathroom, go now . . . On no condition will anyone be able to enter or leave." All of this is to insure that the speakers will not be interrupted.

In four of the trials observed, the judges included the following remarks in their announcement of the closing speeches in which they expressed their beliefs concerning who may speak and when, what may be communicated, and how the hearers should evaluate the content:

(1) "You're about to hear closing arguments, or summations . . . The defense will speak first, and then the Commonwealth . . . which will be submitted to you for your consideration . . . Listen closely, attentively, carefully, attentively, energetically . . . It's important for you to know that . . . statements contain . . . theory, argument . . . but not necessarily evidence. Both sides desire to convince you of their advocacy . . . a connected presentation favorable to his client. Most important, they are *not* part of the evidence and shouldn't be considered as such. The evidence is presented in the trial proper. Evidence ends with the end of the trial . . . Use your God-given common sense and ability to think."

(2) "Nothing that the lawyers say is evidence. It doesn't add to, take away from or change any evidence . . . It's your recollection which governs . . . The order of closing speeches has no special meaning . . . It has nothing to do with persuasiveness. They are permitted to argue to you in a manner which best presents their point of view. If you find their arguments persuasive, follow the argument. They are an attempt to guide your way to an analysis of the evidence."

(3) "Not everything you hear will be fascinating, so it requires your absolute attention."

(4) "It is now time for closing arguments . . . the opportunity to argue to you the weight and facts to be drawn from . . . this very important part of the proceedings . . . [Looks at first speaker] You may close to the jury."[11]

Sometimes the judge will simply nod in the direction of the first speaker, making no comment.

After the closing speeches, the judge charges the jurors by explaining the law which is relevant to the case, and then they are sent back to the jury room to deliberate. The judge leaves the bench soon after. The silent attention in the courtroom ends.

In Chapter 7, the reader will find the quotations which exemplify the features identified as significant by the observer and presented in this chapter. In Chapter 8, specific summations will be discussed.

7. Words Spoken in the Courtroom while Summing Up

The following pages contain quotations that were spoken during the sixty-six closing speeches throughout which I sat near the jury box and, as did the jurors, attended to the speaker and the message. These utterances were recorded on paper as I listened to the speeches, and were selected for one of two reasons. They either demonstrated features of summation which I had already identified as being significant, or they performed the reverse function of signaling a feature which I considered significant and should therefore be identified.

During the forty-seven hours and twenty minutes that I listened to closing speeches, there were many words spoken. From the ones which caught my attention and which I was able to accurately record, I have selected the following quotations to serve as examples of the significant features listed in the proceeding chapter.

The same complexities which were discussed concerning identifying illocutionary force and perlocutionary effect persist for these utterances. Although a quotation might demonstrate one force and have a different effect, there is often overlap so that this same utterance even in the same circumstances might exemplify more than one feature. For example:

"And where's the beef?" Although this utterance appears as an example of a metaphor ('beef' in this play on words of Wendy's commercial being a metaphor for 'evidence'), it also serves as a rhetorical question.

"God-given common sense": This utterance could serve as an example of evoking religion, or as an example of the use of the expression 'common sense'. The category into which each utterance was placed was motivated by the desire to provide appropriate examples of as many of the features as possible.

The quotations are categorized according to the features listed in Chapter 6 and are presented in this chapter in alphabetical order. For example, a reader who is interested in learning what was uttered for nontraditional opening words of a summation may find 'Opening — nontraditional' between 'Onus placed on jurors' and 'Opening — traditional' in the text which follows. Or one might locate 'opening words' under the heading of Their Choice of Words in Chapter 6, and refer to the page referenced there.

The prosecutor in a criminal trial has no client per se, but represents the interests of the state or government. The prosecutor carries the obligation and the burden of proving that the defendant committed the crime of which he or she is accused. The defense attorney represents the accused person, and is under no obligation to prove his/her client innocent, only to defend that person from the charges brought by the prosecution. Since the aims and purposes of the prosecutor and defense attorney differ, it is often relevant to know if an utterance was used for one purpose or the other. Therefore, each quote is followed by either (P) or (D), signifying that the speaker was either a prosecutor or defense attorney.

Writer ellipsis, as usual, is indicated by (. . .), and speaker hesitation or change of topic by a dash (-).

Words Spoken in Summation

American legal system

"We're a government of laws, not men." (P)

"The American system of justice is the envy of the free world." (P)

"I'm asking you to do what the founders of this country demanded; to make the commonwealth prove . . . " (D)

"In this country, we don't have that [communistic] system of justice... And this is the system you would want for a member of your family accused of a crime." (D)

"A system of justice that is just majestic in these United States." (D)

"That's one of the things wrong with our criminal justice system. You're not allowed to write, and you're not allowed to ask questions." (D)

"You become a part of the jury institution, an institution that has a history of eight hundred years." (D)

" . . . ninety-nine guilty men go free — rather than one innocent man go to prison." (D)

"The system looks very strong, but it's very fragile . . . It's ill beyond words." (P)

Apologies

"I've been sarcastic. And if I've offended you, I apologize." (P)

"Frankly, I'll be invading your privacy." (D)

"'Let's fuck 'im up.' — Pardon my language." (D)

"It's none of your business — I don't mean to be rude." (P)

"I don't pick or choose my clients. I get them when they need me." (D)

"Pardon the language: 'threaten to rape a white bitch.'" (D)

"I'm sorry I talked so long. Lawyers have the habit of talking too long." (D)

"I'm just trying to make a point. I trust you'll understand." (D)

"I apologize in advance — I can't remember all the details exactly. I do not intend to mislead you . . . Forgive me if I mislead you." (D)

"I apologize for being so long, and I thank you for your attention." (D)

Reads profanity from testimony: "You'll have to forgive me, but that's the way it was." (D)

Burden of proof

"We do not have the burden of proving complete guilt." (P)

"We have no burden at all." (D)

"The burden of proof on the government never shifts." (D)

"The commonwealth has a burden of proving to you . . . to convince you. And it is the commonwealth's burden to prove to you . . ." (D)

Closing — assertion

"I submit to you that a proper verdict in this case is 'not guilty'." (D)

"You can determine from that evidence that this man is guilty of burglary. Thank you." (P)

"His name is (full name) — and he's not guilty!" (D)

"On that note, when you meet that 'fateful day of judgment', know you have made the right decision." (D)

"If you believe that, then your verdict must be not guilty." (D)

"I trust that the jury will do what's necessary." (D)

"He's got the last speech. But you've got the last word. (Pause) But better than that — you've got the last two words!" (D)

"It won't work anymore. (Full name of accused) knew his accidents were phony. (Full name again) is guilty as charged and as shown by the evidence in the charges. Thank you." (P)

Closing — imperative

"You will bring back the true and correct verdict in this case." (P)

"The name of that, ladies and gentlemen, is first degree murder. You will see that justice is done for the citizens and city of Philadelphia." (P)

"You will review the facts, and all twelve of you — all twelve of you will say: '(Proper name). Not guilty.'" (D)

"Keep that fish on the hook. Find him guilty of every charge." (P)

"Find my client innocent!" (D)

". . . and you'll return a verdict of guilty. Thank you." (P)

"You will have no choice but to bring back a verdict of not guilty." (D)

"Ladies and gentlemen, they have convicted themselves. It remains to you to . . . " bring back a guilty verdict. (P)

"You bring one verdict — and one verdict only — in this case. You say, 'We're not gonna allow the government . . . 'You bring back 'Not guilty.'" (D)

"It is now your job to stand up and tell the government that (full name) is not guilty." (D)

"Ladies and gentlemen, you can *only* return a verdict of not guilty." (D)

"You have in your power to end it. Come back and deliver a verdict of murder in the first degree." (P)

"You will come back from your deliberations and tell the government that they didn't do their duty, and you'll find the defendant not guilty." (D)

"I ask you, ladies and gentlemen, [the two accused murderers] lookin' real cool. Are they shakin' in their boots, or are they not? [Points to them] The bosses! Pin on them, ladies and gentlemen, the label they deserve: 'murderers.'" (P)

"The verdict *must* be not guilty. Thank you." (D)

Closing — request

"I ask you to find Mr. X guilty . . . for first degree murder." (P)

"I ask you on behalf of my client to come back with a verdict of not-guilty for my client. Thank you." (D)

"The commonwealth asks you to find the defendant guilty of all the charges. And then we will ask you to say no more." (P)

"(Proper name), 'Dirty Harry' — anything you wanna call 'im. I ask you to find him not guilty." (D)

"The commonwealth asks you to return a verdict of guilty of murder in the first degree." (P)

"I ask you then to consider the facts that I discussed with you, and return a verdict of first degree murder and possession of an instrument of crime. Thank you very much." (P)

"I ask you to return a verdict of acquittal in this case." (D)

"We are not asking you to guess. We're asking you . . . Then there could be no other verdict than guilty." (P)

"I ask you to reject the testimony of five junkies. I ask you ... I ask you . . . I ask you to return verdicts for all the defendants of *not* guilty." (D)

"If you can explain away all that evidence, then you can find him not guilty . . . I ask you to find him guilty." (P)

"The defense would respectfully ask that you come back with a verdict of not guilty." (D)

Closing — urges

"I urge you to do nothing more than your duty and to find Mr. X not guilty." (D)

Common sense — use your

"Use your heads. Use your common sense." (D)

"You weren't just born yesterday — use your common sense." (D)

"You, as common sense possessed persons, . . . " (P)

"*Please* do not leave your good common sense on the *outside* of the [juryroom] door." (P)

"The one thing we ask of you is not to forget your common sense when you go into that jury room." (P)

"You're common persons. All you're asked to do is apply your common sense." (P)

"Utilize your common sense . . . You've gotta think about this in a common sense way." (P)

"And I would submit that if you were to use your common sense and your reasonableness . . ." (P)

"The very basis of the jury system, the essence of the jury system, is the common sense of those who sit on the jury." (D)

"When you think about common sense, does that fit your common sense? It doesn't fit your common sense." (P)

"It is your common sense which directs you to what makes sense." (P)

"You go through each piece of evidence . . . Use your common sense." (D)

"Just apply your common kitchen sense." (D)

"Consider and apply your own test of common sense." (D)

"Take back to that jury room your good common sense." (D)

"How, ladies and gentlemen, does that appeal to your reason, logic, common sense?" (P)

Compliments jurors

"I'm appealing to your morality and intelligence." (D)

"You are part of justice . . . Something you do will produce an effect." (P)

"I looked over and saw you paying careful attention." (D)

"The fact finding — the fact finding is yours. The jury is the master of the facts." (D)

"You have the power no one else in this courtroom has, including the judge." (D)

"You are supreme in determining the facts . . . " (D)

"I'm not going to stand here and make fools out of any of you." (D)

"You are kings, queens, emperors and empresses — presidents of the United States." (D)

"You can look at it and evaluate it as well as, if not better than I can." (D)

"Your decision is supreme and final." (P)

"Each of you was the kind of person (First name, Last name) wanted to sit in judgment on her." (D)

"Because *you* know who was there, and *you* know who did the shooting!" (P)

Compliments opposing lawyer

"The prosecutor is doing what he is supposed to do." (D)

"Mr. H. He's a great lawyer." (D)

"X (last name of prosecutor) is a decent person — doesn't lie." (D)

Comprehension checks

"I submit you're going to come up with just what I said. Okay? Okay?" (D)

"Had six bullets. Okay?" (P)

"He came here well prepared to do his job, didn't he?" (P)

"I'm wrong, he's right. Okay?" (D)

Courage — jurors told to have

"You just have to say 'Not guilty'. You have to have some courage." (D)

"Please. Someone speak up for the law!" (D)

" . . . I want the other eleven to jump on that person's [juror's] chest." (D)

"One juror — just one — who says, 'I'm not gonna go along with it.'" (D)

"Some of the most interesting verdicts in the country have been 'not guilty'" (D)

Credibility

"We're dealing with believability — credibility. Is it believable that . . . Is it believable that . . . ?" "Is it as unbelievable as?" (D)

"Now ladies and gentlemen; if you believe V. X. [Defendant] was there, then you can believe everything he said." (P)

"Don't believe a police officer just because he's a police officer." (D)

"You ladies; I'm once again going to defer to your credibility." (D)

"That has the ring of truth. That makes sense." (P)

"Not credible. Down right not telling the truth." (D)

Deference to the Court

"May it please the Court." (P)

"With permission of the court." (D)

"Listen carefully to what the judge tells you." (P)

Emotion

"You are not to be swayed by emotion." (P)

"The entire situation is a sad and ugly one." (D)

"I apologize for being overly emotional. I get overly emotional. I can't control myself." (D)

"And I hope your emotion has run away with you." (D)

Hedging

"And I believe the judge will instruct you in this . . . You get the law from the judge. He will instruct, I think." (P)

"I guess what I'm saying to you is . . ." (D)

"I submit to you that you simply cannot . . ." (D)

"The judge will instruct you, I believe, . . ." (P)

"I think you'll see before I finish . . ." (D)

Insults other lawyer

"Detective P. was asked by 'this attorney here'. . ." (P)

"You may have seen the defense self-destruct . . . in the last hour and fifty-five minutes." (P)

"The prosecutor has dismally failed to prove to you anything." (D)

"I'm not going to speak as long as Mr. S." (P)

"I don't know what *their* [opposing counsel and his client] relationship is." (P)

"Mr. L stood up there holier than thou . . . " (D)

Walks over to prosecutor: "I've got news for you. It will blow the whole case over. (Name) is not (Name)!" (D)

"Come on gang, play with a full deck. Play with a full deck on this subject." (D)

". . . And when this prosecutor, and I choose not to praise X, although it's traditional to do that too. X has thrown things into this trial time and time again." (D)

"But my friend Mr. W . . . Mr. W has found that his proofs don't fit his opening speech — an embarrassment that happens to all lawyers. [Smiles] His closing speech was a somewhat different position." (D)

Insults witnesses

"The stink of J.L. will linger in this courtroom for weeks after we've all left it." (D)

About a pimp who testified: "*He's* ashamed that *I'm* Italian. That bum, that east coast distributor of herpes." (D)

"No righteous, moral human being could rely upon the testimony of a man like that." (D)

"Mr. X — and I think I honor him by calling him *Mr.* X." (D)

"If any of you believe X, then you have to live in another place in another time . . . You can see the savagery of the this man — and you can hear it from his own mouth." (D)

Jokes

"Cops aren't dumb. Well, maybe the one in the middle!" (P)

"Good afternoon, ladies and gentlemen. I thank you. I shall be brief - and the judge will be reasonably brief." (P)

"You can never find a cop when you want one." (P)

"You've [jurors] been selected not because of your beauty [smiles] — you demonstrated that you possess common sense." (P)

"That's a kind of a doubt — there's no doubt about it!" (P)

"I don't even know if he has a suit. He's gotta raincoat!" (P)

"I'll be brief. We're limited to thirty-five minutes and the judge has a big hook." [Judge responds: "You exaggerate, Mr. M."] (D)

"Poor X.Y. Poor X.Y. Came in here with one suit — and two Corvettes parked outside." (D)

"Without meaning to be offensive to anyone, the granting of immunity is like restoring someone's virginity." (D)

". . . talking for nine months — enough time to have a baby — and he couldn't remember!" (D)

"Good morning, good afternoon, good evening ladies and gentlemen of the jury." (D)

"It's a problem of staying up late preparing the speech." [Speaker had a frog in his throat; Had to ask for water.] (D)

Metaphors

"A man's home is his castle." (D)

"The defendant is cloaked with innocence." (D)

"It has the 'ring of truth.'" (P)

"Dirty, dirty, dirty Harry. Keep that fish on the hook. Find him guilty of every charge." (P)

"Curiosity killed the cat." (P)

"Now that just doesn't wash." (P)

"There is not one shred of evidence." (D)

"The rules of the game say . . ." (P)

"If false in one, false in all." (D)

"Last night I dreamed I was a butterfly . . ." (P)

"If these two men were standing here trying to sell you something,. . . (P)

"And where's the beef? Where's the beef? . . . Ladies and gentlemen of the jury. I suggest to you that from the evidence, or lack of evidence, where's the beef? Where's the shotgun? Where's the sweater?" (D)

Compares the trial with the Boston Tea Party: "Sometimes we have to protest the abuses of our government." (D)

"Forgive them our Father who art in Washington. Leave these pimps alone." (D)

"What's sauce for the goose is sauce for the gander." (D)

"I grew up in a small town . . . with justice for sale." (D)

"We've been a month. We're almost like family." (D)

"There are within the shifting sands of time, sands which shift." And continues later in the summation, just before the end: "And the sands will begin blowing the day after." (D)

"His lips are in the prosecutor's pocket." (D)

Lawyer sits and reads from 'The Caged Bird' by Maya Angelon: "A free bird floats on the back of the wind . . . freedom from fear, to be safe in one's own home." The bird is a metaphor for the murdered woman. (P)

The arrest of this man places "a black cloud over not only him, but his family. You [the jury] can remove that cloud." (D)

About a man selecting people to kill: "What is he talking about? Weeds in a garden?" (D)

"Can you speculate with eternity? [This metaphor is repeated many times throughout the summation] . . . All our fates are in your hands . . . Regardless of what Mr. F. says, or I say, or Miss C. says, if you're not speculating with eternity . . ." (D)

"Tell them bullshit — and call it Arpege." (D)

"All of William Penn's original city was in their hands." (D)

"D wanted to kill the messenger who brought him bad news." (D)

"That's when Mr. C goes south on us." (D)

Onus placed on jurors

"They're asking *you* to decide." (D)

"It is your sworn duty to convict if . . . " (P)

"*You* have to determine what happened here." (D)

You must judge fairly "so you go home with a clear conscious." (D)

"You now have a sworn duty, even though it may be unpleasant . . ." (P)

"This is a matter of great importance to my client. This is a matter of great importance to the commonwealth." (D)

"You have several jobs to do. You must piece together the evidence." (P)

"You deliberate as a group, but ultimately, you vote as individuals . . . The decision you're going to make will affect my client for the rest of his life." (D)

"All I am asking you to do, all you are duty bound to do, is weigh the evidence." (D)

"Well, ladies and gentlemen, you have the fate of J.B. — a good cop for X years — you have his fate in your hands. Do the right thing." (D)

"This is the most important week of your life." (D)

"I'm not trying to overwhelm you with your duty, but . . ." (D)

"I told you at the outset . . . now I'm going to hold you to your promise that you can follow the law to decide the case." (D)

"In your hands lies the fate of these two men." (D)

"And the only question that remains is what you're going to do about it . . . You've taken an oath like everybody else in this case. And what is you duty?" (D)

"This kind of thing *you* must stop. We will not take it." (D)

". . . and what you promised is that you would not base a case on speculation." (D)

Opening — Nontraditional

"Do you know what the word complete means?" (D)

"You're about to have in your hands the most important responsibility. You are about to hold in your hands the fate of one or three citizens." (D)

"Judge X. Miss Y. Mr. Z. Mr. A. [The chimes atop City Hall strike noon] The bell tolls. It's high noon in more ways than one." (D)

"You're about to have in your hands the most serious responsibility I know of — to pass judgment on another citizen." (D)

"Members of the jury, the question really in this case is who had the gun just before the shooting." (D)

Opening — traditional

"Judge S. Mr. G (Opposing counsel). Ladies and gentlemen of the jury. Good morning ladies and gentlemen." (P)

"Your honor, may I approach the jury?" (D)

"Your honor. If it please the court. Ms. P. (Opposing counsel). Ladies and gentlemen of the jury." (P)

"May it please the court; Counsel for the defendants; Ladies and gentlemen." (P)

"Thank you, Your Honor. Ladies and Gentlemen, at last we're coming to the end." [five week trial] (D)

Patriotism

"Every American doing his thing." (D)

"American people are basically good people." (D)

" . . . massive, overwhelming power of the United States government." (D)

"Some of you may think I'm wavin' the flag, and I'm sorry. But we're not in Russia; we're here." (D)

"I may get accused of flag-waving, but 'Give me liberty or give me death.'" (D)

Pity my poor client

"This peaceful man . . . " (D)

"Find this peaceful, law-abiding character — peaceful, law-abiding citizen . . . " (D)

"*I'm* not nervous here. This is our daily life." But his client was nervous on the unfamiliar witness stand. "I didn't present him to you as an angel . . . We are not here to judge a man's style of living, his morals . . ." (D)

"Who is [defendant]? He's a good husband; a good father." (D)

"(Full name of accused)'s on the line; his wife and kids are on the line . . ." (D)

Presumption of innocence

"The law gives an accused the presumption of innocence." (D)

Qualification

"What we [lawyers] say is not evidence." (D)

"I'm not eloquent enough to stand up here and speak without notes." (P)

"I am aware they [police] are important people in our city. I'm not scolding the police department. But . . . " (D)

"I'm not much of a speech maker . . . I won't speak longer than I must." (D)

Quotes

"'False in one; false in all.'" [First in Latin, then in English] (D)

The quotation on the building of the University of Pennsylvania Law School: "'The known certainty of the law is the safety of all men.'" (D)

Quotes opposing lawyer: "'We acknowledge there was a scheme.'" (P)

"'And, oh what a tangled web we weave, when we practice to deceive.'" (P)

"'The little man who wasn't there, oh how I wish he would go away.'" (P)

Reasonable doubt

"Because everything in life has some element of doubt." (P)

"This does not mean beyond all doubt, or to a mathematical certainty. You can say to yourself, 'I doubt because — ', and you fill in the blanks." (P)

"A reasonable doubt is a doubt for which you have a reason." (D)

"You are not to manufacture a doubt in order to avoid doing an unpleasant chore." (P)

"Not only have we proved our case beyond a reasonable doubt, but beyond *all* doubt." (P)

"Reasonable doubt . . . Not beyond all doubt. Not beyond all doubt to a mathematical certainty." (P)

"Ask yourself, does it start to raise reasonable doubt in your minds?" (D)

" . . . the kind of doubt that would cause you to hesitate in affairs that relate back to you." (D)

"There is such a doubt in this case, you *must* return a verdict of not guilty." (D)

"The judge will explain reasonable doubt. Listen to what he says, because every single word in that definition is important." (D)

"But it must prove its case beyond a reasonable doubt." (D)

Recollection

"Again, it's your recollection that controls." (P)

"It's your memory which is controlling." (D)

"Your collective recollection is supreme and governs." (P)

"To my recollection — I trust to yours . . ." (P)

"You are the trier of fact in this case. It is your recollection that counts . . . You are the soul controllers of the actual facts in this trial." (P)

Refers to deceased as though alive

"Because Robert X is Robert X . . . Because that's the kind of man Robert X is." (D)

Refers to deceased as Mr. (last name)

"Mr. (last name) was a fine man who didn't deserve to die." (D)

Refers to defendant by first name

"My heart goes out to John." [Sarcasm] (P)

Refers to defendant by full name

"I'm certain that Officer X believes in his mind that (first name, last name) committed this crime. And I'm certain that Officer Y believes (first name, last name) committed this crime." (D)

"I short-cutted this trial by not calling (his client's full name) to the stand." (D)

Refers to defendant insultingly

"The defendant is telling you a tale." (P)

"Deciding *what* Mr. M. is guilty of — [Objection sounded by opposing counsel]. *If* he's guilty." (P)

"He'll probably break into my house while I'm trying cases." (P)

Refers to 'evidence' or 'facts' in the case

"That's what I'm here for; to suggest ways of looking at the evidence." (D)

Refers to other lawyer as 'Mr.'

"No, Mr. M. There was no first degree murder here." (D)

"You have been very patient in listening to me. You will be very patient in listening to Mr. [Prosecutor]." (D)

"Mr. C talks in a loud voice; Mr. W in a soft voice. But they [defense attorneys] are all saying the same thing." (P)

Refers to other lawyer with title of power

"I'm not sure what the District Attorney's argument will be." (D)

"How dare the government make an accusation and not produce the witness!" (D)

Refutational arguments

"Mr. G. will probably speak with you about .... Let me speak to you..." (P)

Religion — evokes God's name

"I thank God for Mr. (Client)." (D)

"You can't decide. You can't play God." (P)

"God-given common sense." (P)

"You are not asked ever to find some one innocent. That's left for another time and place." (D)

Rhetorical questions

A lawyer would often supply the answer to his or her own rhetorical question without going outside of the confines of the law. (See utterances marked * below.) However, sometimes the lawyer's comment would be disallowed from the bench. For example, in one instance the lawyer said: "But let me tell you ...", and the judge interrupted with, "Mr. X, you're not allowed to testify in the case."

One of the ways the speaker can avoid directly giving his or her opinion, i.e., 'I think', is by stating a lack of knowledge of the truth of a proposition, i.e., 'I don't know'. But this disclaimer of knowledge can still clearly convey the beliefs of the speaker. (See utterances marked ** below.)

A rhetorical question can also be used to force the opposing lawyer to address an issue in his or her following closing speech."Who's testimony has the ring of truth?" (P)

"What would you do? Eh — excuse me. What would a reasonable man do?" (D)

** "Whose coat could it be? Could it be Mr. W's coat? Why didn't Mr. X see them? . . . I don't know." (D)

* "What's the first thing you do? . . . Take your foot off the break? Maybe." (D)

"Well, if it didn't happen that way, how did it happen?" (D)

"Why would he do that? Does that make any sense to you?" (P)

"Something must have happened here. What did someone do to get here in the first place?" (D)

"Is there reasonable doubt in your mind?" (D)

"Now is that someone who's trying to be evasive?" (P)

** "Do you think . . . ? I think not." (P)

"And isn't it a reasonable assumption . . .?" (P)

"Isn't that what she was supposed to do?" (P)

"Don't you have to be suspicious?" (D)

"Don't you have to worry about their story?" (D)

"Ladies and gentlemen, I'm sure you don't remember what was on the back seat of that car . . . Do you remember the car that you drove in here today?" (D)

** "What does it mean? I don't know what it means." (D)

"A lot of these are rhetorical questions. I'm not asking you. I'm asking you to ask yourself . . . Ask yourself, 'Does that make sense?'" (D)

** "What really happened there? I don't really know. I wasn't there." (D)

* "Who picked these witnesses? Who? You don't pick your witnesses." (P)

* "Yeah, I'm ashamed of you C.D. But interstate commerce? Come on!" (D)

"Venereal disease for high school kids. That's all right, isn't it?" (D)

* "Now ladies and gentlemen, what happens next? Well — nothing happens next." (P)

* "But what do they do? They talk it over." (D)

* "Ladies and gentlemen, is this the conduct of someone who's trying to make a vendetta of this? Or someone who's trying to put a stop to this." (D)

* "Who got caught time and time again? (Full name of accused)." (P)

"Would they come in here and place their hand on a bible and lie — and in such number?" (D)

"Parenthetically you might ask yourself, why did . . . I can't answer you." (D)

* "Did anyone say no? Of course not." (D)

* "She never saw a .45 kept under the mattress? Of course she did." (D)

** "That just doesn't — or does it? — make sense." (P)

* "He's a bum. But who's bum is he? Their bum — not the commonwealth's bum." (P)

* "Was he tryin' to fool you? He wasn't foolin' me." (D)

* "Now was the blue book relevant? Was it relevant? Of course it was." (P)

* "Did Mr. X know? Did he know what was going on in his law firm? Of course. How could *you* not know? How could you not know?" (P)

* "Did she say something — give an instruction to kill somebody? ... And I say absolutely not." (D)

"Where is the evidence we can touch?" (D)

Sarcasm

"*Perverts* — harassed by the bad policemen!" (D)

"Poor Mr. X — the *cockroach*!" (D)

"They've [the policemen] been punished. Not so with the pimps. *They've* been rewarded." (D)

". . . brought here by my learned friend Mr. S [other lawyer]." (D)

"Now who are these two witnesses? These two ladies didn't come off the planet Mars." (D)

"A jury is nothing more than a group of critics . . . Your days are finished. You have done what you came to do." (D)

". . . all the evidence the court *permits* you to see or hear about." (P)

"Get two eminent members of the New Jersey and Pennsylvania bars." (P)

"Now, when she said, 'Bust 'em Freddy', what do ya' think she meant?" (P)

Self-Correction

". . . had told us — had told them." (D)

"As you have saw . . . as you have seen, . . ." (D)

"I was — the testimony, as I recall it . . ." (P)

Talks about "prostitute", corrects to "prosecute". (D)

"Less freedom from — pardon me — *more* freedom from . . ." (D)

"Use your good sense — your *common* sense and good *judgment*." (P)

". . . who in the federal grand jury isn't sayin' nothin' — anything." (P)

"He don't remember. He doesn't remember." (P)

Signals close

"You can rest assured that you've done your duty." (P)

"I'd like to re-cap this very briefly. I know I've been talking a very long time." (D)

"I want to thank you for just surviving. You paid rapt attention . . . The important thing is for you to do your job as a jury, or just say 'the hell with it' . . . Not guilty on all counts — because that's what this case is all about. Do what the law requires you to do; Do you duty, and you will be a happy person . . ." [Speaks of] "to well and truly try these two men." [This speaker seemed to be unwilling to stop. He continued 'closing the closing' with many appropriate closings, one following the other. Finally he said] "I appreciate your indulgence." (D)

"Now I'd like to leave you with just one thought. You cannot disregard the words of the man himself." (D)

". . . and I'm drawing to a close here." (P)

"Members of the jury. In summary, in conclusion, finally . . ." (D)

Slang

"He don't talk too well. He ain't too educated. But he didn't evade you." (D)

"Is that the way a drug deal would go down?" (D)

"That's ridiculous, absurd; it boggles the mind." (D)

Solidarity — 'We' as a team

"You and I understand how difficult . . ." (D)

"Are we going to give her the Academy Award with all the other witnesses in this case?" (P)

"You remember what she said when we got her wiggling on the stand." (D)

"We all hate the IRS." (D)

"In a very real sense, you are us and we are you." (D)

". . . a person from everyday walk of life — like ourselves." (D)

"Ladies and gentlemen, I believe that we all believe in . . ." (D)

"All that a poor lawyer can do is put in a full day — just like you." (D)

Suggests

"I suggest that you're not getting the truth here." (P)

"I suggest to you that they had different customers." (P)

"What I suggest to you is the truth." (P)

"I'm going to suggest five areas." (D)

"I respectfully suggest to you . . ." (D)

"Then I submit to you, ladies and gentlemen, that you are twelve very gullible people . . . I suggest that you may be trying an innocent man." (D)

'Summation' is discussed

"This is the second and last time to speak to you. The defense speaks first, and the commonwealth speaks last." (D)

"I argue first . . . the District Attorney goes last. I won't have the opportunity to answer. I must anticipate [his arguments]." (D)

"Ladies and gentlemen, this is my opportunity to sum up . . . I now truly assume the role of the advocate." (D)

"Members of the jury, this is my opportunity to address you and summarize . . ." to show that "we proved the charges in the indictment. If I were permitted to have a dialogue with you rather than a one-way conversation, . . ." (P)

"What you're hearing today are summations. They're traditional . . . I don't believe in any case that summations have a great effect in changing your opinions . . . Each of us gets to give you a closing speech." (D)

"I just hope that when tomorrow comes and this speech isn't even a memory . . . and I am told even by those who study closing speeches that they are closing arguments — because in your minds, you are arguing with me — thinking, 'Oh, come on now.'. . . But ladies and gentlemen, I would like to argue — and this is really an argument - because you may disagree . . ." (D)

"Closing argument is not a tit for tat . . . Closing arguments are just that. They are not evidence . . . Because I sit here quietly during the defendants' closing arguments, it doesn't mean I agree." (P)

Television is topic

"I'm sure you heard it on television." (P)

"There are no Perry Masons in the courtroom." (D)

"Life doesn't copy Perry Mason. In real life, witnesses lie on the witness stand. Witnesses brazen out their testimony." (D)

"I'm sure we've all heard that on television." (D)

"This is not a television play. Not Perry Mason." (D)

Thanks jurors — in opening

"Ladies and gentlemen of the jury, first off I want to thank you for serving as jurors. It is very important . . ." (P)

"Thank you for listening to me. I have talked longer than I intended to." (D)

"Before I begin my argument I'd like to thank you." (P)

"With permission of the court; members of the jury. To thank you for your patience would be ludicrous. [Second longest trial in the history of Philadelphia: 80 days] If it were possible to thank you for your patience, I would." (D)

Thanks jurors — in closing

"I want to thank you for your attention in this matter." (D)

"Ladies and gentlemen. I thank you once again for your time and attention. Unfortunately, Mr. H speaks last." (D)

"I thank you for your indulgence." (D)

Tone — dramatic

These utterances were considered to be dramatic by me because all of them appeared to have been staged or rehearsed. Many would have been appropriate to a theatrical presentation.

"I am moved by the power of the experience . . . I feel grateful." (D)

" . . . send him home to his family where he was before this experience." (D)

"Imagine what his dreams are like. His dreams of that; But coming down on him not one time, not two times — but perhaps ten times." (P)

"I want to commend you. I have observed you paying strict attention. Our talking is about to end soon. And then — [drops voice] it is your turn to talk in the jury room." (D)

"But sooner or later, the disguise must come off!" (P)

"Our police are human! Our detectives are human! Our prosecutors are human!" (P)

"The Department of Justice never loses when justice is served!" (D)

"They're men. They're decent men. They've performed their duty well. But they made a stupid mistake . . . But Hobbs Act? [Calls out] No!" (D)

"What are we doing here? Is this the guise of cleaning up corruption? Abscam! *Copscam*!" (D)

"I'd hate to think that we go to heaven or hell according to what we could have done." (D)

"All I ask of you, and all (first name, last name) wants of you, is to mete out the same measure of justice . . . We want no more, and expect no less." (D)

"The murderer of (full name of deceased) is still walking the streets of Philadelphia." (D)

"She died for love. She died for love she wouldn't accept — and he wouldn't take no for an answer!" (P)

"Anyone who talks like this is *demented* A mad man! A *mad* man!" (D)

"Ladies and gentlemen, I'm about finished. I've raised my voice. It's not important. What is important is . . . what could have been, and won't be any more. Ask yourself, 'Why would someone have to live in constant fear?' Is that any way to live? Is there any question that the person — after inflicting blows — after the sperm was deposited..." [The lawyer then read a passage from Maya Angelon's 'The Caged Bird'] (P)

"You must find these two defendants not guilty. It's not your right. It's your duty." (D)

"We're talking about first degree murder. We're talking about dying in the electric chair. That's just about as final as you can get!" (D)

Speaker walks over to and stands right behind the two men accused of murder: "Get that tree. Get that tree! We've got two branches. Get the root!" (P)

Witnesses — type of

"He don't talk too well. He ain't too educated. But he didn't evade you." (D)

"He's not a professional witness. He's not used to . . . sitting there." (D)

"She's tryin' to get him off. But don't let her! Let the people at [names address] sleep." (P)

"I was not there. You were not there. Or else you would be witnesses instead of jurors." (P)

"Why can't the police officer, a trained observer, answer without hesitating? . . . Police officers can tell falsehoods . . . The human being in the police officer is now coming out." (D)

"I submit to you that that man was terrifying on the stand." [Objection made by opposing counsel] (P)

"I hope you like Mr. X. But I don't care if you loathe Mr. X." (D)

"We have to take our witnesses where we find them." (D)

"Mr. K is a philander. This man rises to the status of a J.R. Ewing. How does he deceive his wife for three years? He lies for three years. A man who cheats on his wife for three years is a man not to be trusted . . . I could buy him cheap." (D)

Some Quantitative Data

The quantitative data which follow are presented in the spirit of Saville-Troike (1982): "Although an ethnographic approach is quite different from an experimental one, quantitative methods may prove useful (even essential) in some aspects of data collection, especially when variable features of language use are being explored. Quantitative methods are essentially techniques for measuring degree of consistency in behavior, and the amount and nature of variation under different circumstances" (p. 119).

Prosecutor and Defense Attorney Differences

The prosecutors in the cases which I observed in the course of this research entered the courtroom carrying the metaphorical banner of either the State of Pennsylvania or the United States of America. Many of the lawyer/informants in this study, both defenders and prosecutors, expressed the view that the prosecutor usually has the advantage in the courtroom legal battle tried in front of a jury.

This possible advantage of the prosecutor is acknowledged in the Pennsylvania Criminal Practice:

> Because of the possibility that the jury will give special weight to a prosecutor's arguments due to the prestige associated with his office, and because of the fact-finding facilities available to him, the prosecutor in his

> closing address must present only "a disinterested, impartial and fair assessment of the testimony" that has been presented (Wasserbly 1981: Chap. 27-Page 41).

Furthermore, when I served as a juror, I learned that my fellow jurors were not altogether accepting of the concept of the presumption of innocence in spite of cautionary instructions from the judge at the beginning of our trial. I found that the accused was looked upon as one who must explain to the jury why the government had gone to all the trouble and expense of bringing his case to court (Goldberg 1981). Of the thirty-one trials included in this study, only five verdicts went to the defense.

Since the prosecutor and the defense attorney are speaking with difference purposes in mind during summation, I compared how these different purposes might manifest themselves in summation, if at all. Table 1 examines that possibility. All of the features included in this table are exemplified by real world utterances in the beginning of this chapter, in alphabetical order.

TABLE 1

Comparison of the eight features occurring most frequently in the summations of prosecutors and defense attorneys

	PROSECUTOR (N=26)		DEFENSE ATTORNEY (N=40)
100	Traditional opening	.83	Traditional opening
.81	Rhetorical questions	.75	Rhetorical questions
.62	Discusses using '(good) common sense' [.35][a]	.70	Onus placed on jurors
.58	Checks own notes	.68	Discusses or defines 'reasonable doubt' [.35]
.58	Objections made against [.18]	.60	Extensive use of hands [.38]
.58	Refers to 'evidence' or 'facts' in the case	.58	Checks own notes
.56	Onus placed on jurors	.50	Refers to 'evidence' or 'facts' in the case
.50	Jurors very attentive [.28]	.48	Signals close [.35]

a) The number which appears in brackets is the percentage of occurrence of that feature for the other type of lawyer, since it did not appear in the list of the eight most frequent features.

Traditional opening: This feature topped the list for both, which is hardly surprising given that almost everyone, lawyer and non- lawyer alike, knows that 'Ladies and Gentlemen of the jury' (or 'Members of the jury' in our non-sexist generation) knows the formula for beginning a closing speech. Although defense attorneys would sometimes begin their summations without the formalities of an opening, prosecutors never did. (Examples on page 147.)

Rhetorical questions: Since the speaker may not express his or her personal opinion (it is against the law and if done can be cause for mistrial), the rhetorical question permits the speaker to indirectly express an opinion. Therefore, this becomes an invaluable aid to the speaker and, as would be expected, this feature appears frequently in the summations of both prosecutor and defender. (Examples on page 150.)

Discusses using '(good) common sense': This request of the jurors was used almost twice as often by prosecutors. Defenders appear to be less anxious to encourage jurors to think logically about the accusations being made against their clients. (Examples on page 141.)

Checks own notes: Both prosecutors and defenders appeared to check the notes they had prepared for their speeches in equal amount, and to do it with some frequency, even though many informants reported that they didn't use notes. I had the impression that speakers were looking over their notes not only to check what they intended to say, but rather as a device to buy a little time to be certain they hadn't forgotten anything (a concern mentioned by many informants), or to allow a prior statement to 'sink in', or to use silence as a marker to change the focus of the discourse.

Objections made against: Objections to words spoken by the prosecutor in summation were made frequently by defense attorneys. There are legal reasons for this. If the accused is found guilty, a new trial can sometimes be won because of something the prosecutor said in the closing argument. But the defender is often required by law to object at the moment that the words are uttered. Therefore, the defender who objects might be looking ahead to the eventuality that s/he may lose the case and need a reason to have a trial ruled invalid.

Prosecutors objected infrequently. A trial that goes in the favor of the defendant (not guilty) cannot be retried. Therefore, a prosecutor would probably only object if there was something spoken that the prosecutor felt was truly inaccurate and/or prejudicial.

Refers to 'evidence' or 'facts' in the case: The prosecutors referred to the evidence admitted throughout the trial only somewhat more often than did the defense attorneys. (Examples on page 149.)

Onus placed on jurors: More than half of the prosecutors reminded the jurors of their serious responsibility to 'do the right thing'. But almost three quarters of the defenders used this same tactic. However, their approach was a little different, for they were not concerned with the welfare of the community and/or justice per se, but rather the rights of the accused. They wanted to make certain that the jurors took seriously the heavy responsibility of their power to have incarcerated or punished a possibly innocent person. (Examples on page 146.)

Jurors seemingly very attentive: Jurors appeared to give nearly full attention to half of the prosecutors, but did the same for only little more than a quarter of the defenders. The criteria established for attentiveness were: juror looking directly at speaker most of the time with little or no shifting of body in chair. The criteria established for inattentiveness were: looking away from speaker often, gazing at spectators, ceiling, floor, out the window, examining own hands or feet, and/or much shifting and moving about in chair.

However, even though jurors appeared to have been attentive to the summation, the observer could not be certain what was going through the listeners' minds. Just as for an academic lecture or religious sermon, members of the audience may appear to be paying attention while in fact they are entertaining their own thoughts.

There was a notable distinction in the appearance of attentiveness with jurors however, and they were rated 'very attentive', 'moderately attentive', and 'less attentive than at beginning of speech', all three conditions being observable.

There were four prosecutors who lost their cases. For only one were the jurors very attentive throughout, and that speaker was a very pretty woman. For a second speaker, the jury was initially very attentive, but attention dissipated as the speaker continued. The third speaker obtained only moderate attention throughout, and the fourth went from moderate to less than moderate attention.

There were five defense attorneys who won their cases. For two of those speakers, the jurors were very attentive throughout. Two other speakers held the listeners' attention throughout at the moderate level, and a last speaker, who gave a very disorganized closing speech, often fumbling for words, began with moderate attention from the jurors falling to less attention. This appeared to me to be a case which was won on the facts, and that had little to do with the closing speech.

Discusses or defines 'reasonable doubt': This topic occurs in the speeches of defenders almost twice as often as it does in those of prosecutors. Having 'reasonable doubt' is a significant reason for not finding the accused guilty, so it is obviously an excellent tool for the defense. It occurred in the prosecutors speech only in a negative way. (Examples on page 148.)

Extensive use of hands: Defense attorneys did gesticulate more often than did prosecutors. Understanding that gesticulation is often associated with certain ethnic groups, I examined the data to see if there was a correlation. One of the groups I termed Non-ethnic, the other Ethnic. This second group included Black, Irish, Italian, Jewish, and Polish-Americans, those persons I was able to identify in my sample population.

Nine prosecutors out of the twenty-one I observed used their hands extensively while summing up: six Ethnics, three Non-ethnics.

Twenty-three of the thirty-one defenders observed used their hands extensively during summation: fifteen Ethnics and five Non-ethnics. I was not able to place three defenders into either group.

Signals close: Defense attorneys signaled the close of their summations only slightly more often than did prosecutors. But both did find it necessary to lead into the conclusion of the speech event. (Examples on page 152.)

Other Correlations

The reader may find other tables in the appendices of the book representing other correlations between speakers and features:

Appendix D: Percentage of features occurring in ALL summations
Appendix E: Percentage of features occurring in summations of PROSECUTORS
Appendix F: Percentage of features occurring in summations of DEFENSE ATTORNEYS
Appendix G: One lawyer — More than one summation
Appendix H: Summations of winning defense attorneys

Accused Delivers Own Summation

In one case, the defendant Mr. D. served as his own attorney. This elderly black man had been accused of murder. When it came time for his summation, he stood at his chair at the defense table and addressed the jury. He was dressed rather nicely in a felt jacket, was very thin, and appeared as a sympathetic character.

Any accused person has the right to defend him or herself so long as he or she can knowingly do so. But usually the court will appoint a lawyer to this kind of case to be certain the accused is not denied his or her rights. The lawyer who had been appointed to this case sat in the front row of the spectator seats and observed Mr. D's summation.

He began in the expected fashion: "Good morning", he smiled at the jurors. "You've all heard the testimony of each witness." He then read aloud the 6th amendment of the constitution, the right to counsel.

"I have the jury. I have the assistance of a lawyer, but there's one thing lacking: the witness."

As he started to show something to the jurors, the judge interjected, "You may speak to the jury, but you may not show evidence now."

At another moment there was an objection made by the prosecutor, but the judge overruled the lawyer: "Let him make his speech."

He gave a definition of impeach: "Impeach means — misconduct", and speedy trial: "I read to you about speedy trial so you'll know what a speedy trial means." He read about illegal search and seizure, and that a person cannot testify against himself.

"'Shall not be infringed' means 'the right to trespass.'" [Many of his definitions were inaccurate.]

He read aloud a great deal, but he reads hesitatingly. Finally, he looked at the jurors and softly said, "I hope that what I just read you'll keep closely in mind." The jurors *were* listening very attentively.

"I hope you all have got the full understanding of all I've said here. That's all I have to say now. I thank you for your paying attention." He smiled at the jurors, looked up at the judge, and then around the room before he reluctantly sat down. He gave the impression that he did not want to let go of this opportunity to plead for his freedom.

Mr. D. gave the first summation and therefore had no pattern to follow, but he obviously had heard other closing speeches. Although he read much of his speech, many pieces of the puzzle were present and it was a very convincing closing speech.

The prosecutor spoke next, but acknowledged in no way the unique and pathetic appeal made by the accused. This seemed to display an insensitivity to a sensitive situation. He asked the jurors to return a verdict of first degree murder. The jury deliberated just short of three days, and found Mr. D. guilty of third degree murder, a lesser crime than that requested by the prosecution. It appeared to be that Mr. D. did well for himself.

Formation of a Summation

If we were to attempt to construct a format demonstrating the form of what counts as a summation, we must initially state that all parts of a summation are optional, as is the speech itself. A lawyer is not compelled to make a closing speech. However, I saw no instance of a lawyer forgoing the chance to shape a case in the manner which he or she desired.

Agreeing that it would be highly unusual for a lawyer to forfeit this chance at 'the last word', what must be included to count as a closing speech? Again, the answer is — nothing. Although there are many things which a lawyer may not say, there is nothing which s/he must say. Below are listed some instances of what a lawyer cannot say in summation as reported to me by the lawyer-informants.

(1) A lawyer may not express a personal opinion in summation. Therefore, s/he may say:

> "Find my client not guilty."

This is a command for a verdict, not a personal opinion.
But s/he may not say:

> "My client is not guilty."

This expresses the speaker's personal opinion.

(2) The lawyer may not give the jury the impression that there is evidence showing guilt or innocence about which the lawyer knows but for legal reasons cannot tell the jurors. A prosecutor may not say:

> "If I could tell you what I know, you wouldn't hesitate to find the defendant guilty."

(3) The lawyer should not misrepresent the facts, which includes being mistaken or lying.

(4) A prosecutor may not insinuate guilt beca take the witness stand in his own behalf, or opted foi time of arrest which he has, such as the right to counse. remain silent.

Alan Dershowitz, Professor of Law at the Harvard Law Sch with me about another issue which he believes should be cause for a m if discussed in summation. He stated that it is wrong for a prosecuto encourage jurors to find a person guilty on the grounds of sending a message to the community:

> "If you find Mr. X guilty of this crime, you will send a message to those in the community who might be considering doing the same thing that they better not do it."

TABLE 2
Format of Summation

A.	Opening words: (traditional, nontraditional)	
B.	Politeness formulae:	(apologies (compliments (terms of address (thanking
C.	Discussion of legal issues + definition of legal terms - in general: (appeals to intellectual issues)	
D.	Discussion of witnesses, testimony, facts – relevant to specific case:	(appeals to intellectual issues (appeals to emotional issues (refutational arguments
E.	Signals close	
F.	Closing words:	(thanks jurors (asserts, commands, requests, urges verdict)

All parts of the closing speech are optional. C and D may vary in order of presentation, but C never occurs without the presence of D.

Dershowitz considers this inappropriate — that sending a message to the community is not the responsibility of jurors.

The summations in the sixty-six trials I observed spanned a time period from three minutes (one of four closing speeches in a single trial) to two hours and thirty-five minutes, with the average being forty-three minutes. In all of the words spoken during all of these summations, a format for the speech event did develop.

Although we are able to construct a format for summations in general, each summation is unique. In each instance, there are different lawyers, types of defendants, charges, jurors, judges, courtroom systems, seasons of the year, times of the day. Any difference in any one of these factors could cause the same lawyer to sum up in a different manner.

You can never have the same lawyer trying the same case under exactly the same circumstances. A case in point is the lawyer who retries a case. Almost everything is the same (evidence, witnesses, judge, opposing counsel, courtroom) except the jurors. The informants in this study reported that even under these all but identical conditions save the jury, they will give a different closing speech depending on not only the different receivers of the speech event, but perhaps even the way they felt about themselves when they woke up the morning they were to give the speech.

In the next chapter, I will compare what the lawyer-informants told me they do in summation with what I observed them doing. I shall attempt to explain observed differences.

8. What They Say They Do — What They Did

Sixteen, or almost half of the lawyers who were interviewed for Section 1 of this study, were observed in the speech event summation, three of them twice. In their interviews, the lawyers made clear to me what issues were important to them: "This is what I think is important. This is what I do."

In the discussions of their observed summations which follow, I will compare how the lawyer described his or her behavior during the interviews with what I observed them doing or not doing in the courtroom. My reactions to their summations, of course, are my own subjective evaluations. Just as for any performance, which summation is, another viewer might have reacted differently. What I believed to be credible, interesting or sincere in a speaker, might have been interpreted differently by another viewer. But there is always the constant that these are the evaluations of one viewer of the one event of summation.

Sometimes their descriptions and my observations corresponded. Sometimes they did not. As I watched, it became obvious to me that some speakers were more accurate in describing their behavior in summation than others. The focus of this chapter is to examine the degree to which my observations and their self-reports coincided. I shall try to account for observed differences by addressing such issues as: How accurate are people at describing their own behavior in summation? Can we rely on self-report of verbal behavior? Does the knowing about and being able to describe one's behavior in summation make a difference?

Each of the described summations is proceeded by a brief legend. You will learn whether the lawyer was a prosecutor or defense attorney, whether the summation was made in a state or federal courtroom, what the case was about (the crime), what the verdict was, and whether the observation or the interview came first. The code is supplied as information for the reader, so that s/he may place the speech within a meaningful context and better understand what the lawyer may have been trying to accomplish during the summation.

What is not included in the coded legend is the name of the speaker. This information is not relevant to the description and could be, in a few instances, embarrassing for the informant.

The presentation of this code makes no claims for what wins or loses cases. Many different factors enter into a jury verdict, such as evidence, life's experience of each juror, demeanor and likableness of the accused and the witnesses, and perhaps even the impact of the closing speeches of the lawyers. Therefore, any claims made in regard to the following discussion would simply be inaccurate.

Eleven speakers were interviewed before they were observed. Lawyers 8, 9, 12, 14 and 15 were interviewed for the study following my observing a particularly interesting closing speech, or because of court scheduling of trials. Whether the observation proceeded or followed the interview may have some relevance.

When the interview took place before the observation, or when the speaker and I knew one another in other contexts, I felt that sometimes there was an observer-effect. Some lawyers appeared to be performing for me, even seeking eye contact from time to time. One or two of the speakers included in their summations factors which we had discussed in the interview, such as not opening with the traditional formula, or discussing the speech event 'summation' and explaining it to the jurors. One lawyer even referred to the fact that a person studying summations was in the courtroom. Another discussed the fact that 'summation' was a topic of study, and related it to his speech, i.e., "... and I am told even by those who study closing speeches ... "

Even though there may have been some participant-observer effect, I couldn't be certain if it was encouraging or distracting to the speaker. But whichever it was, I deemed it to be minimal, for soon after the lawyer began speaking, he was well into the direct communication with his or her juror audience. Those instances in which I may have had some effect on the speaker in summing up are included in the discussions of the sixteen lawyers which follow. There is also an analysis of this possible effect in Table 3 later in this chapter.

LAWYER 1 Prosecutor: Federal — mail fraud — guilty
Interview first

This speaker described herself during her interview in the following words: "I am clear, I am loud enough, I am not boring, and my delivery conveys conviction in my . . . belief in my position . . . and I am sincere."

When I observed her, I found her description to be accurate. She was clear. Even though I am not a lawyer, I understood every topic she discussed. There were 35 counts against the defendant, and she used a chart on an easel to guide the jurors through the complicated issues. Her voice was very loud and I heard every word she uttered, in contrast to other lawyers who I had to strain to hear.

In the interview she said she didn't use notes. In this case, she did. She also said there was a specific argument she always gives in relation to reasonable doubt, but she didn't.

Although I had not followed the case throughout the entire trial, from her summation I learned a great deal about and understood the case, and her telling of the facts was interesting. I did not find her boring, and I believed what she said.

During the interview, she said, "I do think it's extremely boring to have women show up in court looking exactly like men lawyers. So I generally try to wear a nice dress, nylons and heels . . ." Lawyer 1 arrived in court for the summation wearing a mannish type suit and not a dress. However, there was a dash of femininity — a ruffle at the neck of her blouse. This was a crisp, intelligent, serious lawyer, and her ruffle at the neck seemed like a nod in the direction of defying the tradition of women dressing like men in the courtroom.

LAWYER 2 Defender: State — murder — guilty
Interview first

This lawyer described himself to be "mobile, agile and hostile" during summation. He said his style was, "Preachin' and screamin' — it's neither learned or pretty." That did not accurately describe his behavior during the summation which I observed. For example, the bells in City Hall chimed noon as he began his summation with the very eloquent, "The bell tolls. [Pause] It's high noon in more ways than one." (Shades of John Donne, or the movie High Noon?)

When asked how long he liked to speak, he replied, "Too long, probably." His summation lasted two hours and three minutes, and since the average time for the sixteen observed summations was one hour and five minutes, it could be considered long. He said he never uses metaphors, but during the closing speech, he developed a metaphor about "Can you speculate with eternity?" and wove it in and out of the summation with both skill and poetry.

During the course of observing the closing speeches of black lawyers, I noticed that the attorneys who did not consistently use black English vernacular, or BEV (Labov 1972), would often begin the summation using standard English, which may have been a memorized frozen formula for opening. But then the speaker would switch to BEV further into the closing speech. This speaker was different. He began his closing speech in black English vernacular, and later in the speech switched to standard English.

Lawyer 2, a very interesting older black man, has the physical appearance of being white. He is very sophisticated (observed during our interview and while having dinner with him on one occasion), but during his summation, he gave the impression of wishing to appear far less polished than he is, and thereby perhaps earning the empathy of the jurors, at least half of whom were black. He shared with me his struggles to become a lawyer and develop a law practice in 1949 in New Jersey when, "there may have been all of ten black lawyers throughout the state, because New Jersey had a procedure whereby they very effectively eliminated non-mainstream lawyers." (See Chapter 10 for further discussion of this interview.)

LAWYER 3 Defender: State — murder, rape, arson, burglary — guilty
Interview first

There were many difference between what this lawyer said he does, and what he was observed doing — or not doing. However, the trial observed was a dreadful murder case, and he was speaking in behalf of the accused murderer. He said he likes to speak between thirty to forty-five minutes, but spoke for almost two and a half hours, well beyond the average of one hour, five minutes. He claimed he always talks about what the functions of the various parties are (judge, witnesses, lawyers), but he didn't.

He also expressed a very low level of confidence in jurors to reach the right decision: "I don't assume they can put two and two together and get four." But then he said, "I like to try to let 'em know that I think of them as intelligent human beings who have an important role to play." His closing speech was an almost completely intellectual, logical argument, without passion.

He was right on target, however, when he reported that he likes to "remind the jury of what the witnesses have said that is favorable. Remind the jurors of the credibility factors as it affects each witness who comes along." He discussed each piece of damaging evidence that was presented in testimony, and then proceeded to try to tear it to shreds.

"I do not wax emotional . . . but sometimes I descend to colorful language to describe my 'pitiful client, ambushed by fate.'" And he told the jurors, "The murderer of (first name, last name) is still walking the streets of Philadelphia" [i.e., by locking up my client, you have not caught the murderer]. Towards the end of his closing speech, this lawyer became excited about his arguments, dropped his control, and allowed his emotions to rise for a moment or two. To this observer, this was the most interesting, and convincing, part of the summation.

LAWYER 4 Defender: Federal — Illegal payment to labor union official - hung jury
Interview first

Everything that this lawyer told me he does in summation he did, including the following: use of humor, suggestive questions, using the lectern, reading quotes from the transcript, reasonable doubt argument, and the exact words for opening, "May it please the court, Mr. Prosecutor, Members of the jury."

Because the observed closing speech followed the interview, and because it so exactly matched the description, I wondered if the speaker had not molded the summation to fit the interview. However, from the discussions which I had with this lawyer in the interview, I had the impression that he was very exacting in everything he did. He had made a study of closing speeches in general, and his own in particular.

LAWYER 5 Prosecutor: State — murder — guilty
Observation first

This lawyer reported that she gives "a closing in motion", and she did. She walked back and forth in front of the jury. But at one point in her closing, she sat down, even though she had told me during the interview: "I wouldn't feel comfortable sitting down during any portion of a closing, because I feel that detracts from what should be the force of your closing." However, this closing in a murder trial with two defendants was very long,[12] and she reportedly was not in perfect health throughout the five month trial. She may have been tired during summation. Although she had told me, "I wouldn't go too long", her summation lasted two and a half hours (almost two and a half times longer than the average observed summation), plus a recess.

"Never turn your back on a jury", she reported. Actually, she did, and it seemed to add force to her argument. "Don't answer tit for tat defense's closing. I don't feel that that's a productive thing to do, because I think it detracts from the points you are trying to make." During the summation, she explained the same idea to the jurors: "Closing arguments are just that. They are not evidence ... Closing argument is not a tit for tat."

This was not, in the beginning, a well organized, smoothly presented summation. During the first hour, the speaker seemed unfocussed and tired — without spirit. But after the recess, she returned with energy and conviction, and ended with a strong metaphor. She walked right up behind the accused men and said:

> Get that tree! We've got two branches; get the root . . . I ask you, Ladies and Gentlemen . . . they look real cool — are they shakin' in their boots, or are they not? The bosses! Pin on them, Ladies and Gentlemen, the label they deserve — 'murderers'!

LAWYER 6 Defender — 2 summations:
A) Federal — bribery — guilty
B) State — murder — guilty
Interview first

During the interview, this lawyer stated: "I don't really want them [jurors] to be my friend, or like me. I don't care what they think about me as far as being a decent guy or a bad guy, as long as they have respect for what I do in the courtroom and my client's rights."

He made very frank comments to the jurors during the two closing speeches observed which carried through with this idea. "Your days are finished; You have done what you came to do." "A jury is nothing more than a group of critics." "The important thing is for you to do your job as a jury, or just say 'the hell with it.'"

During the interview, he said: "Never try to offend their space. If you stick your finger right up under their nose, you're asking for trouble . . . that's a form of intimidation." But during one of the closing speeches he did exactly that. He moved right up to the jury box and proceeded to shake his finger in their faces.

He said he very seldom used metaphors, poetry, or quotes, but in one of the summations he used them all, and he did it well. On the other hand, he was precise in knowing how long he likes to talk. He said he liked to talk forty-five minutes to an hour, and indeed he spoke fifty-five minutes in one summation, and an hour and one minute in the other. He said he liked to talk about the duty of a jury, and he did in both summations.

Because this lawyer was observed during two closing speeches, one in federal court, the other in state court, the effect that the contingencies of a case can have on the behavior of a lawyer and the presentation of a closing speech were well demonstrated. This lawyer, although always himself, had two ways of speaking for the two cases: dignified, controlled, and logical for the income tax matter tried in the federal courtroom; emotional and full of passion for the murder case tried in the state courts.

LAWYER 7 Defender — 2 summations:
A) Federal — mail fraud — guilty
B) Federal — perjury to a federal grand jury — guilty
Interview first

Lawyer 7 was observed in the speech event summation twice, both trials in the federal court system for similar matters. This man believed and expressed pride in the fact that he was able to describe his behavior in summation. “I do this better than anyone else. I really have given a great deal of study to it. I’ve perfected it.”

During his speeches, he used well-practiced verbal routines. His opening words in both trials were identical, save one: “You’re about to have in your hands the most serious (important) responsibility.” And later, “. . . ninety-nine guilty men go free, rather than one innocent man go to prison.” During both summations, he discussed the notion of a Scotch Verdict (not proved, rather than not guilty), and the endings were all but identical: “He’s got the last speech — but you’ve got the last word. [Pause] But better than that, you’ve got the last two words.”

During the interview, he reported that the “whole ‘reasonable doubt’ speech is basically the same every time I give it. I like it, I think it’s effective — I’ve improved upon it over the years.” He knows just how long he speaks. He never thanks the jurors. He described his style to be, “A mixture of passion, emotion and logic”, and I found all these elements to be present in the two summations I observed.

There was one discernible difference between the closing speeches for the two trials. The lawyer liked one of his clients very much, but wasn’t too fond of the other.[13] Although his way of speaking and the form of the closing were very much the same, there was an emotional plea made for the favored client that was absent from the second. However, acknowledging that the prosecutor has an advantage, both clients were found guilty by the jurors.

LAWYER 8 Prosecutor: State — murder — guilty
Observation first

This lawyer, the son of a minister, said in the interview that he would instruct new trial lawyers to, "Remember you're talking to twelve people" and "It's an art to talk to people." He also said that he looks at the jury only one time during the trial. This was accurate. During the observed summation, he only looked towards the faces of the jurors once. Every lawyer interviewed, except for this lawyer, stressed looking the jurors in the eyes. However, even without the direct eye contact, I found Lawyer 8 to be a powerful and convincing speaker.

He said he liked to use rhetorical questions ("probably the prosecutor's best friend"), and metaphors, and he employed both of these tools to his advantage.

He said in the interview that he doesn't thank jurors, and he didn't. But he didn't include a passage in the summation which he said he always does: "This is reality. This is not fantasy..." He also claimed to speak between seventeen and twenty-five minutes: "The longer a speech, from a prosecutor's standpoint, the more chances for prosecutorial misconduct. The more chances for an opinion to slip in." However, the summation observed was part of a notorious trial concerning a heinous murder and lasted almost an hour and a half.

In his interview, he told me, "My father was a minister for fifty years . . . I guess [I learned a lot] watching him. He was a very effective speaker." There was no question in my mind that this man had observed his minister father well, and adopted for his own that which he found effective. I thought that his ability to captivate and perhaps thereby persuade an audience was stunning.

LAWYER 9 Prosecutor: Federal — extortion affecting interstate commerce — guilty
Observation first

"To me, it's the most fun and most important part of the case ... I start off in being formal. Then I try to get 'em to smile at me — to like me. And in that sense, I wanna be informal. But I wanna be sincere. I want them to understand that I absolutely, fully, am convinced of the rightness of whatever it is I am arguing . . . it's a matter of sincerity." When I heard this lawyer in summation, I had a complete understanding of the case, and I believed his telling of the facts.

During his interview, he told me that he likes to use humor, and he did. He said he would ridicule what he thought was a ridiculous argument by an opponent, and he also did that. He said he doesn't thank jurors, and he didn't. He told me that his knowledge of summation and himself in summation was acquired through study. He had attended Dale Carnegie sessions in public speaking when a senior in college, and he put great stock in what he termed proper English — like the British use it. "I think if you're going to be a lawyer, you better learn to talk like an educated person . . . " He lectures on closing speeches in the U.S. Attorney's Clinical at Temple University Law School.

This tall, good-looking young man gives the appearance of a church choirboy. His demeanor, to me, bespeaks honesty. That might have been part of the consideration in the appointment of Lawyer 9 as staff director and investigator of very important hearings in Philadelphia in October 1985 related to a tragic fire, where he could be observed on television four days a week for five weeks. In a hearing that purported to be seeking truth, to this observer he was a convincing member of the panel.

LAWYER 10 Defender: Federal — extortion affecting interstate commerce — guilty
Interview first

During his interview, this attorney stated: "Yes, I'm good at it, because I work at it. I think I understand the process of persuasion. I have always been aware of my ability to sell myself." He also said that he doesn't suffer from stage fright or get nervous, but does experience a sensation of anticipation. He claimed that he "responds not at all to those in the courtroom — it's simply a matter of what's going on between me and the jurors."

All of these words seemed to fly out the window when he stood to give his closing speech. This lawyer appeared to be frightened and had a great of difficulty speaking at all. At one point, his voice broke. However, it was an extremely well publicized case, there were five defense lawyers who gave closing speeches, and he spoke just after a captivating speaker — a genuine performance (Lawyer 13). This lawyer was clearly unnerved.

He spoke only twenty-eight minutes, even though in the interview he said he likes to speak for an hour — sometimes two. However, with six closing speeches, five for the defendants plus one for the prosecution, there had to be a consideration of the jurors' attention span. He also paced back and forth in front of the jury like a caged lion, which was contrary to his comments about being impressed with the Loftus studies concerning body movement, about where and how you should position yourself in relation to the jury in the courtroom for the best effect (1974). The interview with this lawyer proceeded the observation by three months, but I sensed that he may have been somewhat distracted by my presence in the courtroom during the first minutes of his summation, until he got into his argument.

There were several features which he said he liked to use which he did. He used charts to good effect, gave very convincing opening and closing thoughts (which he reported he memorizes), and wove his closing speech around an interesting theme in the manner he reported that he had learned from the Irving Younger literature. He appeared to me to gain confidence and move more comfortably through the summation as he approached the end. My reaction to this speech was that the speaker was trying too hard.

LAWYER 11 Defender: State — murder — guilty
Interview first

This lawyer reported in the interview that the value of the summation is to "start the tone of that discussion [deliberations] in one direction or another, and highlight certain points, and give the people who you hope are on your side a way to start arguing for your side." The first words she uttered to begin her observed summation were: "Members of the jury, the question really in this case is who had the gun just before the shooting?" — an immediate focus on what was to be her key issue.

She said she likes to start serious and end serious, "with the frivolous, funny, snotty or snide in the middle." There was only the serious in this murder trial. The lawyer spoke with me from time to time throughout the observation of parts of the trial and between the closing speeches, and indicated that she believed it was a hopeless case for her client. That fact seemed to affect the closing speech. There was no place for the 'frivolous, funny, snotty or snide.' She seemed very angry during the closing speech, standing in front of the jury with her hand on her hip challengingly, and jabbing the index finger of her other hand in the faces of the jurors from time to time.

She said she likes to speak between twenty and thirty minutes, and the summation lasted nineteen minutes. She told me that she suffered from stage fright, and it appeared to me that she did. However, in this instance there may have been research induced effects, for the speaker seemed somewhat distracted by the presence of the researcher. However, her performance may also have been affected by the presence of another lawyer from her law firm who was observing the summation and with whom she consulted frequently.

LAWYER 12 Prosecutor: State — murder — guilty
Observation first

This was the most fascinating speech event which I observed, and one which I would describe as a classic example of the genre. This speaker had no equal in his ability to mesmerize his listeners. His use of words, his stance before the jurors, the manner in which he used his eyes, voice, body, were truly hypnotic. "The strong point would be to try to, in some way, communicate sincerity", this lawyer reported in the interview. I believed that this speaker was very sincere, i.e., that he believed everything that he said to be true, and was deeply committed to his position.

His said he liked to use "the head through the heart" approach. "You must get close to them." He stood right at or very near the rail of the jury box. "You become the thirteenth juror . . . [when they are in the deliberating room] "you are there. You are one of them."

He told me in the interview that, "My objective in summation is to be very extensive and comprehensive, and hopefully have the effect of a long lasting message to the jury." The day that this lawyer gave his summation, every seat in the courtroom was taken. the 'court followers'[14] were there en masse, and even the judge appeared to be listening closely, which is not always the case. There wasn't a sound to be heard in the courtroom during the hour and seven minutes this lawyer spoke.

LAWYER 13 Defender: Federal — extortion affecting interstate commerce — guilty
Interview first

"I regard the trial as only a device to enable you to sum up to the jury." This is a lawyer who loves to talk to a jury, and he does it very well indeed. He was both humorous and entertaining.

"It's my considered opinion that juries react more in line with whether they favor the lawyer rather than the client; and if they trust and like the lawyer, and are entertained in a proper sense, than they will — give the verdict to the lawyer rather than the individual." Several times during this closing speech, the speaker had the audience 'in stitches'. He was quite amusing and the jurors responded. But still, they found his client guilty. The summation could not eradicate the evidence.

"When I have something that is pretty cold against me — then pluck on the heart strings, bring in the priests, the rabbis and the character witnesses, and tell the jury that they've got to believe that *they're* liars in order to convict." The trial which was observed was just this type of situation, but he didn't go that far in the defense of his client, perhaps because he was one of several defense speakers.

During the interview he talked about putting "a little steel in their backbones." And during the summation he said: "One juror — just one — who says, 'I'm not gonna go along with it.'" He said that he likes to challenge the prosecutor in the closing, and he did.

However, he was much more restrained during the summation than he had described himself to be. For example, when asked if he liked to use the lectern during the closing speech, he said: "No. I hate it." But he stood behind and often leaned on the lectern for his entire closing, when other lawyers in the case did not use it.

I felt he was somewhat constrained by the austerity and formality of the federal courtroom. Later I learned that he had used the lectern during his summation because the judge had requested that he do so. This request might have constrained his behavior in general.

LAWYER 14 Defender: State — simple assault and possession of an instrument of crime — not guilty
Observation first

This lawyer appeared to know herself in the act of summing up very well indeed. "I'm very loud, forceful and strong", she said during the interview, and I thought that she was. "I don't like people movin' around a lot . . . It's very distracting; your voice trails off and you look nervous and fidgety. I have an imaginary lectern in front of me — because I'm not movin'." She said she likes to speak between thirty and forty-five minutes, and her closing speech lasted thirty-two minutes. She stood at her desk across the room from the jury, unmoving. You could hear her every word.

While observing Lawyer 14, I made the following notes:

> There is a ring of sincerity — She means it — She's honest about the positive and the negative. She says: "We are dealing in a subculture." She sep-

arates out the people in the case from — "you and me" — reverse solidarity.

"I really love giving summations", she told me. I could feel the confidence that comes from that strong, positive feeling of knowing and loving what you're doing pass right over to the jurors. They found her client not guilty.

LAWYER 15 Prosecutor — 2 summations
A) State — murder — guilty
B) State — murder — guilty
Interview between

"I aim for the head. I don't give an emotional speech because that's not my personality . . . It's not my favorite part of the trial. I don't consider myself an actress. I'm very happy when it's over." This description fit very well my observations of the two summations presented by this lawyer. They were logical, and convincing — but without emotional pleas.

She said she liked to speak between thirty-five and forty minutes. The first summation lasted thirty-eight minutes, the second thirty-one. Both of her speeches seemed to be tightly preplanned.

"The ham may get a little more emotional, a little more flowery. I'm not sure if it gets a different result." You could sense this was not Lawyer 15's favorite part of the trial, but they were both no-nonsense, convincing closing speeches. The jury was attentive during both. However, in one instance she requested the jury to return a verdict of murder in the first degree, and they found the defendant guilty in the third degree, a lesser crime with a less severe punishment.

LAWYER 16 Defender: Federal — bribery — guilty
Observation first

This lawyer reported in the interview that at the end of the closing speech he likes to tell the jurors that, "They are entitled to say that the defendant had been represented by a bad lawyer, or by a lawyer who had done bad things, but they should put that out of their minds — 'that has no bearing on the guilt or innocence of Mr. X.'" He did say this in closing.

"Part of successful advocacy in the trial courtroom is to have command of the courtroom, so that the jurors — and what I strive for — is the jurors look to me and pay attention to me whenever I do something . . . I'm aggressive. I tend to try to keep the jurors interested — and if that means entertained, so be it. As well as informing them." During his summation he pretended to be looking for a dollar bill to illustrate a point. "Have I got a dollar bill?" He then pulled a neatly folded dollar from the pocket of his jacket, a place bills are not usually kept, with a surprised, "here's one!"

"Don't treat the jurors as less than equals", he told me. But during his summation, he said: "You don't have to be a lawyer [pause] by saying 'you don't have to be a lawyer', I don't mean to denigrate. In lots of ways you don't have to be a lawyer."

He said he likes to speak more to the head than the heart, but he didn't. He likes metaphors, and during the closing speech he related a story about a child breaking wind in a schoolroom to illustrate a point. He also reported during the interview that he was the son of a minister, and that he likes to quote from the Bible. "I'm from a small town . . . and I believe what I'm saying." He closed his summation with: "On that note, when you meet that fateful day of judgment . . . know you have made the right decision."

Characteristics of Observed Summations

The discourse of summation was similar to but differed from direct discourse. The lawyers spoke with the jurors as though engaged in a two-way conversation, and even though there was no verbal feedback from the hearers, as an observer I concluded that the lawyers and jurors appeared to be making the same assumptions as to the nature of their relationship. The speakers were acting in terms of Grice's maxims, and the hearers appeared to be cooperative partners. (See page 13 for discussion of Grice and the Cooperative Principle.)

Turn-taking was not an issue, but lawyers did often pause in their presentation at places where a turn might be taken by a partner in discourse, or to shift topics. There were few false starts, fillers, or hesitations as one might expect when engaged in natural discourse. Also, speech tended to occur in full, complete sentences rather than parts of sentences which are characteristic of colloquial speech. There were more repetitions, rhetorical questions and directly quoted material than one would expect in casual discourse.

There was a continuum extending from fixed or frozen forms at one end, such as in opening 'With permission of the court', to spontaneous speech throughout the discourse. However, the spontaneous speech was infrequent, and I had the impression that closing speeches were well thought-out ahead of time even if not formally prepared, and that what appeared to be spontaneous speech was actually pre-planned.

Character of the Speakers

Coordinated with the characteristics of the discourse were the shadings of the speaker's personality and his or her way of speaking which permeated the entire closing speech. When the lawyer finally stopped talking and sat down, I had the feeling that I knew not only something about the case being tried, but I also knew a lot about the lawyer trying the case.

In almost all instances, the speakers took into account the type of case they were speaking about, the audience to which they were speaking (judge and jury), and often the closing speech of opposing counsel which proceeded their speech, or anticipation of the one which would follow.

Evaluating the Speeches

Since in many instances I had not followed the entire case but arrived in court only for summation, one of the criteria I used for evaluating summations was what I learned about the trial during summation. If I learned what the case was about, something about the persons involved, had a good idea of what the decision of the jurors was going to be based on, and if I had my own view of guilt or innocence of the accused, I knew that the speaker had done much of what he or she needed to do.

Even though the jurors are present throughout the proceedings, they too need the pieces of the trial to be placed into an integrated whole during summation. Testimony is submitted into a trial without concern for chronology, for witnesses often testify according to when they are available. Also, the proceedings are constantly interrupted by objections, side-bar conferences, lunch, rest and end of day recesses. Trials often last for weeks, and jurors can forget much of what was entered as evidence in the early days. Therefore, the juror also needs a 'telling of the tale' during summation which will bring together the various parts of the trial into a meaningful whole. As informant Preiser reported:

> The trial is like a jigsaw puzzle. It has a bunch of little tiny pieces of evidence all coming in at different times, and really meaningless to a jury. And when you put it together in the summation, it becomes a great big painting. A beautiful painting is what you want them to see.

A second criterion was credibility. Did I believe that the lawyer was telling the truth, or was the speaker trying to pull the wool over the jurors' eyes — and ears? And did the lawyer believe in what he or she was saying?

My evaluation of the summation was absolutely unrelated to the consequent verdict. In fact, I never remained in or returned to the courtroom to learn what verdict was returned.[15] It was not important to my response to the speech event. I learned about the verdict either in subsequent conversation with a speaker or judge, from newspaper accounts of the trial, or when I was interviewing jurors after deliberation for Section 3 of this study.

Self-Report: Observation

In order to explore the degree to which speakers were able to accurately report their behavior in summation, and to search for possible correlations, the nineteen closing speeches given by observed, interviewed lawyers are analyzed in Table 3.

What first becomes obvious in Table 3 is that all the prosecutors enjoyed the verdict agreeing with their position. Furthermore, the only positive defense verdicts were those in which an attorney gave a single defense summation. The informants reported that it is more difficult to win a not guilty for your client in a case with multiple defendants.

According to Table 3, it did not seem to matter which came first, the interview or the observation, even though the speaker knew that I was in the courtroom, and for what purpose. There were self-report differences of all degrees, and verdicts in both directions for both conditions A and B. Lawyer 15 seemed to be unaffected by the interview which came between her two observed summations.

The lawyers who displayed many differences between their self-reported behavior and the performance did so in both federal and state court. Those who had a close correspondence between self-report and the observation were also represented in both courts. The lawyers who spoke for shorter periods of time than stated were those who were one of multiple summations. When you are not the only person to sum up for the defense, you must give some consideration to the attention span of the jurors. The only lawyer who greatly exceeded his self-reported time in a trial with multiple summations was a lawyer who several of my informants told me to be one who often has difficulty terminating speech.

The three lawyers who exceeded their self-reported times by an hour

TABLE 3
Speakers and their Speeches

a Position	b Lawyer	c Speech	d Court	e Crime	f Verdict	g Difference	h Time
P	1	A	F	Mail fraud	+	Almost none	+ :11
P	5	B	S	Murder	+	Many	+1:20
P	8	B	S	Murder, rape	+	Several	+1:00
P	9	B	F	Extortion	+	Almost none	Exact
P	12	A	S	Murder	+	Almost none	Exact
P	15A	Btw	S	Murder	+	Almost none	Exact
P	15B	Btw	S	Murder	+	Almost none	Exact
D	4	A	F	Union payoff	+	Almost none	Exact
D	14	B	S	Assault	+	Almost none	Exact
D	3	A	S	Murder, rape	−	Many	+1:45
D	7B	A	F	Perjury	−	Almost none	Exact
D(m)	2	A	S	Murder	−	Several	Exact
D(m)	6A	A	F	Bribery	−	Almost none	Exact
D(m)	6B	A	S	Murder	−	Several	Exact
D(m)	7A	A	F	Mail fraud	−	Almost none	Exact
D(m)	10	A	F	Extortion	−	Many	− :32
D(m)	11	A	S	Murder	−	Almost none	Exact
D(m)	13	A	F	Extortion	−	Several	− :23
D(m)	16	B	F	Bribery	−	Several	+ :25

a) D = Defense attorney
P = Prosecutor
D(m) = one of multiple defense summations in trial

b) Numbers in chart match lawyer numbers in proceeding text

c) A = Speech observed after the interview
B = Speech observed before the interview
Btw = Interview between two speeches

d) F = Federal court S = State court

e) Crime with which defendant is accused

f) + = Verdict agreed with arguments of speaker
− = Verdict opposed to arguments of speaker

g) Differences between self-stated behavior of speakers and researcher observations
Almost none (0 to 2)
Several (3 to 5)
Many (more than 5)

h) Difference in stated preferred time of speaking (+ or −), or Exact (within five minutes) or more were all involved in complex, infamous murder trials. Lawyer 1, who spoke somewhat longer than she likes to, had to explain to the jurors a case with 35 charges against the defendant.

In eleven of the nineteen summations (58%), there was almost complete agreement between self-report and observation. Another five summations varied in only several matters, such as the speakers not saying things they claimed they always do, or using options such as metaphor when they reported that they never do, or speaking more or less than they stated they like to. All of these differences could have been case-dependent, i.e., a certain kind of case demanding a somewhat different summation.

In only three instances (16%), were there many differences between the self-report and the observation. Only one of these speakers, Lawyer 5, won the case, but that crime (murder for hire) was so horrendous and the circumstances that prevailed throughout the trial so unusual, that I believe the verdict was unrelated to the closing speeches.

A Special Case

The trial in which I observed Lawyer 5 sum up lasted five months, the second longer trial in the history of Philadelphia. This prosecutor, a young, small (less than a hundred pounds) woman had been harassed by her male opponents with no relief from the judge throughout the trial. Even during her summation, one of the defense lawyers would stand and call out insulting comments such as:

> Hey, hey, hey! Wait a minute. I object. Forget that. That's what she's been doin' for 105 days.
>
> Your honor, there's no way to curb this woman.
>
> She's taking three hours for this nonsense. [Followed by loud applause by all the defendant spectators. Judge sits silently.]

The judge sustained all of these rude objections. The defense attorneys whispered and laughed together, and spoke to spectators in the courtroom throughout her summation. This behavior of defense counsel during the trial and the closing speech might have affected both the delivery of the prosecutor's summation, and the decision by the jurors.

The prosecutor began her summation in a less than forceful manner, and seemed to be tired and without enthusiasm for the task. She requested a recess after speaking for an hour and twenty-one minutes. When she returned, she spoke with renewed energy and delivered a first rate summation for another hour and fourteen minutes. (See LAWYER 5 earlier in this chapter.)

The jurors, perhaps irritated by the behavior of the defense counsel and believing that the woman lawyer had been treated unfairly, paid rapt attention to her summation. They found in her favor after deliberating only two and a half hours in this five month long trial. Since the defense summations were also very interesting and convincing, I think this case may demonstrate how verdicts are reached apart from closing speeches.

On the other hand, this could be an instance of closing speeches being judged in important part in terms of the audience's view of the speakers. As a consequence of the behavior of the defense attorneys throughout the trial, the prosecutor had the advantage of the sympathy of the jurors, and her summation may have sustained that sympathetic predisposition. The good efforts of the defense attorneys may have been diminished by their rude behavior.

Same Speaker — Multiple Summations

The instances of multiple summations of Lawyers 6, 7, and 15 in Table 3 provide interesting information. Lawyers 7 and 15 described their behavior to me, and then went into the courtroom twice, and on both occasions did what they said they do. However, both of their trials were for the same or similar crimes, and both took place in the same type of court. Lawyer 7 summed up in a federal courtroom for mail fraud and perjury, Lawyer 15 in a state courtroom for two murder charges.

Lawyer 6 presents us with information along another dimension. His two trials were for very different charges, one bribery and the other murder, and were tried in different kinds of courts. The bribery trial was held in the modern, austere atmosphere of the federal courthouse, and the murder trial took place in a much older, slightly seedy, traditional City Hall courtroom.

His description of his behavior in summation held true in the atmosphere of the federal court, with almost no discrepancies between observed and self-reported behavior. He was unemotional, factual, and aimed for the head not the heart, his behavior agreeing with what he reported in the interview: "The heart I don't know too much about."

When I observed him in the murder trial, I found out that he knew plenty about the heart. He was quite emotional, breaking many of his own rules, full of passion for a passionate issue. He had two ways of speaking, and could do both well even though he described himself as performing in only one way. This lawyer demonstrated that perhaps some lawyers are better at giving closing speeches than they are at reporting about how they do it. But here again, a different kind of case required a different kind of summation, and this lawyer was flexible enough to do it well both ways.

In addition to multiple summations of the interviewed and observed lawyers presented in Table 3, in the course of collecting data for Section 3 of this study, I observed two other lawyers who I did not interview deliver three summations each. Fourteen of the trials observed for Section 3 were held in a courtroom where only 'career criminals' are tried.[16] These are persons who are repeat offenders of crimes other than murder, i.e., burglary, rape, assault, car theft. The jurors for these cases do not know that the accused are recidivists. The same prosecutors are assigned to cases in this courtroom over a period of time, so that a regular spectator would see the same prosecutors more than once.

I observed Lawyer A try three cases, armed robbery, burglary, and a granny-squad robbery, for all of which he earned a guilty verdict. However, all three summations were perfunctory, and I did not consider this lawyer to be in the same category as the thirty-four interviewed lawyers. There were only two features which were common to all three summations: traditional opening, and imploring jurors to use their 'common sense'. You could see the lawyer adjust the closing to fit the facts of a particular case. Attention from the jurors was moderate in two cases, very attentive dropping to less attentive for the third.

It is important to recognize that if the prosecutor enjoys an advantage in most instances, in Career Criminal Court s/he more than enjoys the advantage. The persons who appeared as defendants in this court were, by and large, an unsavory looking group, charged with the type of crimes ordinary citizens like the jurors fall victim to. The evidence wins most of these cases.

Lawyer B, also a prosecutor in Career Criminal Court during the months I was observing there, offered a more interesting case for consideration. He won two of his trials, but lost the third, all robbery charges. Several features were common to all three summations: traditional opening, rhetorical questions, a reasonable doubt discussion, and imploring the jurors to use 'common sense'. All three summations lasted about half an hour, closely matching the average for prosecutors in this courtroom, which was thirty-seven minutes.

Studying that third case for differences in his presentation offered very few clues. Did he do anything that was different in the third summation? He enumerated items, and used his hands extensively, hardly causes for obtaining a different verdict. Therefore, I looked at the summation of the opposing counsel, Lawyer C.

This summation for a case won was one of the weakest of any observed. The speaker performed as though it was his first summation and he didn't know exactly how to do it. He fumbled for words from time to time, threw his hands up in frustration at his inability to express himself at other times. I did not find him credible, and felt the hour he spoke to be interminable. Some of the comments I noted while observing him demonstrate what I viewed as a weak summation:

> He opens: "This is the last opportunity I will have to talk to you. Many of you will say 'Thank God.'"
> Trivial arguments
> Keeps apologizing — too humble
> Not very confident. Stumbling a lot. Weak.
> Hands in pockets. Sloppy in appearance and demeanor.
> He says: "Mr. B [Lawyer B, his opponent] He's a great lawyer."
> Jury is not enthralled
> He stands in front of jury box. His notes are across the courtroom on his table. He keeps walking back and forth across the courtroom to check them. Very distracting.
> Stops speaking and reads to himself for at least a full minute.
> Jury is very inattentive
> Many of the students [visiting the courtroom] are sleeping
> Another very long pause while he searches through his notes
> Says: "I'd like to recap this very briefly. I know I've been talking a very long time."
> Hands now in back pockets
> I wrote: I think you could talk your client into a *guilty* verdict!

The verdict went his way, but I did not believe that it was the quality of the summation which won the case. I was surprised to learn later that this was an experienced trial lawyer. Perhaps he had assumed the role of an inexperienced lawyer to win the sympathy of the jurors, which he may have done. However, I also learned after this trial that the prosecution evidence was not strong, so the facts in this case may have been the true determinant.

Defense Summations in Winning Cases

There were only five trials in which the verdict was in favor of the defendant in this study. The summations in two of these cases are analyzed in Table 3, Lawyers 4 and 14. The summation in a third trial was discussed just above, that of Lawyer C, which serves as an example of a weak summation. The summation of a fourth lawyer in a trial with a defense verdict was mentioned in Chapter 1. That summation was a fascinating performance by defense Lawyer D, but all my efforts to interview this lawyer failed.

However, considering the trial of which this fourth summation was a part, I can't be certain that the verdict was closely related to his summation, although it may have been. The defendant was an older Black man who was accused of murder. The man who was killed was known to the defendant, and had at an earlier time tried to kill the defendant with a knife, badly wounding him. The accused sat at the defense table throughout the trial between his lawyer and his daughter, who was also a lawyer. To this viewer, he was a very sympathetic figure.

In the summation, Lawyer D presented his client as "a peaceful man . . . I thank God for Mr. Z." He said, "He don't talk too well. He ain't too educated. But he didn't evade you [on the witness stand]." The lawyer, who began in standard English and then changed to BEV, talked about the accused's military service record in Korea, "serving America." He used a metaphor about a man in Czechoslovakia, quoted Oliver Wendell Holmes, and related a parable from Aesop's Fables.

At one point he cried out: "I am moved by the power of the experience", and ended soon after requesting that the jurors, "send him home to his family where he was before this experience." That's exactly what the jury did.

Of course I can't know if this very emotional, dramatic, highly entertaining closing speech made any difference to the jury's decision. But I do know that the prosecutor felt cheated out of the verdict; that the correct verdict was clearly 'guilty'. I later learned that there were complaints registered against the judge for irregularities which the prosecutor felt occurred during the trial.

The fifth summation is a second example of a weak defense closing speech in a defense verdict trial. However, I decided not to interview the speaker, Lawyer E, and that decision may indicate how the judgment of goodness of summation, if you will, is unrelated to the verdict.

Lawyer E seemed very unsure of himself, and had memorized parts of his speech, which he kept forgetting. When he forgot, he would connect inappropriate pieces of memorized sentences together, and end up with utterances such as, "Take upon your — own common sense." Sometimes he would delete prepositions: "He's not a professional witness. He's not used ( ) sitting there."

Three noticeable events happened during his summation. (1) When he began, "Good morning Ladies and Gentlemen", the jurors audibly responded, "Good morning Mr. E." They did not respond to the same greeting from the prosecutor. I think the jurors liked Lawyer E, and empathized with him. (2) The prosecutor walked to and drank from the water fountain during Lawyer E's summation. This was rude and did not go unnoticed by the jurors. (3) The jurors paid very close attention throughout the summation. I think they were trying to figure out what this lawyer was attempting to tell them. This seemed to have been an instance of a jury having already made up its mind before closing speeches, and seeking verification during the summation.

There were only two features which occurred in all five of these summations: rhetorical questions and traditional opening statements. There were another three features which appeared in four of them: extensive use of hands, appeals to patriotism, and a discussion of the American legal system. The average time of these closings speeches was forty minutes, the shortest being thirty-two, the longest fifty-five, while the average for defense attorneys in state courts was forty-six minutes.

Summary

In only slightly more than half of the observations did the self-report concur with the observation. However, many of the discrepancies were case dependent. Specific aspects of any one trial can alter the speech event, such as the type of jurors, the judge presiding in the case, who are and what was said by the other lawyers in the courtroom. All those contingencies must be taken into account when evaluating different linguistic behaviors by the same lawyer.

Perhaps the self-reports should (and many did) carry the proviso, "Under ideal circumstances, this is the way I would like to behave in summation." However, while in the act of summing up, I do not believe that lawyers are aware of many aspects of their behavior to which jurors respond and are therefore significant. Even their self-critiques given just after delivering a summation spoke only to content, not verbal behavior. For this dimension, other than a strong awareness of how long they like to or did speak, they are often imperfect self-reporters.

During the interviews, some were better able to describe their behavior than others. Did it make a difference if they could? Using the information presented in Table 3 as evidence, we see that other than Lawyer 5, who was involved in an exceptional trial, the lawyers who displayed many differences between self-report and observed behavior were involved in cases where the verdict went against them.

What also is clear in Table 3 is that the two defense attorneys who delivered the sole defense summation in a trial, and which earned a positive verdict against presumed odds as defenders, both described their behavior in summation without a single exception.

For the summation of Lawyer 7B, all the same conditions prevailed except the verdict. That lawyer reported that he did not like his client in this case. That must make a difference.

From my observation of the two winning defense lawyers, and the information gained about them from their interviews, I am convinced that the time invested in self-analysis, in self-assessment of one's behavior during summation, is necessary for the lawyer to realize his or her strengths, and how and when, and when not to use them. There is always the question of judgment — when to appear humble, when to be outrageously outspoken, when to use BEV, when not to. These should not be spontaneous reactions but rather under the control of the speaker because of self-knowledge earned through analysis of summation.

SECTION 3: The Receiver

9. What Jurors Believe the Summation Means to Them

Persuasion is defined by Costopoulos (1972: 384) to be "an act of influencing the minds of others by arguments or reasons, by appeals to both feeling and intellect; it is the art of leading another man's will to a particular choice, or course of conduct." He continues, "No one doubts this is what trial lawyers do every day in the courtroom."

Costopoulos reports that trial lawyers agree that the closing argument, along with the opening argument and the examination of witnesses, must be considered an art and not a science. "The effective use of language and voice is critical. Language is the medium. And voice — need it be said — is the most persuasive means of communication known."

The third part of this study explores the question of how persuasive lawyers are perceived to be by the jurors during the speech event summation. This is a difficult task. Although jurors may report that they were affected by the summation, either negatively or positively, and that they changed their minds after hearing a summation, what is actually being reported is what a particular juror *believed* the summation meant to his or her decision. In fact, this decision may have been a result of the way the defense attorney dressed throughout the trial, the prejudices felt for or against the defendant, or even the facts in the case.

Subjects

A scientifically valid study of whether jurors are or are not persuaded by the summation is not possible within the real world. If jurors could retire to the jury room and determine the verdict having heard everything *except* the summations, and then retire a second time hearing everything *including* the summations, all else kept constant, and if they could be questioned following both deliberations, we could design an experimental study with internal and external validity, one which would allow us to generalize about the effect of summation on juror decisions beyond a singular research project.

An alternative to this design would be one in which mock jurors participate in either a mock or real trial. However, since the mock juror has removed from him the onerous responsibility of determining another person's fate, one surely has altered the emotional and rational responses of that mock juror. (See discussion of mock trials in Chapter 10.)

Much of past research concerning language in the courtroom has been carried out on mock juries (Hastie, Penrod and Pennington 1983; O'Barr 1982; O'Barr and Lind 1981). These mock juries are usually comprised of undergraduate and/or law students. In the real world of the Philadelphia court system, it is unusual to have more than one or two persons with a college or even a partial college education sitting on any one jury. In the twenty-one juries included in this part of the study, two of the juries contained no one who reported exposure to education beyond the twelfth grade. Also, the cross section of age, color and social class that exists for actual juries is probably rarely if ever achieved with mock juries. Therefore, research studies using mock juries must elicit different kinds of responses from the different kinds of subjects.

This study is unique in that actual jurors in real cases were used as subjects. It is also unique in that 223 jurors served as informants, which is an extremely large number of respondents for a research project using actual jurors as subjects. (See Chapter 1, page 9 for a complete discussion of this study.)

Method

What could be done, and was done, was ask the jurors through the use of a questionnaire what they *believed* that piece of speech, the summation, meant to their decisions. The questionnaire was presented to the jurors immediately after they returned the verdict and had been excused from their jury service. A slightly different questionnaire was completed by alternate jurors after they were excused, just before the other twelve jurors began to deliberate.

Sometimes they completed the questionnaire while they were still in the jury box, and at other times after they had returned to the juryroom, depending on the desires of the presiding judge. The enthusiasm with which the jurors answered the questions was directly proportionate to the enthusiasm expressed by the judge for the research enterprise.

This also affected alternate jurors. Some judges were willing to ask the alternates to participate in the experiment, and some were not. Sometimes there would be only one or no alternates, as they may have replaced regular jurors who, for one reason or another, could not continue their jury service. Thirty-five alternate jurors participated in the research, in addition to the two hundred and twenty-three regular jurors.

Questionnaire

There were two questionnaires developed to obtain the data for this part of the study. The first questionnaire (Appendix B) was presented to those jurors who completed their jury duty fully by deliberating to verdict.

The second questionnaire (Appendix C) was completed by alternate jurors just as they were excused from jury duty. This questionnaire was identical to the first except for the deletion of two questions, 6 and 13, both of which concerned what transpired in the jury room during deliberations.

These questions read:

6. Was the Prosecutor's closing speech discussed in the jury room?
7. Was the Defense Attorney's closing speech discussed in the jury room?

The questionnaires contain one set of questions relating to the closing speech of the prosecutor, and an identical set for the closing speech of the defense attorney. The rationale behind all of the questions was to explore from a variety of points of view the issue of what summations mean to juror decisions.

Questions 7 and 14 (6 and 12 on the alternate questionnaire) explored a somewhat different issue. These two paired questions read:

6 (7) If it were possible, would you like to know the Prosecutor better and have him or her as a friend?

12 (14) If it were possible, would you like to know the Defense Attorney better and have him or her as a friend?

These questions tested a point maintained in the literature (Geoghan 1978, Mills and Aronson 1965, Outerbridge 1978) and concurred with by 26 of the 32 informants who stated that they believe there is a relationship between liking someone and believing him or her.

The last several questions collected demographic information concerning the informants.

Questionnaires were completed by twenty-one sets of state jurors: 223 'complete' jurors plus 35 alternates, totaling 258 respondents. No questionnaires were completed by jurors in the federal courts. The longest deliberation recorded was three days (guilty verdict), the shortest only twenty minutes (not guilty.)

Data Analysis

Chi-square tests were performed on the data obtained from the questionnaires. A chi-square with a probability of .05 or less was considered statistically significant, indicating that the relationship found would occur by chance at most only 5 percent of the time. Means were also calculated for comparative purposes.

Results

Significance was established for the following juror responses: (Alternate juror responses are not included in this data)

Results from ALL Jurors

(1) The jurors reported that they REMEMBERED more of the *prosecutor's* summation than that of the defense attorney's. ($p < .005$)

(2) The jurors reported that they thought the summation of the *prosecutor* was more INTERESTING than the summation given by the defense attorney. ($p < .001$)

(3) The jurors reported that they thought the *defense attorney* spoke TOO LONG. ($p < .001$)

(4) The jurors reported that they BELIEVED more of what the *prosecutor* said in his or her summation than of what the defense attorney said. ($p < .001$)

(5) The jurors reported that they would like to KNOW the *prosecutor* better. ($p < .01$)

Results from ALL Jurors in NOT-GUILTY Decisions

No significant differences were found.

Results from ALL Jurors in regard to WINNERS and LOSERS

- o A lawyer is defined to be a winner if the decision of the jury is in agreement with his or her argument.
- o A lawyer is defined to be a loser if the decision of the jury is against his or her argument.

(6) The jurors reported that they REMEMBERED more of the summation delivered by the *winning* lawyer. ($p < .01$)

(7) The jurors reported that they found the summation of the *winning* lawyer more INTERESTING. ($p < .001$)

(8) The jurors reported that the *losing* lawyers spoke TOO LONG, the *winners* just the right amount of time. ($p < .001$)

(9) The jurors reported that they BELIEVED more of what the *winning* lawyer said in his or her summation than of what the losing lawyer said in summation. ($p < .001$)

(10) The jurors reported that they would like to KNOW the *winners* better. ($p < .025$)

In regard to results (3) and (8), inspection of the data indicates that in 12 cases out of 21, the defense attorney(s) did speak longer that the prosecutor. The average time the prosecution took for closing speeches was 37 minutes, and the average time for the defense was 46 minutes, or 25% longer.

Since only 4 of the 21 cases included in the juror-survey part of the study produced not guilty verdicts, the data on those defense attorneys who won these cases are limited. In these not-guilty verdicts, 2 of the 4 defense attorneys spoke longer that the prosecutors. (See Table 3 and Appendix H for more information on winning defense summations.)

I observed that concluding (ending the closing speech) seemed to be a problem for some speakers. Sometimes attorneys seemed to be afraid to stop, displaying a reluctance to let go of this their last opportunity to persuade. For example, at the end of one closing speech in a very long and complicated murder trial, the defense attorney attempted to conclude. The following statements were spoken almost in sequence:

> "I want to thank you for surviving. You paid rapt attention."
>
> "The important thing is for you to do your job as a jury. Or just say 'the hell with it'."

> You must come back with a verdict of "not guilty on all counts. Because that's what this case is all about."
>
> "Do what the law requires you to do. Do your duty and you will be a happy person."

Then, apparently finished speaking, he opened a new topic and talked about the fact that he will not be able to rebut the prosecutor's closing speech, followed by:

> "I thank you, ladies and gentlemen."
>
> "And I ask you to find both of these defendants not guilty as charged."
>
> And finally: "I appreciate your indulgence."

According to the significance found in questions (1) through (5), it appears that the attorney defending the accused against charges made by the government is at a distinct disadvantage, always fighting an uphill battle. The prosecutor, who enters the courtroom carrying the banner of either the City of Philadelphia or the United States of America, must be assumed to have an advantage in the legal battle.

The data presented in (5) and (10) appear to support the proposition that there is a relationship between liking a lawyer and deciding in his or her favor, a position which was repeatedly expressed by the trial attorneys interviewed. However, it might be an other-way relationship. The jurors may like the lawyer better who represents the side of the case which agrees with their own evaluations of the same.

Most interesting, perhaps, is what was *not* found. No significance was established in relation to prosecutors or defense attorneys (winners or losers) and whether or not a juror claimed that he or she changed his or her opinion after hearing summations.

Other results:

If it were possible, would you like to know the (lawyer) better and have him or her as a friend? (The number in parentheses indicates the number of respondents)

	Prosecutor (208)	Defense Attorney (245)[17]
Yes	.77	.65
No	.23	.35

Did you believe what he or she said?

	Prosecutor (211)	Defense Attorney (265)[17]
Almost everything	.44	.14
Enough of it	.52	.56
Almost nothing	.04	.30

Did you change your opinion after hearing the (lawyer's) closing speech?

	Prosecutor (215)	Defense Attorney (259)[17]
Yes	.14	.11
No	.82	.85
I don't remember	.04	.04

Note that 88% of 214 complete jurors who responded reported that they thought the closing speeches *were* important. The most frequently given reasons as to *why* they believed the closing speech was important were:

1. It refreshes your memory
2. It clarifies the issues and pulls the pieces together
3. It gives a good summary of the entire trial

Results from Questionnaires Completed by Alternate Jurors

After the judge charges the jurors, repeating the laws which apply in the case, the alternate jurors are thanked for their service and excused. Their jury duty is terminated.

Alternate jurors were then interviewed by me. They were very cooperative, as they were pleased to be able to finally express their opinions. Jurors are not permitted to discuss the case they are hearing with anyone (other jurors, family and friends included) until after all the evidence is in and they begin to deliberate. Because alternates never get to deliberate with their fellow jurors, there is a great sense of incompleteness. They are barred from discussing to conclusion a case to which they have often devoted great attention, and sometimes weeks of time.

Thirty-five alternate jurors completed questionnaires for this part of the study and statistical significance was established for the following responses:

Results from ALTERNATE Jurors

(1) The alternate jurors reported that they thought the *defense attorney* spoke TOO LONG. ($p < .005$)

(2) The alternate jurors reported that they BELIEVED more of what the *prosecutor* said in his or her summation than of what the defense attorney said. ($p < .05$)

It is noted that significance was found for these same two issues for ALL jurors. See (3) and (4) on pages 162-163.

The questionnaire which the alternates completed was without the questions which could only be answered after having deliberated, but did include an additional question:

Would you have voted — or are you leaning towards: (N=34)

a. guilty	24
b. not guilty	6
c. undecided or no answer	4

When comparing the alternate responses to this question with the verdict reached by the jurors after deliberating, there were interesting and revealing discrepancies.

In five instances, the alternates indicated they would have voted guilty when the deliberated verdict was not guilty.

In three instances, the alternates indicated they would have voted not guilty when the deliberated verdict was guilty.

This evidence seems to indicate that the response to the closing speech immediately after hearing it is much stronger than after jurors have discussed it as a group, and blended it with the evidence and testimony. It appears that the immediate dramatic effects of closing speeches are mitigated through the process of reasoned discussion. (See Chapter 11 for more discussion of this important finding.)

There is support for this conclusion in Hovland, Janis and Kelley (1953:30). They reported the findings of a Hovland and Weiss study: "The effect of the source [speaker] is maximal at the time of the communication but decreases with the passage of time more rapidly than the effects of the content [message]."

One of the alternate jurors wrote on his questionnaire, "I would have to talk to other people" before reaching his decision. Indeed, the design of the trial process may be very wise. Deliberation is necessary to equalize and fit together into a comprehensive whole the various pieces of the puzzle to which the decision-markers are exposed throughout the trial. The above information would seem to indicate that discussions between lawyers and alternate jurors, a practice engaged in by some lawyers in an attempt to get a preview of the verdict, can often be misleading.

Conclusion

The tone of a criminal trial, obviously, is extremely serious. No one charged with the responsibility of another person's freedom takes this obligation lightly. Jury after jury of citizens from many segments of the population were observed paying the strictest attention to every word that was spoken in the courtroom. Even side-bar conferences (which are quiet conversations supposedly spoken outside of the hearing of jurors) were attended to very closely, with most jurors straining to pick up a word or two to help them along their difficult way.

However, the limitations of an opinion survey are many. The reader must maintain a constant awareness that even though jurors, with all good intentions, may wish to convey their reasons for deciding a case, they may not be able to separate out the actual factors which were primary in the complicated human process of decision-making.

The reader must also bear in mind that the jurors were answering questions about how they came to their decision after having been instructed by the judge during the charge to decide the case only on the evidence. Their responses might have been colored by this fact.

> If the individual happened to listen to a persuasive speech, and then said something that indicated a change in cognitions, the inclination would be to attribute the change to the speech. Actually, there could have been many reasons for the change, but determining the exact causes of cognition change is always difficult (Bettinghaus 1980:8).

Therefore, the conclusions of this part of the study, with perhaps the potential of being quite valuable to trial lawyers, are presented with a caveat.

10. Other Related Issues

Presented here is information relating to language in the courtroom in general, and to summation specifically, which was gleaned from sources other than the lawyer-informant interviews in Section 1, the observations of those informants discussed in Section 2, or from the jurors who participated in Section 3. These topics are discussed because they are germane to the issue under study.

Summation in Mock Trials

During the time that this study was in progress, I was invited by one of the interviewees to participate as a juror in a mock trial. This was a very fruitful experience, as I had also served as a juror in an actual trial, and serving as a mock juror gave good information for comparative purposes.

The trial was conducted as part of an annual educational opportunity for lawyers. It is sponsored by The Academy of Advocacy, A Non-Profit Institute to Enhance the Quality of Litigated Justice. The director of the program is S. Gerald Litvin, one of the interviewees for this study, and the trial is part of a week long program held annually at the Villanova Law School, Villanova, Pennsylvania.

The case presented involved a civil matter and was tried four times simultaneously, in four different courtrooms, with four different 'casts of characters'. The jurors were assigned to a courtroom, and then a voir dire was conducted by the lawyers appointed to the job. The process of voir dire permits the lawyers, and in some instances judges, to question perspective jurors with the purpose of detecting conscious or subconscious preconceptions or biases which might interfere with someone performing as a fair and impartial juror. Many questions were put to us as potential jurors, but as this entire exercise is a learning experience for the lawyers, no one was excused.

Although the program was very well executed, there was never a moment when the jurors were not aware that this was 'let's pretend'. During the deliberation discussions, in spite of the earnestness with which the mock jurors faced their job, they were aware that when four o'clock came around, they would all go home, no matter what the stage of deliberations. The jury upon which I sat had a difficult time deciding upon what was a complex case, and didn't have time to complete the deliberation. However, the tenor of the deliberations was serious, and the jurors dedicated to the task at hand — no less so than the jury upon which I sat in Philadelphia City Hall in 1981.

There are three factors concerning mock trials to which one must attend. First of all, there was always the awareness that the decision the jury reached affected not one person. There was never a sense of the serious responsibility felt by actual jurors knowing that what they believed, what they did, could have real consequences for a fellow human.

Second of all, the type of jurors was quite different from that of the actual Philadelphia jurors. Almost all of the mock jurors were college educated, and well-off enough so that they could arrange to be free on a workday to participate in the program. Several were law students or the spouses or children of lawyers. This jury was far more informed than any actual jury is likely to be.

Thirdly, the trial itself was condensed, with many important pieces of the trial reduced or eliminated because of the one-day time requirement. There was much that would have been brought to light and/or developed in an actual trial that was not. The witnesses were professional actors, a far cry from what so many witnesses really are, and the attorneys were new to their roles as trial lawyers, lacking the finesse which so many experienced attorneys exhibit.[18]

It must be acknowledged that these same factors will affect in a significant way any research that employs mock jurors, or jurors from actual juror pools deciding a mock or condensed real trial. This researcher presents this information as a caveat to be considered when evaluating all mock trial research.

University of Pennsylvania Law School Class Observed

During the course of this research, I was invited to attend a class in trial practice procedure (named Trial of an Issue of Fact) at the University of Pennsylvania Law School. This course is offered once a year, meets for thirteen sessions of two hours each, with one two-hour lecture devoted to closing speeches. I observed that session.

The first hour began with comments by the lecturer David Rudovsky, an experienced trial lawyer, who was at the time of this writing the First Assistant Defender for the Defender Association of Philadelphia. This organization offers, without cost, defense counsel for the indigent. This includes needy persons with non-American citizenship finding themselves in criminal legal difficulty in this country. Mr. Rudovsky was also one of the informants in this study.

After general comments about closing speeches by Mr. Rudovsky, and a brief question and answer period, several of the students took turns standing at the lectern in the front of the lecture hall, with 'Judge Rudovsky' sitting to one side, and gave closing speeches for an assigned case. The preparation of the summation had been the homework assignment that week. Four out of the class of approximately 20 students participated.

The students each had approximately ten minutes to present their arguments, some taking more, some less. One student read his entire closing. Another young man was quite a dynamic speaker, but apparently disobeyed the laws about what one may or may not say in a closing speech. Each of the presentations was followed by a verbal evaluation by Rudovsky, and questions from fellow students.

The lecturer stressed the point that the speaker may not give a personal opinion: "It's not what you think, or what the state thinks, but 'that's what the evidence shows, that's what we've proven.' Especially the prosecutor, who can get a mistrial."

About objections: "You've got to know the law on objections before you even argue a case. One of the disadvantages of objecting is that the jury thinks you're interrupting; and maybe the objection gets overruled."

When a student made a mistake concerning reasonable doubt, Rudovsky said: "It's embarrassing to be corrected by the judge in front of the jury; 'That's an incorrect statement of the law.' And then your credibility is diminished somewhat before the jury. Correspondingly, when you are able to say accurately, 'This is what the judge will charge on this', then the jury hears it from the judge in exactly the same words that you've provided. Your credibility is enhanced."

The language and/or behavior of the students during their summations prompted the following comments from Mr. Rudovsky:

> The responding person has to be a little more flexible. You don't know quite which way he's going to go, and you have to respond directly to what he says.
>
> If you're a defense lawyer, if you appeal too much to sympathy, that can be turned around against you.
>
> The defender is really being ambiguous — and the prosecutor should use that. Make a point out of his being ambiguous . . . Whatever the case, civil or criminal, the person going second really has to rebut. More than just argue affirmatively, you've gotta take their best shot and turn it around . . . It's more than just thinking, 'This is what I'm gonna say. I don't care what my opponent says. This is what I'm gonna do.'
>
> Stay away from legalese. You can lose people that way. I think you also lose people by reading . . . you lose that personal contact with the jury.

After better than a hour of this activity, the two other sections of the course joined with this one in another lecture hall and the students became observers of a demonstration of closing speeches. The first person to sum up in the presented case was a defense lawyer, who spoke nine minutes. He was followed by an actual Philadelphia Assistant District Attorney, who spoke for a much longer time. This concluded the students' study and practice of closing speeches at the University of Pennsylvania Law School for that school year.

The session was well done and one can imagine that the students left better informed about closing speeches than when they arrived. Granted that it was not possible for all students to have a turn at speaking, I believe that the students would benefit more from having another six students in each section present instead of observing the demonstration summations. Although they were interesting, it seems more instructive to *do* it rather than *watch* someone else do it — especially in a nonrealistic setting.

Sherzer (1983) reports that the Kuna, when learning and teaching 'Kuna ways of speaking', both verbal and nonverbal skills, are "intimately involved in the actual practice of these skills." They learn through a combination of observation, participation, and verbal explanation. According to the information provided by the informants in this study, this appears to be an appropriate combination for learning 'lawyer ways of speaking'.

As the Law School of the University of Pennsylvania is situated in a metropolitan area, it should be required of the students, in addition to the session in the classroom, that they attend at least one trial in the Philadelphia or federal courts and observe actual closing speeches. Since Philadelphia has so many courtrooms, almost all of them in daily use, and is the seat of a federal district, the opportunities for students are numerous and immediately available.

They could also select the type of case (civil or criminal) which interests them most. This would provide real knowledge about the consequential speech event summation, which the trial lawyer must present every time a case goes to court. It would also preclude the problem Justice Frank identified (see Chapter 1), of having practicing lawyers who have never been inside a courtroom.

Three Other Studies With Corroborating Evidence

1. In a study examining note-taking by jurors in the United States District Court for the Eastern District of Pennsylvania, sponsored by the Philadelphia Bar Association and for which I served as research director, the responses to three questions provide further evidence in the matter of closing speeches (Walter and Heim 1985).

1) What was most important in your reaching your decision in this case? (301 jurors responded)

The law as it was given to us by the judge	35%
The facts presented by the witnesses	59%
The closing speeches of the lawyers	06%

According to these responses, closing speeches had little effect on juror decisions. However, even though it appears that summation played a very small part, the responses to this question *might* be biased data. In the charge from the court, which the jurors heard prior to filling out the questionnaire, the jurors were encouraged to rely more on the law and evidence, and less on the closing arguments of the lawyers. A common jury instruction will include information such as:

> You should be guided by each lawyer's arguments to the extent they are supported by the evidence and insofar as they aid you in applying your own reason and common sense. However, you are not required to accept the arguments of either lawyer. It is for you and you alone to decide the case based on the evidence as it was presented from the witness stand and in accordance with the instructions which I am now giving you.
> (Taken from the charge of Judge Marvin Halbert, Court of Common Pleas, Philadelphia.)

Because there is a strong implication in the charge that the closing speech is 'low man on the totem pole', the responses of the jurors may have been influenced by their not wanting anyone to think that they were not following the instructions of the court. Garfinkel, in his discussion of juror attitudes (1967:113), states that when interviewing jurors after a verdict about how they reached their decision, "regardless of the procedures that were actually followed, as these were learned by the interviewer from other sources, jurors identified them with procedures depicted in the official line", i.e., instructions from the judge. Hence, it is possible that the jurors in this study may well have been more influenced by the closing speeches than they cared to admit.

Moreover, there is evidence that the effects of summation are strongest immediately following the delivery of closing speeches, and that those effects are then mitigated during deliberations when they are meshed together with evidence and law through discussion. (See the results from alternate jurors in Chapter 9.)

2) When did you take the most notes?
(228 jurors responded, some marking more than one class)

While the lawyers were questioning the witnesses	65.3%
During the judge's charge	14.8%
During the opening speeches	10.3%
During the closing speeches	9.6%

Most of the notes were taken by the jurors during the questioning of witnesses, with a very substantial drop to the judge's charge, and a further drop to the speeches. Very few jurors reported that they took notes during the attorneys' opening and closing speeches.

3) When did you take the fewest notes?
(228 jurors responded, but some marked more than one class)

During the closing speeches	45.1%
During the opening speeches	31.4%
During the judge's charge	21.2%
While the lawyers were questioning the witnesses	2.3%

The responses to questions 2 and 3 are, not unexpectedly, almost a mirror image of one another. The results of these two questions lend evidence to the hypothesis that during closing and opening speeches, and often when the judge is charging the jury, there is a direct interaction transpiring between the speaker (lawyer or judge) and the hearers (jurors). The speaker usually looks directly at the jurors and thereby demands their attention, as though they were two individuals engaged in a two-way conversation. The jurors are being addressed directly, and their attention is required. The Cooperative Principle (Chapter 1) is operative.

However, when a lawyer is questioning a witness, the lawyer as the sender of the message and the witness as receiver are the ones who are engaged in the linguistic exchange. The jurors at this moment are overhearers, or third parties to a conversation between two other persons. Their attention is requested, but in an indirect fashion, as spectators of rather than participants in a speech event. authorised participants.

When they are overhearers to a conversation, the jurors are freer to take notes, and they did. But when they are directly engaged in the interaction, when the lawyer or the judge is speaking to them, it might seem uncooperative, or even rude, to look away from the the speaker to take notes. The responses to questions 2) and 3) reflect this exactly, and indicate that the jurors gave the lawyers their full attention during both opening and closing speeches.

2. In a second and ongoing jury research project, the focus of study is the civil jury system in the United States. This project, for which I also serve as research director, is sponsored by the Roscoe Pound Foundation, the research arm of the Association of Trial Lawyers of America. Ultimately, this study will be included in a book on the civil jury written in collaboration with John Guinther. The results reported below account for slightly more then half of the anticipated juror responses.

In exploring the question of whether civil jurors understand the issues of the trials in which they participate as fact-finders, the following three questions which relate to closing speeches were included:

1) Which statement best describes your feelings about the closing speech of the PLAINTIFF'S lawyer:
(172 jurors have responded thus far)

It caused me to change my opinion about the case	5%
It didn't change my opinion about the case	95%

2) Which statement best describes your feelings about the closing speech(es) of the DEFENSE lawyer(s):
(176 jurors have responded thus far)

It caused me to change my opinion about the case	7%
It didn't change my opinion about the case	93%

3) In making your decision about the case, what was MOST important to you?
(202 jurors have responded thus far)

The FACTS as told to you by the witnesses	47%
The LAW as explained to you by the judge	41%
The FACTS and LAW together	6%
The CLOSING SPEECHES given by the lawyers	4%
The LAW and CLOSING SPEECHES	1%
All three	1%

Once again, we have jurors stating in very strong numbers that they did not change their opinions after hearing the closing speeches, and that these speeches were not very important to their verdict decisions. Even taking into account the comments by judges which admonish jurors not to place too much emphasis on closing speeches, and the possible influence that admonition might have on conscientious jurors when questioned on this same issue, one cannot ignore the consistent and dramatic percentages every study has produced.

3. In another study of juror decision making, Vinson (1985) reports that, "80 to 90 percent of all jurors come to a decision during or immediately after the opening statements." However, continues Vinson, even though people come to quick decisions, that doesn't mean they won't change their minds. "But they usually would rather not, and if you haven't hooked your jurors early, it may be hard to get them later" (p. 72). If this is a valid finding, and if the purpose of the closing speech is to persuade the jurors, then the lawyer certainly must be engaged in an uphill battle during summation.

Although these figures are startling and, if valid, would put a different light on closing speeches, I note that I have never found this research referenced, nor do I know that it has ever been published. Yet these figures are widely quoted in the legal community. It is not without interest that Vinson, who describes himself as a behavioral scientist, is engaged in selling his services to assist with juror selection, and writes that "The problem of persuading jurors is in part a problem of selecting jurors who are persuadable . . . if the case is important, guesswork won't do" (p. 76). I would urge the interested reader to attempt to locate and examine the data carefully before accepting this study as valid.

The results from Study 2 discussed above do lend some support to Vinson's claim.

Other Sources of Information

'Court followers' are a group of elderly and/or retired persons, mostly men, who make a profession of observing trials. They arrive in court every day that it is in session (some preferring federal court, others state), comb through the court lists of what is transpiring in which courtrooms, and then select for the day's viewing, by their definition, the 'best' trials and the 'best closing speeches'.

They know a great deal about the quality of the courtroom charisma of many trial lawyers, and are opinionated and loyal followers. I consulted with them concerning their lists of outstanding speakers. If a lawyer who I had previously determined to observe and interview was on their list, I was assured that I had made a correct evaluation.

However, they had many names on their list of speakers, and I learned that court followers were less selective than I needed to be. When one is observing trials as frequently as they are, and knowing how infrequently outstanding lawyers go to court, out of necessity of assuring them an interesting day, their list has to include more than the very best. Therefore, I used their input for confirmation rather than for new information.

Many jurors like to share their jury experience after the trial is over (Goldberg 1981), and lawyers often pursue this resource, where it is legal to do so, to help them improve their courtroom performance. One of the lawyer-informants in this study recently reported a conversation with a juror who served on a jury which found the two defendants guilty. That juror conveyed the following about his fellow jurors:

1) The jurors believed the defendants must have been guilty, otherwise why would they have been charged?
2) The judge must have thought they were guilty too because she always sustained the objections made by the prosecutor, and overruled the objections made by the defense lawyers.
3) The defense lawyers took too long to try the case.
4) The more conservative people on the jury wanted to find the defendants not guilty, and the more educated, liberal jurors wanted to find them guilty.

Statements 1) and 2) put a heavy cloud over the concept so basic to the success of our judicial system — the presumption of innocence. Statement 3) indicates that time is a dimension to be taken seriously by lawyers in the courtroom; perhaps less is more. Statement 4) puts the issue of jury selection services in question.

Cross-Cultural Comparisons

There is an increasing interest in cross-cultural study of disputation. Frake (1972) discussed litigation as one kind of Yakan talk in his study "'Struck by Speech': The Yakan Concept of Litigation", the Yakan being Philippine Moslems who live on the island of Basilan located off the southern tip of Zamboanga Peninsula. In this study, he contrasts Yakan with the Subanun, "pagan swidden agriculturists inhabiting the interior of Zamboanga Peninsula on the island of Mindanao" (p. 127).

He claims that a striking difference between Subanun and Yakan litigation is the place of the activity in the overall structure of cultural scenes. The Subanun settle trivial disputes in scenes of formal festivities, whereas the Yakan settle relatively serious disputes in informal settings. "This difference is crucial to any functional interpretations of litigation in the two societies. Participation in litigation has different meanings and different consequences in the two societies because of it" (p. 129).

It would be accurate to say that litigation in Philadelphia is distinct from both the Subanun and the Yakan practices, as serious disputes are settled in formal settings. That leaves one dimension of this comparative structure to be accounted for, i.e., trivial disputes in informal settings. Ethnographers may find that this scene exists in other cultures, but there may also be an example of it in our own; Traffic Court is the place where minor disputes, such as parking tickets, are resolved informally. A clerk calls out to the group of complainants gathered there, "If you think your ticket was wrongly given, raise you hands, give your ticket to the clerk — and you're all excused."

Talk Never Dies: The Language of Huli Disputes (Goldman 1983) is another example of a sociolinguistic analysis of talk in disputation. Disputes and dispute-management procedures for the Huli of Papua New Guinea are defined and analyzed through the activity talk. Speech is the resource and the topic by which disputants interpret and negotiate each other's actions, as it is in our own culture. However, summation may not be a tool for the Huli disputants. Goldman states that dispute is an open state of talk, and that "There is a marked absence of opening and closing rituals" (p. 15). There is no discussion in his study of anything similar to a summation.

Women Trial Lawyers

The number of experienced, female trial lawyers is small but growing as the number of women in lawyering in general increases. However, few have been in the trial field long enough to have gained prominence. The American College of Trial Lawyers, an organization which recognizes excellence in trial advocacy and requires fifteen years at the bar before consideration for membership, in 1984 listed only four women as colleagues out of a total membersship of 3,827.

See 'Lawyer 5' and 'A Special Case' in Chapter 8 for more information concerning how women are sometimes treated during summation by other lawyers and judges. Also, see Chapter 3, item 3.3, 'Women in the act of summing up'.

Black Trial Lawyers

Below are excerpts from an interview with Raymond A. Brown, Newark, who related to the ethnographer what it was like for a black male to become a lawyer in New Jersey in 1949:

> I graduated from Florida A and M in 1938-39, and Fordham Law School finally in 1948.
>
> I was a new black lawyer in 1949. In New Jersey then, there may have been all of ten black lawyers throughout the state, because New Jersey had a procedure whereby they very effectively eliminated non-mainstream lawyers. You had to have a year's clerkship before you took the bar [examination]. New Jersey had at that time, and up until 1953, two categories of lawyers, analogous to the barristers and solicitors of England. Attorneys who could only try cases on a trial level could not go into the appellate court, and therefore counselors-at-law, who were necessarily few, were the only ones who could get a clerkship, and they could only have two clerks at a time.
>
> I can speak for New Jersey. I don't know what New York had at the time — but nearly all the states did at one time — because until around 1915-1916, everybody read law, and very few people went to law school. And then in New Jersey, up until 1949, you could take the bar without any college or any law school — if you could read law and pass the bar.
>
> In 1949, a new constitution — which was effective in 1949 — required that you be a graduate of law school, and that you have a year's clerkship. And needless to say, that year's clerkship was almost without pay. So again you restricted on an economic basis. And so as a new, black lawyer in the com-

> munity, I couldn't get a clerkship, until I wandered across the one Jewish guy who decided that he would give me a break, because he helped (there were no black lawyers) and he, pro bono, helped the local NAACP chapter. So he took me in, Ray Chasan took me in, and entered a clerkship. Worked on the docks, did a clerkship — and he very often, very kindly, forgave me days when I didn't certify.
>
> But then when I came out, I had nothing. I lived in a low income, black housing project, with one child, and another one on the way when I started, and I had no office . . .
> [His son now practices law with him.]

The Old Bailey

The Central Criminal Court in London, called The Old Bailey, was a place I visited on three different occasions during the course of observing summations. Because the American legal system has developed from and is based on English law, it was of interest to me to see how much or little the American way of summing up differs from or remains constant to the British way.

The courts in England are open to the public just as they are in this country. Visitors are invited to sit in the small, elevated galleries of the four courtrooms of the old, original part of the Old Bailey, as long as there are seats.

The similarities are immediately recognizable, for there is the judge sitting at his elevated position, the clerks sitting near him (I saw only male judges and lawyers), the lawyers, the accused — all the same persons you would find in a criminal trial in this country. Because of the media exchange between America and England, there are few visual surprises.

There are interesting differences. First of all, the rooms themselves are splendid to behold, especially the famous courtroom number one, where the more serious criminal cases are tried. The most immediate difference to meet the American eye is the one of costuming. Only the judge in this courtroom was observed wearing a red robe. He is a High Court judge, known as the 'red judge,' and tries the more serious cases.

The barristers and solicitors are separated by seating, just as they are by occupation,[19] yet the prosecutor and the defense attorney sit side by side on the same bench. The accused is seated in the dock, which is large, elevated, enclosed to waist level, and contains stairs which exit directly below to the prison cells. The police custodians sit in the dock with the accused.

"In each court can be found a man or woman sitting unobtrusively writing every word that is spoken" (Morecroft et al. 1984). This person, called the 'shorthand writer', transcribes the proceedings of the case by hand in pen and ink. There was no dictating or recording apparatus visible in courtroom number one. The woman writing in booklet after booklet had a second bottle of ink at her elbow, at the ready when the first went dry.

It is noted however that in other courtrooms in the Old Bailey, there were stenographers sitting before machines which were recording the proceedings while the person in charge stared off into space.

The positioning of the witness stand, which was side by side with the jury box, was extremely interesting. This meant that when a witness was testifying, the jurors were unable to see the face of the speaker. Only the two jurors at the end of both rows could see the witness, and only in profile. The jurors were seated facing the lawyers, as was the witness stand. Therefore, the question is raised, how can jurors examine the face of a testifying witness for clues as to the veracity of testimony?

When the speakers stood to give their closing arguments, other than the garb of wig and black robe which all barristers are required to wear, there were few discernible differences. There was the opening: "Members of the jury", although one lawyer started right in, just as some lawyers did in the Pennsylvania courts. There was the rhetorical question: "But how did it go on?" There were the repetitions, and the checking of ones own notes, just as did many of the lawyers in this study. However, jurors took notes freely, which can only be done at the discretion of the judge in federal and state courts in this country (Walter and Heim 1985).

Using the same language in a system which is the parent of the American derivative, one would expect similarities. But the differences in the use of English were obvious time and time again. For example, in the formality of expression, "You may be prepared to consider another possibility." Or the emotional constraint, as in words of closing, "We submit that the case has not been proved to the high level required." And always the Received Pronunciation of British English to remind us of the differences which so often fall on the American ear, with or without justification, as a form of erudition.

Outside of the visitors' gallery doors in the Old Bailey, there is often a sign on a standing holder which signifies what is transpiring in the courtroom. There might be one or two words handwritten in ink on a placard. One sign read, 'Summing Up'.

Inside of all four of the public galleries which I visited, there was one sign only posted. In its own fashion, this notice made clear the value of the *lawyers'* closing speeches to the English court system:

> Members of the Public are Requested to Refrain as far as Possible From Moving About When the Judge Is Summing Up

Textbook for Studying Summation

Although many practicing courtroom lawyers and legal scholars have written many words about 'how to give a closing speech' (Bailey 1979, Baldwin 1984, Belli 1979, Cartwright 1978, Crawford 1983, Holmes 1982, Jeans 1975, Keeton 1973, Mauet 1980, Smith 1982, Stein 1979), there is a text written by Ray Moses (1985) which I consider worthy of examination by lawyers interested in studying the speech genre summation. It should be read not only for its quality, which is consistently high, but it is also an excellent and current sample of the type of text which is available.

Jury Argument in Criminal Cases: A Trial Lawyer's Guide is a text which considers the genre summation rather than just the event. In the early chapters, the book addresses itself to the prosecutor and the possible objections to his or her arguments, and then to the permissible prosecution arguments.

There are two chapters on the preparation and delivery of the closing argument which relate, in exquisite detail, how to go about it. Moses then takes the essential core arguments, i.e., reasonable doubt, burden of proof, Call to Arms!, etc., and gives examples of them. Most are less than brilliant, but they certainly do provide food for thought and recipes upon which to improve.

There are two chapters devoted to sample arguments for the prosecution and defense relevant to the two issues of guilt and punishment.

Although not the most effective way to learn how to give a closing speech, reading the texts of fascinating summations can be quite informative. Moses writes:

> Caution must be exercised not to blindly imitate others. Mimicry makes one appear as a fool. Yet, the reader can count on learning something from each of these examples. Much of human behavior originates with our observation of others. This is particularly true of trial lawyers. We borrow from one another. If it works, it doesn't matter that the thought was not original (p. 7-1).

It is difficult to believe that there is not something to be learned from reading the closing speeches of the likes of Melvin Belli and F. Lee Bailey, two of the nine speakers of whom he gives samples. But, then again, how many lawyers will ever during their career at the bar have the opportunity to either prosecute or defend persons like Patricia Campbell Hearst, John W. Hinkley, Jr., or Sirhan Bishara Sirhan?

The great weakness of the text is the detailed to distraction, and often inappropriate, instructions for speakers in the Preparation and Delivery chapters. However, Mr. Moses is very much on target when he writes about persuasion through legal oratory, or factors in legal argumentation, or:

> The most candid among us will recognize that there are very few great prosecutors or criminal defense lawyers. In modern times, we could probably count them on the fingers of one or two hands. There may be one or two among the readers of this manual. Chances are that it's not you (p. 3-6).

But then he gives instructions for posture such as:

> The advocate should stand erectly on the balls of his feet. For a comfortable stationary stance, line the chin up with the left heel, with the hands at the side (p. 4-6).

If speakers had to worry about such picayune matters when standing to address the jury, there would probably be far fewer trial lawyers.

In the overall, the materials are well presented, well documented, full of good ideas, and with more than a sideways glance in the direction of reality in the courtroom. For example, when writing about the length of the argument, he says:

> Knowing when to stop is important to the persuasive impact of a jury argument. Time is an important commodity to jurors. Trial lawyers who pay attention to their audience can sense that juncture in time when the jurors are no longer paying attention.
>
> The advocate makes his impression, if he is going to make one, in the first half hour, sometimes in the first fifteen minutes of summation. The average well-intentioned American juror has an attention span of little more than twenty minutes (p. 3-31).

The bibliography is excellent, as is the indexing. The reader is easily able to find analogies (and metaphors) for a host of topics, such as confession, juror's role, presumption of innocence, or prior crimes, to mention only a few. And the examples of the topics are well detailed, such as under the heading of Reasonable Doubt, one can select analogies having to do with:

> Alphabet, bubble, Doubting Thomas, fresh bread, Ivory soap, jigsaw puzzle, second opinion, termite free house, unhooking life support system, and others.

Summation as Literature

If it is agreed that one can learn something from reading the texts of great closing speeches, perhaps one of the most interesting books from which to read is *The Law as Literature*, edited by Ephraim London (1960). Within its pages are the summations of Daniel Webster in the trial of John Francis Knapp for the murder of Joseph White, the closing address in the Nuremberg trial, and one of the very best, Clarence Darrow in summation in the Sweet case.

This closing speech demonstrates how much of the summation is traditional and continues even to this date from when Mr. Darrow spoke in 1926 on behalf of Dr. Sweet, a successful, black gynecologist who was accused of murder in Detroit. Dr. Sweet was defending his home against a white mob which did not want a black family living in their neighborhood, and took to arms to try to evict them. A white man was killed in the riot when Dr. Sweet, his two brothers — one a dentist, the other a student — and seven friends tried to protect his rightful home.

Obviously, much is different in our country today, just as much is different in the courts. However, as I read through the text of Mr. Darrow's closing speech, I found much there that is still observed in the courts of the 1980s. For example, the traditional opening differed only in that Mr. Darrow said, "If the court please, *gentlemen* of the jury." In 1926, only men served as jurors.

There were the rhetorical questions, compliments for jurors and opposing counsel, the 'we' and 'us' of solidarity:

> Colored people living right here in the city of Detroit are intellectually the equals and some of them superior to most of us. Is that true? Some of them are people of more character and learning than most of us (p. 350).

Darrow also answered his own rhetorical questions:

> Who was he? He was a conspirator in as foul a conspiracy as was ever hatched in a community; in a conspiracy to drive from their homes a little family of black people. Not only that, but to destroy those blacks and their home. Now, let me see whether I am right. What do we know of Breiner [the man killed in the attack on the house]? He lived two blocks from the

> Sweet home... (p. 354).

Clarence Darrow was an artist at using emotional pleas to persuade his jurors. But his emotionalism was balanced by his being a highly credible source:

> All right, gentlemen, call them something else. These blacks have been called many names along down through the ages, but there have been those through the sad years who believed in justice and mercy and charity and love and kindliness, and there have been those who believed that a black man should have some rights, even in a country where he was brought in chains. There are those even crazy enough to hope and dream that sometime he will come from under this cloud and take his place amongst the people of the world. If he does, it will be through his courage and his culture. It will be by his intelligence and his scholarship and his effort, and I say, gentlemen of the jury, no honest, right-feeling man, whether on a jury or anywhere else, would place anything in his way in this great struggle behind him and before him (p. 357).

Mr. Darrow was forthright in saying much that others dared not say in 1926. Notice that he ends by placing the onus to do the right thing squarely on the jurors' shoulders, just as did so many lawyers in this study.

Darrow too seemed reluctant to stop talking, and explained to the jurors, "I always fear results. When life or liberty is in the hands of a lawyer, he realizes the terrible responsibility that is on him, and he fears that some word will be left unspoken, or some thought will be forgotten" (p. 363). He talked about the American jury system and apologized for speaking too long, and signaled the close: "I shall not talk to you much longer. I am sorry I talked so long. But this case is close to my heart" (p. 369). And finally, he requests in the closing:

> This case is about to end, gentlemen. To them, it is life. Not one of their color sits on this jury. Their fate is in the hands of twelve whites. Their eyes are fixed on you, their hearts go out to you, and their hopes hang on your verdict.
>
> This is all. I ask you, on behalf of this defendant, on behalf of these helpless ones who turn to you, and more than that — on behalf of this great state, and this great city which must face this problem, and face it fairly — I ask you, in the name of progress and of the human race, to return a verdict of Not Guilty in this case! (p. 374).

The next day, the jury returned its verdict of not guilty. But the Sweets never moved back into their house, and the editor ended with this note: "Today, thirty-one years later [1957], both white and colored live in the neighborhood" (p. 375).

Reading this summation even in 1985 is an extraordinary experience. One can well imagine the emotion in the courtroom When Mr. Darrow dared to put the following rhetorical questions to his jurors in 1926:

> First, there was Dr. Sweet. Gentlemen, a white man does pretty well when he does what Dr. Sweet did. A white boy who can start in with nothing, and put himself through college, study medicine, take postgraduate work in Europe, earning every penny of it as he goes along, shoveling snow and coal, and working as a bellhop on boats, working at every kind of employment that he can get to make his way; is some fellow. But Dr. Sweet has the handicap of the color of his face. And there is no handicap more terrible than that. Supposing you had your choice, right here this minute, would you rather lose your eyesight or become colored? Would you rather lose your hearing or become a Negro? Would you rather go out there on the street and have your leg cut off by a streetcar, or have a black skin? (p. 370).

To be sure, there are few Clarence Darrows among the ranks of courtroom lawyers of any era. He was an artist as well as a lawyer. But the impact of the reading of this speech sets forth the best example of what one can do with this way of speaking in the courtroom.

Tapes for Studying Summation

There were two sets of cassettes which I heard and believed to to be of value for the lawyer studying summation. Herald Price Fahringer (one of the interviewees in this study) and Irving Younger were both recorded while delivering speeches about language and law.

Mr. Fahringer was specifically addressing the issue of summation in a speech delivered at at a 1982 Criminal Defense Litigation Seminar for an American Law Institute-American Bar Association (ALI-ABA) course of study.

During the interview with Mr. Fahringer, I discussed the possibility that some of the comments made on his tapes might be more appropriate for experienced trial lawyers summing up in complicated, lengthy trials. What about summations in single issue, less complicated, very often one or two day trials, which so many attorneys spend their careers trying on a day to day basis? Mr. Fahringer maintained that his comments applied to all summations, for every trial was significant in its own right.

The cassettes of Irving Younger were three in a series on jury selection, which were produced in 1984 by The Professional Education Group, Inc. I had intended to interview Mr. Younger for this study, but due to his ill health, I was not able to schedule a meeting. However, as Mr. Younger is such an outstanding persuader in his own right, several of his recorded comments on various issues are included below.

About *persuasion*:

> Essentially our profession is the use of words. We're men and women of letters — that's what we are. It's the spoken word and the written word. We are professionals at speaking. (Tape 2:2)
>
> You must interest the jury . . . It's not comedy. It's not entertainment as such. Your task as a trial lawyer is to persuade. You cannot persuade if they're not listening. And they can't listen — it's just not possible for human nature to pay attention — if they don't find it interesting. So that you have a professional obligation to be interesting to that jury. (Tape 3:1)
>
> [Don't use notes because] it detracts from the eye contact which is probably the single most important thing you have going for you when it comes to persuading the jury. (Tape 1:2)
>
> [You should pay attention to how you dress, or the jurors will think] 'He's careless. He doesn't pay attention to details.' And if jurors think that about you, you're on the way to losing . . . It doesn't communicate to the jury that kind of infinite self-assurance that is the hallmark of successful work in front of a jury. (Tape 1:1)
>
> In the last analysis, at the heart of it, the secret of winning cases with a jury is to make the jury trust you . . . If they trust you, you will win the case! (Tape 3:1)
>
> In my view . . . a trial, among all the other things that it is, is an exercise in education. The lawyer knows about the case, the jurors do not — by definition — at the start. And one of the things that a lawyer must do . . . is educate the jury. If you can't teach the jury about the case, there is no chance of winning their verdict. Educating them is not all that there is to it. You gotta persuade . . . but everything rests on information that jurors must have about the case. (Tape 2:2)

Mr. Younger, a practicing trial lawyer and professor of law until recently at the Cornell Law School and now at the Georgetown Law Center, had the following to say about *law professors*:

> The teachers of procedure say it [about jury selection] because they believe it. And they believe it because for the most part they have never tried a case. Indeed, for the most part, they have never practiced law. And as a matter of fact, the higher you go in the pecking order, the more nearly you come to the very first drawer, the elite of law schools, the more likely

> it is to be true that the teacher has never practiced. An extraordinary, and in my view, scandalous situation. (Tape 1:1)

About *rhetorical questions*:

> The nature of the English language is such that any declarative sentence can be turned into an interrogative sentence. Any statement can be made a question. That is to say, you may question jurors — not to get an answer. [What is important is] communicating information to the jurors. The answer is unimportant. It's the question that's important, because the question contains a piece of information that you want the jury to have . . . The jurors, having heard the question, now know something about the case. (Tape 2:2)

About *humor*:

> No jokes — no humor — in the courtroom. It is totally out of place . . . Just take it as an absolute rule: you cannot make jokes in a courtroom when there are jurors older than you. Only if you are older than every one of the jurors can you use humor — and then, very delicately. The situation is a serious one in court — no matter the nature of the case. (Tape 3:2)

About *selecting a jury*:

> If you are *not* looking for an impartial, unbiased, and open-minded jury [and you shouldn't be], what kind of jury are you looking for? And the answer, of course — as every one of us who's ever tried a case knows — is that you are looking for a biased, prejudiced, close-minded jury, absolutely incapable of deciding this case fairly. You're looking for the jury that is capable of deciding the case in only one way — and that way is *your* way. So what you want is a jury of six to twelve bigots. People who cannot conceive of any result other than a result favorable to you . . . That is the purpose of jury selection . . . The magic of the system . . . is that it's in the clash of the opposites, in the contest between the advocates, that things seem to work well. (Tape 1:1)

About *jury selection services*

> The social scientist will produce a very persuasive result, in the sense that the profile of the ideal juror that the sociologist comes up with, after doing his sampling . . . is invariably identical with the profile you would have come up with simply on the basis of intuition and common sense.
>
> But it's very reassuring to the client to have the 'scientist' tell him that the lawyer knows what he's doing — and very reassuring to the lawyer to have the scientist tell you that the seat-of-your-pants is telling you the truth. (Tape 2:1)

11. Conclusions

In Section 1 of this study, the lawyer-informants told us that the summation is very important to the trial process. In Section 2, I observed discrepancies between what lawyers say they do in summation and what they did, and consequently, I questioned their ability to describe their own behavior in summation. In Section 3, the jurors told us in very clear terms that the summation did not make a difference to their verdict decisions. This opinion is confirmed by other jury studies which were discussed in Chapter 10.

How do we make sense of these opposing views of the same event? What is a good closing speech, what is its value, and why do lawyers put so much time and effort into a speech event which may not serve their stated purpose of winning a case?

What is a Good Closing Speech?

The answer to the question of what is a good closing speech, and of how we determine competence in delivering one will depend upon whom is responding. The lawyers reported repeatedly in their interviews that a good summation is one which wins the case for them, and that one of the key ingredients of the speech would be convincing arguments, i.e., arguments that would make the jurors do what they want them to do. They reported that much of what they do and say during the trial, including summation, is directed towards getting the jurors to like them so that they will be more receptive to their ideas.

The answer was only somewhat different when asked how they would identify competence at summation in another lawyer. Since they have all heard and used many of the politeness formulae, opening and closing routines, and different ways of requesting or demanding a verdict, to what are they responding when they say, "Lawyer X really gave a good closing speech today"? Their answers always centered around persuasion through good arguments, i.e., "Her arguments were brilliant", or "He really persuaded those jurors — he had them in his pocket."

The lawyer-informants reported that they believed there was a connection between competence and outcome. "Good, I guess, is measured in success", said one lawyer. Whenever informants spoke with me after a summation about 'doing it better', they invariably talked about forgotten arguments — ones that should have been included, ones that could have made a difference. Repeating informant Fitzpatrick:

> The fear is that you will leave out something that you should have mentioned that would convince one juror, who will then go the other way . . . The fear I have is not that I won't be able to talk, or my mind will go blank, or I'll start stuttering . . . it's that you'll pick the wrong approach — you'll say the wrong thing.

I note that no lawyer ever admitted to me that s/he said the wrong thing during summation.

As an observer, I deemed a good summation one which informed me about the case, held my interest, and convinced me that the speaker was *credible*. I often arrived in the courtroom just before closing speeches, and knew little or nothing about the case. I considered this an advantage in evaluating them, for if it was a good summation, by the time the lawyer sat down I knew a lot about the case, about the people involved in the case, and the outcome which s/he believed should follow from the arguments. Even if I didn't agree with the speaker's conclusion, I held a good opinion of the 'telling of the tale'.

What became obvious to me was that a lawyer who delivers a good closing speech knows far more than how to fill the sequential slots which constitute the format of a summation (Table 2). He or she has knowledge of the law; the ability to choose content that would be effective given the facts of the case, the attributes of the accused, and the general character of the jury; an awareness that summation is a performance, and that his or her way of speaking might make a difference.

Whether a summation was part of a winning or losing case was irrelevant to my evaluation of the speech event, which is demonstrated by two facts: (1) I never stayed to hear the verdict unless I was in court to interview the jurors for Section 3 of this study, and (2) there were many lawyers, including two defense attorneys, who delivered summations in trials in which the verdict went for their client, but who I decided not to interview. These summations were not good, the speakers not exceptional. Who won or lost the trial was unrelated to my reaction to the speech.

It is difficult to specify what jurors think a good summation is or isn't, but we do know that they evaluate summation as a speech event apart from the verdict. They often noted that they thought the speech of one lawyer was very interesting, and that they believed the speaker, but then decided the case in the opposite direction. The evidence collected in this study indicates that jurors respond to the speech as a performance, but that it is not usually vital to their decision in the case.

One of the most revealing pieces of information which was identified in this study was the results of discussion with alternate jurors. These jurors, with whom I spoke just after they had heard the closing speeches and were excused from jury service, reacted to them strongly. But the jurors who sat through deliberations of the same trials, and discussed the case through group interaction, had a different view of them. The effects of the closing speeches were mitigated through discussion, and the summation took its rightful place along side of the evidence and applicable law in the case.

The jurors seemed to take seriously the admonition from the judge not to place too much weight on closing speeches, which s/he stressed were the opinions of the lawyers, not evidence. From the results presented in Chapters 9 and 10, I think it is clear that most jurors heed the judge's charge and give the closing speech equal but not extra weight.

Contradictory Evidence

Although lawyers reported that winning the case was the main point of summation, there is much evidence that the speaker may have other purposes in mind as well when giving a closing speech.

Several informants spoke to me about needing or wanting an audience in the courtroom to perform better during summation. If the intention of the lawyer is solely to persuade the jurors, why is the presence or absence of third parties a concern of the speaker?

Lawyers prepare their closing speeches in detail even when they have little or no hope of winning the case. Why all this effort for a lost cause?

In the appellate courts, when the purpose of argument is to reverse a prior judicial decision, the arguments often are limited by the court to ten minutes. In this type of argument, the stated purpose is to win, and the argument is addressed to informed jurors, i.e., judges. This summation is different.

If the evidence is valid that 80-90% of the jurors make up their minds about the case after opening speeches, which many lawyers believe it is, again, why so much effort invested in summation, and what is its real value?

Finally, as I learned in this study, weak closing speeches do not necessarily lose cases. A trial can be won apart from the summation.

What a Summation can do

During the past three years, many hours were spent in courtrooms, judge's chambers, lawyer's offices, law and linguistic libraries. Culling through the accumulated information conveyed to me by lawyer-informants, from observations of and conversations with courtroom speakers and listeners, and from what jurors reported in interview and questionnaire, I conclude that the following can be achieved with a good summation:

A summation can win a case. If the evidence is unclear or not strong, if the accused is a sympathetic person who has never been in trouble before (that the jurors know about), if it is what the informants describe as a close case, and if the jurors find the lawyer credible, if any or all of these conditions prevail, the summation may win the case.

A summation can favorably impress the client who has paid the lawyer to represent him or her. The client might feel cheated or poorly represented if the lawyer did not do his or her best for them in the closing speech.

A summation can make a favorable impression on the other lawyers in the case, or other lawyers in the courtroom. Many of the cases which are brought to an attorney's office are those which are referred from other lawyers. How other lawyers view the speaker is important for building or maintaining a reputation and, hence, a law practice.

How a lawyer behaves during a trial, including summation, can make a favorable impression on the judge. A judge who holds a high opinion of a lawyer may deal more reasonably with him in future non-trial matters, such as sentencing, appeals, or bench decisions. Therefore, lawyers refrain from saying some things in summation which might sway the jurors, but might also offend the judge.

In cases in which the press or television reporters are present in the courtroom, good summations may be reported about in the local, and even national media. Good reputation in the community can be won or maintained with good behavior in summation.

On a more personal level, lawyers often invite their friends and family to hear closing speeches, and a good summation can win admiration from those about whom the lawyer cares.

A good summation brings personal gratification to the speaker. It feels good.

All of the above can accrue to the speaker who delivers a good summation. It should also be noted that if a closing speech is perceived to be weak, it could reverse all or any of them. Knowing this, we know the real value of summation.

Summation is a multi-functional speech event which must be performed according to certain shared standards. The information gathered in this study does not indicate a strong connection between summation and juror verdict decisions, or consequent outcomes of trials. The connection seems to be between reputation among others, and reputation in one's own mind.

A summation is a speech event that all persons involved in a courtroom trial expect, an event by which we are entertained and informed when it is well done, and would be disappointed if it were ommitted. Quoting Dell Hymes, "It is as if it were the lawyer's one aria in the opera of the trial" (personal communication).

Suggestions for Future Research

As everything in a trial is achieved through the spoken word, future research into language in the courtroom offers a fertile field for exploration. Below are listed some suggested areas for investigation, most related to summation.

1. The metaphors which lawyers have for and use during summation are replete with information about what summation means to them, of how they comprehend this speech event through other events, and how this knowledge affects their behavior in the act of summation. A lawyer often holds multiple metaphors for summation. An investigation of what these metaphors are and how they interrelate with behavior could be important in further understanding of both speaker and event.

2. There is a slowly growing cross-cultural literature on disputation in dissimilar cultures. This literature could be expanded so that we can determine if summation occurs in other cultures, and if it does, how does it compare

with regard to its impact on litigation? Who decides the outcomes of disputes, how is one able to appeal to and influence those with the power to determine outcomes, what is the part played by speech in general in litigation?

3. Speech which occurs during a trial is recorded by a stenographer. The resultant transcription, called the court record, is available to anyone and sold by the page. The records are usually purchased by lawyers who wish to study a trial, perhaps for the purpose of appealing the verdict and, as the cost is relatively expensive, they will buy only the pages which are vital to their concerns.

Before 1981, closing speeches were not necessarily transcribed in the Pennsylvania State Courts. "The decision to have them recorded is discretionary with the court. It is, however, common practice to record closing arguments in murder cases" (Wasserbly 1981). With the adoption of Pennsylvania Rule of Criminal Procedure 9030 in April of 1981, "In court cases, after a defendant has been held for court, proceedings in open court shall be recorded." This includes, of course, summation.

Transcribed closing speeches were not used in this research for the areas explored here were the linguistic rather than legal dimensions of summation. Transcriptions tell us *what* was said, but not *how* it was said. In relation to the four categories of features discussed on pages 128-133, transcriptions do provide us with data concerning the choice of words used (1), and the topics for argument (4). However, they tell us nothing of the features apart from words (2), or of hearer response (3). Nor do they inform us of the physical context in which the summation took place.

However, for research purposes other than those addressed in this study, transcription as analysis is an area of interest. What is recorded and what is deleted, what is filtered in and out by transcribers during summation could be insightful in terms of what the trained stenographer has been taught, or determines for him or herself, is important.

4. Appellate courts are those which review appeals from lawyers and have the power to reverse lower court decisions. When a lawyer sums up to this court, the arguments are made not to naive jurors, but to judges who as former lawyers are educated in the law. Therefore, many emotional issues are deleted and the focus is truly on argument. How do these two types of summations differ, and what do they share? From a comparison of what is deleted because it does not persuade judges, we might learn what lawyers

believe is persuasive for jurors.

5. The focus of the analysis of the data in Section 1 was a description of summation in the words of the users. However, this is not the only analysis which could be performed on the same data. The question may occur to many: are there connections between the responses of any one lawyer? Is a lawyer who feels one way about a feature of summation likely to feel a particular way with regard to another, or were the responses random with little or no relatedness? By correlating lawyer responses with interview questions, we might learn that there are patterns of views of summation by individual lawyers; that a lawyer who responds one way on one issue is likely to respond in a predictable way on another.

6. Interviews with alternate jurors excused just before deliberation are a potentially rich source of information for learning about juror response to events of the trial, such as summation. These jurors often have strong views on everything that occurred during the trial; knowledge of what jurors do and do not do, say and do not say during the hours they spend together before deliberation; and most have an opinion on the verdict. Beyond that, after devoting themselves to the trial for some period of time, they are frustrated by not being able to finish what they came to do. They are willing and knowledgeable informants. By comparing their responses with those of jurors who complete deliberations, we would be able to absract away much valuable information, including what happens during deliberation. This mine has hardly been tapped.

7. As stated on the first page of this book, everything that happens during a courtroom trial occurs through the spoken word. Only the judge's charge, questioning of witnesses, and now summation, have been the focus of linguistic research. On every weekday in every city in this country, courtrooms abound with speech, there for the hearing by any linguist. There are many speech genres remaining to be examined in the language rich environment of the courtroom.

APPENDIX A: Questions for Interviews with Lawyers

1. What is the value of the summation to the trial process?
1a. Would the outcome of the trial be different without the summation?

2. What are you trying to do during your closing speech?
What's the key purpose?

3. How did you learn to make a closing speech?
Any formal instruction?

4. Have you given much time to studying closing arguments, either by reading transcripts or observing in courtrooms?
4a. How do you decide who to watch?
How do you determine who's good at it?

5. When do you begin working on the summation?

6. Do you include the client in the preparation of the summation?

7. Are there standard routines or pieces of information that you always include in your closing speech?
7a. Do you have a standard opening? Closing?

8. If you were teaching a young lawyer how to deliver a closing speech, what would you tell him or her? What makes a summation good? What weakens it?

9. What kind of people do you like to have sit on the jury?
9a. Do you have a high or low regard for jurors in general? Are they "your team" or "the opponent"?

10. Do you address one particular juror, all of them, or a few?

11. Do you aim for the head or the heart?
The intellectual or emotional side of the jurors.

12. Are you good at it? ......at making closing speeches?

13. If there are several attorneys representing several clients, when do you prefer to give your summation; first, middle, last, doesn't matter?

14. How would you describe your personal style?

15. Do you respond positively or negatively to the concept of 'audience'?
15a. Do you suffer from stage fright? Do you get nervous?

16. Do you like to use exhibits, large charts, overhead projector — props?

17. Do you like to use a lectern? Notes?

18. Do you like to use metaphors, stories, poetry, (bible) quotations? Are you a 'phrase-maker'?

19. Do you think there is a relationship between liking someone and believing them? Do you try to get (want) the jury to like you?
20. Do you memorize any portion of your closing speech?
21. How much time do you like to take for your closing speech?
22. Are you attentive to the way you dress for court on the day you deliver your summation? If yes, in what way?
23. (For women) Does being female in a traditionally male arena make any difference to you during the trial? During summation?
24. How do you feel about jurors taking notes during the trial?
25. (For men) What do you think about female trial lawyers?
26. Do you use humor during your summation?
27. Do you ever disparage your opponent during the summation?
28. How many summations do you deliver a year?

APPENDIX B: Questionnaire Completed by Jurors

As part of a research study of closing speeches, would you please answer the following questions?

Questions relating to the closing speech of the Prosecutor:

1. How much do you remember of his or her closing speech?
   a. a lot b. some of it c. almost nothing
2. Was the Prosecutors's closing speech:
   a. interesting b. boring c. sometimes interesting, sometimes boring
3. Was the Prosecutor's closing speech:
   a. too long b. too short c. just the right length
4. Did you believe what he or she said?
   a. almost everything b. enough of it c. almost nothing
5. Did you change your opinion after hearing the Prosecutor's closing speech?
   a. yes b. no c. I don't remember
6. Was the Prosecutor's closing speech discussed in the jury room?
   a. yes b. no c. I don't remember
7. If it were possible, would you like to know the Prosecutor better and have him or her as a friend?
   a. yes b. no

Questions relating to the closing speech of the Defense Attorney:

8. How much do you remember of his or her closing speech?
   a. a lot b. some of it c. almost nothing
9. Was the Defense Attorney's closing speech:
   a. interesting b. boring c. sometimes interesting, sometimes boring
10. Was the Defense Attorney's closing speech:
    a. too long b. too short c. just the right length
11. Did you believe what he or she said?
    a. almost everything b. enough of it c. almost nothing
12. Did you change your opinion after hearing the Defense Attorney's closing speech?
    a. yes b. no c. I don't remember
13. Was the Defense Attorney's closing speech discussed in the jury room?
    a. yes b. no c. I don't remember
14. If it were possible, would you like to know the Defense Attorney better and have him or her as a friend?
    a. yes b. no

15. Check the statement which best expresses your opinion:
    a. I think closing speeches ARE important for jury trials.
    b. I think closing speeches are NOT important for jury trials.
    c. I am NOT CERTAIN if closing speeches are important for jury trials.
16. If you had been permitted to take written notes during the trial, would you have wanted to?
    a. yes b. no c. I'm not certain
17. How old are you?
18. Are you? a. male b. female
19. What was the last grade of school you completed?

If you answered yes to 15a. (if you think the speeches ARE important), please tell me why.

APPENDIX C: Questionnaire Completed by Alternate Jurors

As part of a research study of closing speeches to jurors, would you please answer the following questions?

Questions relating to the closing speech of the Prosecutor:

1. How much do you remember of his or her closing speech?
   a. a lot b. some of it c. almost nothing
2. Was the Prosecutors's closing speech:
   a. interesting b. boring c. sometimes interesting sometimes boring
3. Was the Prosecutor's closing speech:
   a. too long b. too short c. just the right length
4. Did you believe what he or she said?
   a. almost everything b. enough of it c. almost nothing
5. Did you change your opinion after hearing the Prosecutor's closing speech?
   a. yes b. no c. I don't remember
6. If it were possible, would you like to know the Prosecutor better and have him or her as a friend?
   a. yes b. no

Questions relating to the closing speech of the Defense Attorney:

7. How much do you remember of his or her closing speech?
   a. a lot b. some of it c. almost nothing
8. Was the Defense Attorney's closing speech:
   a. interesting b. boring c. sometimes interesting, sometimes boring
9. Was the Defense Attorney's closing speech:
   a. too long b. too short c. just the right length
10. Did you believe what he or she said?
    a. almost everything b. enough of it c. almost nothing
11. Did you change your opinion after hearing the Defense Attorney's closing speech?
    a. yes b. no c. I don't remember
12. If it were possible, would you like to know the defense attorney better and have him or her as a friend?
    a. yes b. no
13. Would you have voted — or are you leaning towards:
    a. guilty b. not guilty

14. Check the statement which best expresses your opinion:
    a. I think closing speeches ARE important for jury trials.
    b. I think closing speeches are NOT important for jury trials.
    c. I am NOT CERTAIN if closing speeches are important for jury trials.
15. If you had been allowed to take written notes during the trial, would you have wanted to?
    a. yes b. no c. I'm not certain
16. How old are you?
17. Are you? a. male b. female
18. What was the last grade of school you completed?

If you answered yes to 14a. (if you think the speeches ARE important), please tell me why.

APPENDIX D:

Percentage of Features Occurring in ALL Summations (25% and greater) N=66

89%	Traditional opening
77%	Rhetorical questions
65%	Onus placed on jurors
58%	Checks own notes
55%	Discusses or defines 'reasonable doubt'
53%	Refers to 'evidence' or 'facts' in the case
52%	Uses hands extensively
45%	Discusses using '(good) common sense'
	Metaphors
	Signals close
41%	Thanks jurors (in closing)
38%	Thanks jurors (in opening)
36%	Jurors very attentive
	Requests verdict in closing
	Speaker stands at rail of jury box
35%	Refers to defendant by full name
	Repetitions
33%	Direct quotes
	Objections made against
	Reads testimony or documents aloud
32%	Argument: Type of witnesses
	Describes crime
	Discusses the 'American legal system'
	Imperative for verdict in closing
	Uses charts, photographs, exhibits, maps
30%	Jurors paying less attention than at start of summation
	Reviews testimony of witnesses
	Tone of speaker: Direct
29%	Compliments jurors
27%	Apologizes for rudeness or obscenities
	Enumerates items
26%	Body movement much in evidence
	Disparages opponent
	Tone of summation: Very believable
	Suggests possible arguments to be made by opponent

The Following Features Occurred Only Once

- No discernible closing
- Referred to the deceased in present tense, as though alive
- Sat in witness box during summation
- Speaker never looked at jurors' faces
- Tone of speaker: Defensive

APPENDIX E: Percentage of Features Occurring in Summations of PROSECUTORS (25% and greater) N=26

100%	Traditional opening
81%	Rhetorical questions
62%	Discusses using '(good) common sense'
58%	Checks own notes
	Objections made against
	Refers to 'evidence' or 'facts' in the case
56%	Onus placed on jurors
50%	Jurors very attentive
42%	Direct quotes
	Not too distant and moving
	Requests verdict in closing
	Thanks jurors (in closing)
	Thanks jurors (in opening)
	Uses charts, photographs, exhibits, maps
38%	Describes crime
	Disparages opponent
	Extensive use of hands
	Metaphors
	Reads testimony or documents aloud
35%	Body movement much in evidence
	Discusses or defines 'reasonable doubt'
	Jokes used
	Signals close
	Speaker stands at rail of jury box
31%	Enumerates items
	Hand props used (i.e., pencils, glasses)
	Imperative for verdict in closing
	Repetitions
	Reviews testimony of witnesses
27%	Compliments jurors
	Tone of summation: Very believable

APPENDIX F:
Percentage of Features Occurring in Summations of DEFENSE ATTORNEYS (25% and greater) N=40

83%	Traditional opening
75%	Rhetorical questions
70%	Onus placed on jurors
68%	Discusses or defines 'reasonable doubt'
60%	Extensive use of hands
58%	Checks own notes
50%	Refers to 'evidence' or 'facts' in the case
48%	Signals close
45%	Metaphors
43%	Refers to defendant by full name
40%	Discusses the 'American legal system'
	Thanks jurors (in closing)
38%	Argument: Type of witnesses
	Speaker stands at rail of jury box
	Suggests possible arguments to be made by opponent
35%	Discusses using '(good) common sense'
	Jurors paying less attention than at start
	Repetitions
	Tone of speaker: Direct
33%	Discusses or defines 'presumption of innocence'
	Imperative for verdict in closing
	Requests verdict in closing
	Thanks jurors (in opening)
30%	Apologizes for rudeness or obscenities
	Compliments jurors
	Jurors moderately attentive
	Qualification expressed in opening
	Reads testimony or documents aloud
28%	Describes crime
	Direct quotes
	Jurors very attentive
	Not too distant and moving
	Reviews testimony of witnesses
25%	Enumerates items
	Implies 'pity my poor client'
	Not too distant and stationary
	Refers to the defendant as 'Mr — '

Refers to the prosecutor with term of authority or power
(i.e., Counselor, Prosecutor, the Commonwealth)
Tone of speaker: Timid
Tone of summation: Very believable
Uses charts, photographs, exhibits, maps

APPENDIX G:
One lawyer — More than one closing speech

Five of the lawyers in the sample were observed during more than one closing speech. Below are listed the features which reoccurred in their speeches and, therefore, might be considered factors with which that particular speaker is comfortable.

LAWYER A: Prosecutor — Three summations

Features which occurred in all three summations:

Discusses using '(good) common sense'
Traditional opening

Features which occurred in two of the summations:

Discusses opponent's arguments
Discusses or defines: Burden of proof
Reasonable doubt
Disparages other lawyer
Humor
Metaphors
Objections made against
Onus placed on jurors
Refers to 'evidence' or 'facts' in the case
Rhetorical questions
Signals close
Speaker stands at rail of jury box
Thanks jurors (in opening)

LAWYER B: Prosecutor — Three summations

Features which occurred in all three summations:

Discusses or defines: Reasonable doubt
Discusses using '(good) common sense'
Rhetorical questions
Traditional opening

Features which occurred in two of the summations:

Jurors very attentive at start
Jurors paying less attention than at start
Requests verdict in closing

Repetitions
Speaker stands at rail of jury box
Tone of speaker: Intense

LAWYER C: Prosecutor — Two summations

Features which occurred in both summations:

Describes crime
Discusses using '(good) common sense'
Follow the rules of law as judge presents them
Hand prop used (pencil)
Objections made against
Onus placed on jurors
Refers to deceased by full name
Rhetorical questions
Speaker stationary
Tone of speaker: Direct
Logical
Tone of summation: Very believable
Traditional opening

LAWYER D: Defense Attorney — Two summations

Features which occurred in both summations:

Checks own notes
Discusses or defines: Reasonable doubt
Discusses using '(good) common sense'
Follow the rules of law as judge presents them
Hand prop used (eyeglasses)
Metaphors
Onus placed on jurors
Patriotism
Qualification in opening
Refers to defendant as 'Mr'
Refers to 'evidence' or 'facts' in the case
Rhetorical questions
Signals close
Tone of speaker: Direct
Tone of summation: Very believable
Thanks jurors (in closing)
Traditional opening

LAWYER E: Defense Attorney — Two summations

Features which occurred in both summations:

Defendant doesn't have to testify
Discusses or defines: Presumption of innocence
Reasonable doubt
Scotch verdict
Discusses the 'American legal system'
Encourages — 'have courage!'
Hand prop used (eyeglasses)
Metaphors
Onus placed on jurors
Patriotism
Refers to defendant by full name
Rhetorical questions
Signals close
Stands at lectern
Television mentioned
Type of witnesses

APPENDIX H: Summations of Defense Attorneys in Winning Cases

LAWYER 1: Not guilty verdict. Duration: 40 minutes

(1) *Their Choice of Words*

Compliments jurors
Direct quotes
Insults other lawyer
Metaphors
Refers to defendant by full name
Repetitions
Rhetorical questions
Thanks jurors (in closing)
Traditional opening

(2) *Apart from words*

Extensive use of hands
Stance: Not too distant from jurors — stationary

(3) *Hearer response*
Juror response: Jurors very attentive

Observer response: Tone of speaker — Dramatic
Impassioned

(4) *Topics for Argument*

Appeals to emotional issues
- Patriotism
- Pity my poor client
- Religion — invokes God's name

Appeals to intellectual issues
- American legal system
- Refers to evidence or facts in the case

Legal definition (or discusses)
- Burden of proof

LAWYER 2: Not guilty verdict. Duration: 25 minutes

(1) *Their Choice of Words*

Imperative for verdict in closing

Memorized material used
Reads testimony aloud
Rhetorical questions
Traditional opening

(2) *Apart from words*

Body movement — lots of
Checks own notes
Extensive use of hands
Objections made against
Silence: Loses train of thought
Stance: Not too distant from jurors — and moving

(3) *Hearer response*

Juror response: Jurors very attentive

Observer response: Tone of speaker — Angry
Brusque
Impassioned

(4) *Topics for Argument*

Appeals to emotional issues
Discusses using 'good common sense'
Onus placed on jurors

Appeals to intellectual issues
Refers to evidence or facts in the case

Legal definition (or discusses)
Burden of proof
Reasonable doubt

LAWYER 3: Not guilty verdict. Duration: 32 minutes

(1) *Their Choice of Words*

Apologizes for obscenities
Refers to the defendant as 'Mr.'
Request for verdict in closing
Rhetorical questions
Traditional opening

(2) *Apart from words*

Extensive use of hands
Stance: Far across the room

(3) *Hearer response*

Juror response: Jurors very attentive

Observer response: Tone of speaker — Direct
Tone of summation — Very believable

(4) *Topics for Argument*

Appeals to emotional issues
Patriotism
Qualification set forth in opening
Solidarity: 'We' — You and I are a team
Television mentioned

Appeals to intellectual issues
American legal system
Type of witnesses

Legal definition (or discusses)
Burden of proof

LAWYER 4: Not guilty verdict. Duration: 55 minutes

(1) *Their Choice of Words*

Apologizes for: Length of summation
Obscenities
Compliments opposing lawyer
Enumerations
Refers to opposing lawyer as Commonwealth, Counsel
Repetitions
Rhetorical questions
Suggests verdict
Thanks jurors (in opening)
Thanks jurors (in closing)
Traditional opening

(2) *Apart from words*

Checks own notes
Extensive use of hands
Silence: Loses train of thought
Stance: Stands far across the room — moving

(3) *Hearer response*

Juror response: Jurors less than very attentive

Observer response: Tone of speaker — Informal
Unsure of self

(4) *Topics for Argument*

Appeals to emotional issues
  Onus placed on jurors
  Patriotism
  Qualification set forth in opening
Appeals to intellectual issues
  American legal system
  Reviews witnesses through testimony
  Type of witnesses
Legal definition (or discusses)
  Presumption of innocence
  Reasonable doubt
Refutational argument
  Suggests opponent's arguments

LAWYER 5: Hung Jury. Duration: 50 minutes

(1) *Their Choice of Words*

Apologizes for length of summation
Direct quotes
Enumerations
Imperative for verdict in closing
Insults (disparages) opposing lawyer
Jokes
Metaphors
Reads testimony aloud
Refers to defendant: By last name
'My client'
Refers to opposing lawyer: 'Mr.'
Prosecutor
Repetitions
Rhetorical questions
Self-correction
Signals close
Suggests verdict
Thanks jurors (in opening)
Traditional opening

(2) *Apart from words*

Charts used
Checks own notes
Stance: Stands at lectern

(3) *Hearer response*

Juror response: Jurors moderately attentive

Observer response: Tone of speaker — Direct
Tone of summation — Very believable

(4) *Topics for Argument*

Appeals to emotional issues
- Onus placed on jurors
- Patriotism
- Pity my poor client
- Qualification set forth in opening
- Television mentioned

Appeals to intellectual issues
- American legal system
- Refers to evidence or facts in the case
- Reviews witnesses through testimony

Legal definition (or discusses)
- Reasonable doubt

There were two features which occurred in all five defense closing speeches in 'winning' cases:

Rhetorical questions
Traditional opening

There were three features which occurred in four of the defense closing speeches in 'winning' cases:

Appeal to patriotism
Discussion of the American legal system
Extensive use of hands

There were seven features which occurred in three of the defense closing speeches in 'winning' cases:

Checks own notes
Discusses burden of proof
Discusses reasonable doubt
Jurors very attentive
Onus placed on jurors
Qualification set forth in opening
Refers to evidence or facts in the case

The average time of a summation by a defense attorney in a winning case was 40.4 minutes.

NOTES

1. The voir dire is a process in which prospective jurors are questioned by judge and/ or lawyers in an attempt to identify and thereby, in theory, to eliminate potentially biased jurors.
2. Official transcripts of closing speeches are available for purchase from courtroom stenographers. However, these were not used for this study for the reasons discussed on page 123. Also see page 226.
3. I use as a definition of 'code' a "language, or dialect, or style of language" (Brown and Yule 1983: 38).
4. 'Summing up' is an expression used by lawyers to mean 'give a summation'.
5. For a more complete linguistic discussion of 'conversational implicature', see Levinson (1983), Chapter 3.
6. Appellate courts are those which hear appeals and which may or may not reverse the decisions of lower courts. The decision makers in these courts, and the persons to whom the lawyers appeal, are judges rather than jurors.
7. Note that he uses 'say' rather than 'ask', because rhetorical questions are really disguised statements conveying some piece of information and are not requests for response.
8. One juror accepted 'You didn't hear that, did you?' as a true question, and hence, responded.
9. I have recently been informed that some judges can and will now permit audio taping in their courtrooms during a trial.
10. Speech act theory is an extremely interesting issue in relation to the general theory of language usage, and the discussion above presents only some concepts of Austin. For a further and more complete discussion of speech act theory see: Cole and Morgan (1975), Levinson (1983) Chapter 5, Morgan (1978), or Searle (1969) Chapter 8.
11. 'Close to the jury' is a standard expression used by lawyers and judges signifying 'give a closing speech.'
12. This was the second longest trial in the history of Philadelphia. The jury required only 2 1/2 hours to decide this 5 month trial.
13. Learned through personal communication.
14. See Chapter 10 for a discussion of court followers.
15. This lack of interest in the verdict seemed to puzzle some of the observed attorneys.
16. The first prosecutor observed in Career Criminal Court was elected District Attorney of Philadelphia as this was being written.

17. This number, which is greater than the number of jurors in the study, reflects multiple defendants (hence multiple lawyers) in a single trial.
18. However, I observed in actual trial an experienced attorney wearing the mantle of the unpolished, inexperienced lawyer much to his advantage (see p. 185.) I also observed a powerful and convincing summation which I later discovered was that attorney's first closing speech.
19. Solicitors advise clients, represent them before lower courts, and prepare cases for the barristers, who alone have the privilege of pleading cases in the higher courts.

BIBLIOGRAPHY

Aiken, Ray J.
1960. Let's Not Oversimplify Legal Language. *Rocky Mountain Law Review* 32:358-364.

Alschuler, Albert W.
1980. Courtroom Misconduct by Prosecutors and Trial Judges. In Yale Kamisar, Wayne R. LaFave and Jerold H. Israel, *Modern Criminal Procedure*. St. Paul: West Publishing Company.

American College of Trial Lawyers.
1983. *Roster, Bylaws, Code of Trial Conduct*. South Bend, Indiana: Carleton Graphics.

Andrews, Lori B.
1984. Exhibit A: Language. Special Edition: You the Jury. *Psychology Today*, February 1984: 28-33.

Argyle, Michael.
1980. Verbal and non-verbal communication. In John Corner and Jeremy Hawthorn (eds.), *Communication Studies*. London: Edward Arnold.

Atkinson, J. Maxwell and Paul Drew.
1979. *Order in Court*. Atlantic Highlands, New Jersey: Humanities Press.

Austin, J.L.
1962. *How to Do Things with Words*. London: Oxford University Press.

Bailey, F. Lee.
1979. *Opening and Closing Arguments in a Criminal Trial*. Minneapolis, Minn: National Practice Institute — Continuing Legal Education.

Bailey, F. Lee.
1982. *To be a Trial Lawyer*. Marshfield, Mass.: Telshare Publishing.

Baldwin, Scott.
1984. Jury Argument: How to Prepare and Present A Winning Closing Argument. *Trial* 20.4: 58-64.

Bauman, Richard and Joel Sherzer (eds.).
1974. *Explorations in the Ethnography of Speaking*. London: Cambridge University Press.

Bell, Allan.
1984. Language style as audience design. *Language in Society* 13.2: 145-204.

Belli, Melvin M.
1979. Techniques of final argument. *Trial Diplomacy Journal*, Winter: 34-39.

Bettinghaus, Erwin P.
1980 (1930). *Persuasive Communication*. Third Edition. New York: Holt, Rinehart and Winston.

Birdwhistell, Ray L.
1970. *Kinesics and context: Essays on body motion communication*. Philadelphia: University of Pennsylvania Press.

Black, Mary and Duane Metzger.
1965. Ethnographic description and the study of the law. *American Anthropologist* 67.6,pt.2: 141-165.

Bowers, J.W.
1964. Some Correlates of Language Intensity. *Quarterly Journal of Speech* 50: 415-420.

Bricker, Victoria R.
1974. The Ethnographic Context of Some Traditional Mayan Speech Genres. In Richard Bauman and Joel Sherzer (eds.), *Explorations in the Ethnography of Speaking*. New York: Cambridge University Press.

Briggs, Charles L.
1984. Learning to ask: Native metacommunicative competence and the incompetence of fieldworkers. *Language in Society* 13.1: 1-28.

Brown, Gillian and George Yule.
1983. *Discourse Analysis*. Cambridge: Cambridge University Press.

Carrigan, Jim R.
1982. My Approach to Closing Argument for the Plaintiff. In Grace W. Holmes (ed.), *Opening Statements and Closing Arguments*. Ann Arbor, Michigan: The Institute of Continuing Legal Education.

Cartwright, Robert E.
1978. Winning psychological principles in summation. *Trial Diplomacy Journal*, Spring 1978: 31-39.

Cole, Peter and Jerry L. Morgan (eds.).
1975. *Syntax and Semantics: Speech Acts, vol. 3*. New York: Academic Press.

Colson, Bill.
1982. Arguing Expert Testimony in the Summation. In Grace W. Holmes (ed.), *Opening Statements and Closing Arguments*. Ann Arbor, Michigan: The Institute of Continuing Legal Education.

Conley, John, William M. O'Barr and E. Allan Lind.
1978. The Power of Language: Presentational Style in the Courtroom. *Duke Law Journal* 78: 1375-1399.

Connolly, Paul R.
1982. Persuasion in the Closing Argument: The Defendant's Approach. In Grace W. Holmes (ed.), *Opening Statements and Closing Arguments*. Ann Arbor, Michigan: The Institute of Continuing Legal Education.

Costopoulos, William C.
1972. Commentaries: Persuasion in the Courtroom. *Duquesne Law Review* 10: 384-409.

Crawford, Richard J.
1983. Closing Argument: High Noon at the Penthouse Corral. *Trial Diplomacy Journal* 5.4: 12-17.

Crystal, David.
1971. Prosodic and Paralinguistic Correlates of Social Categories. In Edward Ardener (ed.), *Social Anthropology and Language*. London: Tavistock Publications.

Cutler, A.S.
1949. *Successful Trial Tactics*. New York: Prentice Hall.

Danet, Brenda.
1980a. "Baby" or "fetus"? Language and the construction of reality in a manslaughter trial. *Semiotica* 32: 187-219.

Danet, Brenda.
1980b. Language in the legal process. *Law and Society Review* 14: 445-564.

Danet, Brenda.
1980c. Language in the Courtroom. In Howard Giles, Philip Smith and Peter Robinson (eds.), *Social Psychology and Language: Proceedings of an International Conference*. Oxford: Pergamon.

Danet, Brenda, Kenneth B. Hoffman, Nicole C. Kermish, H. Jeffrey Rafn, Deborah G. Stayman.
1976. An Ethnography of Questioning in the Courtroom. In Roger W. Shuy and Anna Shnukal (eds.), *Language Use and the Uses of Language*. Washington, D.C.: Georgetown University Press.

Danet, Brenda and Nicole C. Kermish.
1977. *Courtroom Questioning: A Sociolinguistic Perspective*. Jerusalem: The Communications Institute The Hebrew University of Jerusalem.

Darrow, Clarence.
1960 (1926). Summation in the Sweet Case. In Ephraim London (ed.), *The Law as Literature*. New York: Simon and Schuster.

Davis, James H., Robert M. Bray, and Robert W. Holt.
1977. The Empirical Study of Decision Processes in Juries. In June Louin Tapp and Felice J. Levin (eds.), *Law, Justice and the Individual in Society: Psychology and Legal Issues*. New York: Holt, Rinehart and Winston.

Davison, Alice.
1976. Linguistic Analysis and the Law. In Roger W. Shuy and Anna Shnukal (eds.), *Language Use and the Uses of Language*. Washington, D.C.: Georgetown University Press.

Duranti, Alessandro.
1983. Somoan speechmaking across social events: One genre in and out of a 'fono'. *Language in Society* 12.1: 1-22.

Ellen, R.F.
1984. *Ethnographic Research*. London: Academic Press.

Elwork, Amiram, Bruce Dennis Sales, and David Suggs.
1981. The Trial: A Research Review. In Bruce Dennis Sales (ed.), *The Trial Process*. New York: Plenum Press.

Erickson, Bonnie, E. Allan Lind, Bruce Johnson, and William M. O'Barr.
1978. Speech Style and Impression Formation in a Court Setting: The Effects of 'Powerful' and 'Powerless' Speech. *Journal of Experimental Social Psychology* 14: 266-279.

Erlanger, Howard S.
1970. Jury Research in America: Its Past and Future. *Law and Society Review* 4.3: 345-370.

Fahringer, Herald Price.
1982. Closing Argument. *The Criminal Defense Litigation Seminar* Cassette two. The American Law Institute.

Fishman, Joshua A.
1983. Epistemology, Methodology and Ideology in the Sociolinguistic Enterprise. *Language Learning* 33.5: 33-47.

Flango, Victor E.
1980. Would jurors do a better job if they could take notes? *Judicature* 63.9: 436-443.

Fontes, Norman E. and Robert W. Bundens.
1980. Persuasion during the Trial Process. In Michael E. Roloff and Gerald R. Miller (eds.), *Persuasion: New Directions in Theory and Research*. Beverly Hills: Sage.

Frake, Charles O.
1964. How to ask for a drink in Subanun. In John J. Gumperz and Dell Hymes (eds.), The Ethnography of Communication. *American Anthropologist* 66.6,pt.2: 127-132.

Frake, Charles O.
1972 (1969). "Struck by Speech": The Yakan Concept of Litigation. In John J. Gumperz and Dell Hymes (eds.), *Directions in Sociolinguistics: The Ethnography of Communication*. New York: Holt, Rinehart and Winston.

Frank, Jerome.
1966 (1949). *Courts on Trial: Myth and Reality in American Justice*. New York: Atheneum.

Galanter, Marc, Lawrence M. Friedman, Thomas Raiser and Howard Hines.
1974. The Future of Law and Social Science Research. *The North Carolina Law Review* 52.5: 1060-1089.

Garfinkel, Harold.
1967. Some rules of correct decision making that jurors respect. In *Studies in Ethnomethodology*. Englewood Cliffs, New Jersey: Prentice-Hall.

Geoghan, William F.X., Jr.
1978. The Plaintiff's Approach in Closing Argument. In Grace W. Holmes, (ed.), *Persuasion: The Key to Success in Trial*. Ann Arbor, Michigan: The Institute of Continuing Legal Education.

Giles, Howard and Peter F. Powesland.
1975. *Speech Style and Social Evaluation*. London: Academic Press.

Goffman, Erving.
1980 (1959). Introduction to the presentation of self in everyday life. In John Corner and Jeremy Hawthorn (eds.), *Communication Studies*. London: Edward Arnold.

Goldberg, Bettyruth Walter.
1981. The Trials of a Juror. *The Pennsylvania Gazette* 79.6:19-25. (Also see Walter)

Goldman, Laurence.
1983. *Talk Never Dies: The Language of Huli Disputes*. London: Tavistock Publications.

Goodenough, Ward G.
1957. Cultural Anthropology and Linguistics. In P. L. Garvin (ed.), *Report of the Seventh Annual Round Table Meeting on Linguistics and Language Study*. Georgetown University Monograph Series on Language and Linguistics 9: 167-173.

Greene, Hon. Henry F.
1982. Memorandum to Attorneys. Washington, D.C.

Gregory, Michael and Susanne Carroll.
1978. *Language and Situation: Language Varieties and their Social Contexts*. London: Routledge & Kegan.

Grice, H.P.
1975. Logic and conversation. In Peter Cole and Jerry L. Morgan (eds.), *Syntax and Semantics* Vol. 3. New York: Academic Press.

Gumperz, John J.
1964. Linguistic and Social Interaction in Two Communities. In John J. Gumperz and Dell Hymes (eds.), The Ethnography of Communication. *American Anthropologist* 66.6,pt.2: 137-153.

Gumperz, John J.
1972. Introduction. In John J. Gumperz and Dell Hymes (eds.), *Directions in Sociolinguistics: The Ethnography of Communication*. New York: Holt, Rinehart and Winston.

Hager, John W.
1959. Let's Simplify Legal Language. *Rocky Mountain Law Review* 32:74-86.

Hansell, Donald Wade.
1963. The Persuasive Elements in Summation Speeches of Twenty Contemporary Jury Trials. Ph.D. dissertation, University of Denver.

Hastie, Ried, Steven D. Penrod and Nancy Pennington.
1983. *Inside the Jury*. Cambridge, Massachusetts: Harvard University Press.

Hastie, Reid, Steven D. Penrod and Nancy Pennington.
1983. What Goes on in a Jury Deliberation. *American Bar Association Journal* 69: 1848-1853.

Hayes, Harold B.
1972. Applying Persuasion Techniques to Trial Proceedings. *South Carolina Law Review* 24.3: 380-397.

Holmes, Grace W.
1982. *Opening Statements and Closing Arguments*. Ann Arbor, Michigan: The Institute of Continuing Legal Education.

Hovland, Carl I., Irving L. Janis and Harold H. Kelley.
1953. *Communication and Persuasion: Psychological Studies of Opinion Change*. New Haven: Yale University Press.

Hudson, R.A.
1980. *Sociolinguistics*. Cambridge: Cambridge University Press.

Hymes, Dell.
1962. The Ethnography of Speaking. In T. Gladwin and W.C. Sturtevant (eds.), *Anthropology and Human Behavior*. Washington, D.C.: The Anthropological Society of Washington.

Hymes, Dell.
1964. Introduction: Towards Ethnographies of Communication. In John J. Gumperz and Dell Hymes (eds.), The Ethnography of Communication. *American Anthropologist* 66.6,pt.2: 1-34.

Hymes, Dell.
1967. Models of the Interaction of Language and Social Setting. *Journal of Social Issues* 23.2: 8-28.

Hymes, Dell.
1972. Models of the Interaction of Language and Social Life. In John J. Gumperz and Dell Hymes (eds.), *Directions in Sociolinguistics: The Ethnography of Communication*. New York: Holt, Rinehart and Winston.

Hymes, Dell.
1974. *Foundations in Sociolinguistics: An Ethnographic Approach*. Philadelphia: University of Pennsylvania Press.

Hymes, Dell.
1974. Ways of Speaking. In Richard Bauman and Joel Sherzer (eds.), *Explorations in the Ethnography of Speaking*. New York: Cambridge University Press.

Hymes, Dell.
1975. Breakthrough into Performance. In Dan Ben-Amos and Kenneth S. Goldstein (eds.), *Folklore: Performance and Communication*. The Hague: Mouton.

Hymes, Dell.
1977. Discovering Oral Performance and Measured Verse in American Indian Narrative. *New Literary History* 8:431-57.

Janis, Irving L. and Carl I. Hovland.
1959. Summary and Implications for Future Research. In Irving L. Janis, Carl I. Hovland, et al. (eds.), *Personality and Persuasibility*. New Haven: Yale University Press.

Jeans, James W.
1975. *Trial Advocacy*. St. Paul, Minn.: West Publishing Co.

Kalven, Jr., Harry and Hans Zeisel.
1966. *The American Jury*. Boston: Little, Brown.

Keeton, Robert E.
1973. *Trial Tactics and Methods*, 2d. ed. Boston: Little, Brown.

Kevelson, Roberta.
1982. Language and Legal Speech Acts: Decisions. In Robert J. Di Pietro (ed.), *Linguistics and the Professions*. Norwood, N.J.: Ablex.

Labov, William.
1972. *Language in the Inner City: Studies in the Black English Vernacular*. Philadelphia: University of Pennsylvania Press.

Lakoff, George and Mark Johnson.
1980. *Metaphors We Live By*. Chicago and London: The University of Chicago Press.

Laver, John and Peter Trudgill.
1979. Phonetic and linguistic markers in speech. In Klaus R. Scherer and Howard Giles (eds.), *Social Markers in Speech*. Cambridge: Cambridge University Press.

Levinson, Stephen C.
1983. *Pragmatics*. Cambridge: Cambridge University Press.

Lind, E. Allen and William M. O'Barr.
1979. The Social Significance of Speech in the Courtroom. In Howard Giles and Robert St Clair (eds.), *Language and Social Psychology*. Oxford: Basil Blackwell.

Lind, E. Allen and Laurens Walker.
1979. Theory Testing, Theory Development, and Laboratory Research on Legal Issues. *Law and Human Behavior* 3.1/2: 5-19.

Loftus, Elizabeth.
1974. Reconstructing memory: the incredible eye-witness. *Psychology Today* 8:117-119.

London, Ephraim, ed.
1960. *The Law as Literature*. New York: Simon and Schuster.

Malinowski, Bronislaw.
1970 (1926). *Crime and Custom in Savage Society*. London: Routledge and Kegan Paul.

Mauet, Thomas A.
1980. *Fundamentals of Trial Techniques*. Boston: Little, Brown.

Maynard, Douglas W.
1983. Language in the Court: Review Essay. *American Bar Foundation Research Journal* 1: 211-222.

Mellinkoff, David.
1963. *The Language of the Law*. Boston: Little, Brown.

Mey, Jacob L.
1985. *Whose Language: A Study in Linguistic Pragmatics*. Amsterdam: John Benjamins Publishing Company.

Mills, Judson.
1966. Opinion Change as a Function of the Communicator's Desire to Influence and Liking for the Audience. *Journal of Experimental Social Psychology* 2: 152-159.

Mills, Judson and E. Aronson.
1965. Opinion Change as a Function of the Communicator's Attractiveness and Desire to Influence. *Journal of Personality and Social Psychology* 1.2: 173-177.

Mills, Judson and J.M. Jellison.
1967. Effect on opinion change of how desirable the communication is to the audience the communicator addressed. *Journal of Personality and Social Psychology* 5: 459-463.

Milroy, James.
1984. Sociolinguistic Methodology and the Identification of Speakers' Voices in Legal Proceedings. In Peter Trudgill (ed.), *Applied Sociolinguistics*. London: Academic Press.

Milroy, Lesley.
1980. *Language and Social Networks*. Oxford: Basil Blackwell.

Morecroft, John, Cornelius Coughlin, George Glenton, Ernest Spring, and Ronald Gerelli.
1984. *The Old Bailey*. London: The Corporation of London.

Morgan, J.L.
1978. Two Types of Convention in Indirect Speech Acts. In Peter Cole (ed.), *Syntax and Semantics: Pragmatics, vol. 9*. New York: Academic Press.

Moses, Ray.
1985. *Jury Argument in Criminal Cases: A Trial Lawyer's Guide*. Houston, Texas: Azimuth Press.

Nader, Laura.
1965. The anthropological study of law. *American Anthropologist* 67.2,pt.2: 3-32.

Naifeh, Steven and Gregory White Smith.
1983. *The Best Lawyers in America*. New York: Seaview/Putnam.

O'Barr, William M.
1981. The language of the law. In Charles A. Ferguson and Shirley Brice Heath (eds.), *Language in the USA*. New York: Cambridge University Press.

O'Barr, William M.
1982. *Linguistic Evidence*. New York: Academic Press.

O'Barr, William M. and John M. Conley.
1976. When a Juror Watches a Lawyer. *Barrister* 3.3: 8-11, 33.

O'Barr, William M. and E. Allen Lind.
1981. Ethnography and experimentation — partners in legal research. In B.D. Sales (ed.), *The Trial Process*. New York: Plenum.

Opening and Closing Arguments.
1985. Pennsylvania Bar Institute: The Continuing Legal Education Arm of the Pennsylvania Bar Association.

Outerbridge, Ian W.
1978. The Defendant's Approach in Closing Argument. In Grace W. Holmes, (ed.), *Persuasion: The Key to Success in Trial*. Ann Arbor, Michigan: The Institute of Continuing Legal Education.

Packel, Leonard and Delores B. Spina.
1984. *Trial Advocacy: A Systematic Approach*. Philadelphia: American Law Institute — American Bar Association.

Parkinson, Michael G.
1981. Verbal Behavior and Courtroom Success. *Communication Education* 30: 22-32.

Pelto, Pertti J. and Gretl H. Pelto.
1978. *Anthropological Research: The Structure of Inquiry*, 2d. ed. New York: Cambridge University Press.

Pride, J.B.
Customs and Cases of Verbal Behaviour. In Edwin Ardener (ed.), *Social Anthropology and Language*.

Prince, Ellen F.
1984. Language and the law: Reference, stress, and context. In Deborah Schiffrin, (ed.), *Meaning, Form, and Use in Context: Linguistic Applications*. Washington, D.C.: Georgetown University Press.

Probert, Walter.
1959. Law and Persuasion: The Language-Behavior of Lawyers. *University of Pennsylvania Law Review* 108: 35-58.

Report on the Committee on Juries of the Judicial Council of the Second Circuit.
1984. New York: Manuscript.

Rosenthal, Douglas E.
1976. Evaluating the Competence of Lawyers. *Law and Society Review* 11: 257-286.

Saks, Michael J. and Reid Hastie.
1978. *Social Psychology in Court*. New York: Van Nostrand Reinhold.

Salmond, Anne.
1982. Theoretical Landscapes: On Cross-Cultural Conceptions of Knowledge. In David Parkin (ed.), *Semantic Anthropology*. London: Academic Press.

Sams, Jr., Murray.
1982. Closing Argument: New Answers to Some Old Problems. In Grace W. Holmes (ed.), *Opening Statements and Closings Arguments*. Ann Arbor, Michigan: The Institute of Continuing Legal Education.

Saville-Troike, Muriel.
1982. *The Ethnography of Communication*. Oxford: Basil Blackwell.

Scherer, Klaus R.
1979. Voice and Speech Correlates of Perceived Social Influence in Simulated Juries. In Howard Giles and Robert St Clair (eds.), *Language and Social Psychology*. Oxford: Basil Blackwell.

Searle, J.R.
1969. *Speech Acts*. Cambridge: Cambridge University Press.

Shepherd, John C.
1982. Closing Argument: The Defendant's Last Chance. In Grace W. Holmes (ed.), *Opening Statements and Closings Arguments*. Ann Arbor, Michigan: The Institute of Continuing Legal Education.

Sherzer, Joel.
1983. *Kuna Ways of Speaking*. Austin: University of Texas Press.

Smith, Lawrence J.
1982. *Art of Advocacy — Summation*. New York: Matthew Bender.

Statistical Abstract of the United States.
1986. Government Publications Department.

Stein, Jacob A.
1979 (1969). *Closing Argument: The Art and the Law*. Wilmette, Illinois: Callaghan & Co.

Vinson, Donald E.
1985. How to Persuade Jurors. *American Bar Association Journal*. October: 72-76.

Walter, Bettyruth and Robert C. Heim.
1985. *Note-Taking by Jurors in the Federal Courts*. A Research Project Sponsored by the Philadelphia Bar Association. Philadelphia: Manuscript. (Also see Goldberg)

Wasserbly, Richard S.
1981. *Pennsylvania Criminal Practice, Vol. 2*. Wilmette, Illinois: Callaghan & Co.

Weld, H.P. and E.R. Danzig.
1940. A study of the way in which a verdict is reached by a jury. *American Journal of Psychology* 53: 518-536.

Weld, H.P. and Merrill Roff.
1938. A Study in the Formation of Opinion Based upon Legal Evidence. *American Journal of Psychology* 51.4: 609-628.

Wolfson, Nessa.
1976. Speech events and natural speech; some implications for sociolinguistic methodology. *Language in Society* 5: 189-209.

Younger, Irving.
1976. In praise of simplicity. *American Bar Association Journal* 62: 632-634.

Younger, Irving.
1984. *Jury Selection*. Three cassettes. Minneapolis, Minnesota: The Professional Education Group, Inc.

Zeisel, Hans.
1973. Reflections on Experimental Techniques in the Law. *The Journal of Legal Studies* Vol. II (1): 107-124.

Zeisel, Hans and Alice M. Padawer-Singer.
1974. The Selection of Topics and Methods for Law and Social Science Research. *The North Carolina Law Review* 52.5: 974-999.

SUBJECT INDEX

ATTORNEY INDEX

Below are listed the pages on which quotations by or discussion of the attorneys who were interviewed for this study are identified by name. A lawyer who appears with few page references may have been quoted extensively, but without his or her name. The determination to use or not use names was solely that of the author, and based on the desire not to risk embarrassment to her sincere and forthright informants.